"At a time when many Christians—and many evangelicals in particular—are discovering or rediscovering 'the mystery of God,' there's an urgent need for discernment. Steven Boyer and Christopher Hall's 'theology for knowing the unknowable' is a gift to the church."

—**John Wilson**, editor, *Books & Culture*

"Here at last is a clear, precise, and careful treatment of mystery in Christian life and theology. Boyer and Hall chart a middle course between the cliffs of rationalism and the whirlpool of irrationalism, bringing readers safely through to the spiritual homeland, to lives hidden with Christ in God. There is no mystery mongering here. When Boyer and Hall appeal to mystery, they are not obfuscating but opening up and clarifying vast ranges of theology and spirituality."

—**Fred Sanders**, Biola University

"This book is a gem. Boyer and Hall display the beauty of historic Christian orthodoxy in clear, elegant prose. Skillfully avoiding the twin plagues of arrogant rationalism and anti-intellectual irrationalism, they demonstrate the tremendous potential of the concept of mystery to illuminate central doctrines and practices of the Christian faith. Scholars, pastors, and students alike will reap rich rewards from this outstanding contribution to contemporary evangelical theology."

—**Jeffrey P. Greenman**, Wheaton College

The
MYSTERY
of
GOD

The

MYSTERY

of

GOD

Theology *for* Knowing *the* Unknowable

STEVEN D. BOYER *and*
CHRISTOPHER A. HALL

Baker Academic

a division of Baker Publishing Group
Grand Rapids, Michigan

Published by Baker Academic
a division of Baker Publishing Group
P.O. Box 6287, Grand Rapids, MI 49516-6287
www.bakeracademic.com

Printed in the United States of America

Library of Congress Cataloging-in-Publication Data

Boyer, Steven D., 1962–
    The mystery of God : theology for knowing the unknowable / Steven D. Boyer and Christopher A. Hall.
        p.   cm.
    Includes bibliographical references and indexes.
    ISBN 978-0-8010-2773-4 (pbk.)
    1. Mystery 2. God (Christianity) I. Hall, Christopher A. (Christopher Alan), 1950– II. Title.
    BT127.5.B69 2012
    230—dc23
                                       2012016490

In keeping with biblical principles of creation stewardship, Baker Publishing Group advocates the responsible use of our natural resources. As a member of the Green Press Initiative, our company uses recycled paper when possible. The text paper of this book is composed in part of post-consumer waste.

12   13   14   15   16   17   18   7   6   5   4   3   2   1

To

Heidi Elise Boyer

and

Debbie Hall,
in whom the mystery of God
is so fittingly embodied

Contents

Introduction

The Landscape on a Sunny Day

This book is the work of two authors, and we have endeavored throughout to speak with a single authorial voice. Nevertheless, it seems wise to begin with a short anecdote that comes from just one of us, and that introduces a line of thinking that we will be building on quite a bit in the pages that follow.

A Morning Walk

Like many people, I (Steve) deeply enjoy a peaceful walk on a clear, fresh morning. Since I lived for a time only a couple miles north of the university where I teach, I have often had opportunity for such walks on my way to the office. On one occasion not long ago, I took advantage of such an opportunity, and I found that the pleasure of my stroll that spring morning was so intense that I could barely give attention to the business that the day at the office would include. My senses were bombarded on every side by magnificent invitations to distraction. It was still fairly early, so a delicious coolness was everywhere, even though the day was already bright with streaming sunshine. The song of birds was unbroken and loud enough that my children had already complained about being awakened by it. The air was so fresh and so thick with the scents of a spring morning that I wanted to savor each breath like a bite of a nourishing meal.

Of course, there was a great deal to see on such a bright morning: squirrels running skillfully along telephone wires, small birds pecking in the grass for a bit of breakfast, children waiting for a bus to take them to school, an elderly woman working in her garden before the day became too hot, a man in a tie climbing into his automobile, a procession of cyclists in their colorful biking attire. My path took me past a local golf course, where I could see several clusters of golfers enjoying the clear day, some of them teeing off not twenty yards from where I walked, others in the distance on other fairways or greens. The trees on the golf course, both nearby and farther away, displayed (when one attended closely) more subtle shades of green than one would have thought possible, with the combination of colors constantly changing as the leaves danced and sparkled in the morning sun. A little farther on, I passed a local school's quarter-mile jogging track, around which three or four runners were proceeding at varying paces, one of them with a black Labrador as an escort. In the middle of the track, the school's football team was just finishing up a morning scrimmage, and I could tell by the dirty uniforms and the coach's red face that they had been hard at work for some time before my arrival.

As I began to approach the campus of my institution, I proceeded south along a fence (on my left) that bordered an open field, and for the first time I found myself under the wide-open sky. I absentmindedly watched the antics of playful birds above me and off to the right (the west), and I marveled at the size and brilliance of the blue expanse in which they cavorted. Coming to the end of the fence, I turned left (east) toward the school, and I found that I could no longer attend to the birds, for the brightness of the sun directly in front of me and above me required me to keep my eyes lowered to the horizon for a few moments until I came to another stand of trees.

Now, at this point, an odd thought occurred to me. I realized that this morning's walk—a little over a mile so far, supremely pleasant, and filled with sights made all the more interesting by their ordinariness—had not included any steadfast attention to one very evident element in this lovely spring day. It was not that this element was unavailable or inaccessible. On the contrary, its ready accessibility was precisely what kept me from attending to it. It also was not that I had overlooked it or taken it for granted, for its presence was a very conscious part of my enjoyment of the day. And yet, though I delighted in it, and though it was available for inspection, I never once looked at it, or even tried to.

The neglected item was the sun. I had, of course, been aware of its rays: I had felt their warmth and had seen the shadows that they cast. And I knew that the bright sun in the sky was the source of those rays: indeed, I remembered telling my wife as I left the house what a "beautiful *sunny* day" it was, and how pleasant the walk would be as a result. If I had been asked, I could have pointed (with eyes lowered) to the spot in the sky where the sun was currently blazing. Yet I knew all of this, and enjoyed it, without ever looking directly at the sun itself.

As I thought about it, and while I was still under the open sky, I offhandedly stole a quick glance upward to look at the sun directly. This was foolish, of course. Even that momentary flash of the sun's brilliance hurt my dazed eyes, and I had to blink and rub them for a moment before looking around again. When I did look around, I found that I could not quite see clearly for a few moments: the negative image of the sun's disk continued to haunt my vision like a ghost.

By the time I reached the trees a little farther up the road, my eyes were back to normal. The trees themselves helped, by providing a leafy filter through which the sun could shine, but not in its full force. Looking up, one could glimpse tiny bits of the sun for just a split second between the constantly dancing leaves. And even with such protection, the brightness was not always pleasant.

Surely, I thought, this is a rather ironic situation. Not only is the sun a key element in a pleasant spring morning, but it is also the one element that allows me to see all of the other elements that contribute to the pleasantness. On a cloudy day I could not have seen the cyclists or the Labrador or the multiple shades of green nearly so well; in the dark I could not have seen them at all. Yet the very thing that allows me to see this beautiful spring morning cannot itself be seen. This is something of a surprise, isn't it? The sun makes things visible, but it is not visible itself, at least not to ordinary looking. On the contrary, the only way I had found to look *at* the sun was in fact to *hide* the sun behind ever-shifting leaves that could give me just the tiniest, most fragmentary glimpses of what I could not bear to gaze upon.

Theology and the Sun We Cannot See

Both of the authors of this book have found an experience like this one to be instructive. Of course, our book itself is a work of Christian theology, not one of solar astronomy or of nature lore. But we think that the scenario described above is worth a bit of theological reflection (and perhaps even a reenactment on some beautiful spring morning!), and we are not the first to think so. Perhaps most famously in recent memory, it was in a rich theological context that C. S. Lewis observed, "We believe that the sun is in the sky at midday in summer not because we can clearly see the sun (in fact, we cannot) but because we can see everything else."[1] Lewis's point was clear: there may be certain things that are themselves too great to understand but that nevertheless enable us to understand lesser things with remarkable clarity.

Lewis's image seems to be especially apt when we consider the Christian doctrine of God. Christians from the very beginning have insisted that the God they worship is the one, true, living God—the God who is not one "thing" among others, but the source and end of every "thing" that exists; the God of whom no image may be made, since every image falls short; the God whose thoughts are not our thoughts, whose ways are not our ways. "All the gods of the nations are idols," declares the psalmist, "but the Lord made the heavens"

1. C. S. Lewis, *Miracles: A Preliminary Study* (1947; repr., New York: Touchstone, 1996), 145.

(Ps. 96:5). This Creator "lives in unapproachable light" (1 Tim. 6:16); before him both heaven and earth flee away, and no place is found for them (Rev. 20:11); this God ominously announces, "No one may see me and live" (Exod. 33:20). This is a God whom philosophers, theologians, and ordinary Christians have recognized as "incomprehensible," "inscrutable," "hidden," "past finding out."

Yet this God is also the center of all things, the fount of life, the God of all truth, the Father of lights, the Light that enlightens every person. How can Life be the occasion of death, or Light dwell in dazzling darkness, or Truth be beyond understanding? Yet such paradoxical formulations have been used to describe God from the beginning. In an early twentieth-century study of the universal human experience of God, German philosopher of religion Rudolf Otto summarized this very paradox when he described God with the Latin phrase *mysterium tremendum et fascinans*, which may be roughly translated as "mystery that overwhelms and yet attracts."[2] There seems to be something profoundly right about this characterization of God, especially in its insistence that God is, in some quite remarkable sense, a *mystery*. The full meaning and import of this term will be the subject of the rest of this book, but we can recognize right from the outset that to speak of God in this way is to speak of him as blinding, crushing, devastating, overpowering. To approach God is to approach an unfathomable depth of reality and truth that, like the sun in the sky, is too intense, too bright to look at, but that nevertheless brings meaning and coherence and beauty to everything else. God is a mystery.

The task of this book is to investigate this notion of divine mystery and to investigate it in a way that is explicitly theological. To describe our goal in this way might strike some readers as odd. Isn't theology, someone might ask, the attempt to *overcome* mystery? Aren't theologians exactly the people whom we ask to solve the perplexing puzzles and oddities of religious life, so that we can all understand God better?

There is a kernel of truth to this intuition, for we do indeed expect theologians to help us to know God better. But there are confusions here as well. One of the confusions has to do with the notion that a "mystery" is primarily a puzzle or a riddle that has to be solved. This is a very understandable assumption, since the term "mystery" is used in a bewildering variety of ways, even when one considers only its religious or ecclesiastical applications. In chapter 1, we will explore this variety of meanings and try to make clear the sense in which we are using the term in this book. For the moment, let us say simply that the "mystery" that the Creator must be, by virtue of his status as Creator, cannot in the nature of the case be "solved," like a puzzle. The mystery of God is not a question to which we must find an answer; it is itself the answer—and an answer into which we are invited to enter ever more fully in Christ.

---

2. Rudolf Otto, *The Idea of the Holy: An Inquiry into the Non-rational Factor in the Idea of the Divine and Its Relation to the Rational*, 2nd ed., trans. John W. Harvey (London: Oxford University Press, 1950), esp. 12–40.

A second confusion, and one not unrelated to the first, concerns not the nature of mystery but the nature of theology. Particularly in the modern West, where Theology (note the capital *T*) may be best known as one discipline among many others in the curriculum of academic institutions, it is not at all uncommon to treat theologians as those who seek the right answers to religious or theological questions, just as we treat historians as those who seek answers to historical questions or mathematicians as those who seek answers to mathematical questions. Ours is a culture of technicians, whose task it is to understand a problem in order to solve it. Not understanding a problem—that is, having a *mystery* on our hands—means that we will not know how to fix it. Or even if the inquiry is not directed toward a problem that needs to be fixed, still we want to *understand* it as clearly and distinctly as we can. And theologians often find themselves fitted into this mold, especially by students and others who are curious about religion and who want to understand and master it as they have understood and mastered other areas of knowledge.

But we would do well to consider "theology" from another angle. The word "theology" comes originally from two Greek words, *theos* and *logos*. Consider the latter first. *Logos* is the Greek word for "word." It can refer to the word on a page, or the word whispered in the ear, or the word formulated in the mind but unexpressed. Of course, a word is not simply an arbitrary arrangement of sounds or letters. "Book" is a word because it *means* something: the thing you are currently reading. And "pook" is not a word because it does not mean anything (except in some privately developed language, in which it becomes a word precisely by being assigned a meaning). So *logos* refers not simply to the word as written or spoken or thought, but to the *meaning* of the word. Indeed, since meaning often attaches to words only in particular contexts or clauses or sentences, *logos* implies not just a meaningful word, but a larger meaningful setting in which meaningful words have their meaning. This larger setting could be a sentence, or a paragraph, or an essay, or a focused body of literature. Thus *logos* is extended to refer not just to a meaningful word about something, but also to the whole mass of words that come together to form a coherent arena of discourse that one might study—for instance, "socio-*logy*," which is the study of social forces, or "psycho-*logy*," which is the study of the inner person (Greek, *psyche*).

But now let us go one step further. *Logos* refers not only to a word, or to the meaning of the word, or to the larger world of discourse that supports that meaning, but also to the human faculty that is able to grasp that meaning—to reason or rationality. This connection is revealed in the link between the Greek *logos* and our English word "logic." It is no accident that many human cultures have regarded our capacity to reason, to perceive and work with meaning, as a defining trait of humanity. As we begin to reason, to think in an integrated or coherent fashion, about a thing, we bring to bear on that thing what is central to our humanness. We apply *ourselves* to it in a way that brings out the fullest understanding, appreciation, and response. The word *logos* suggests this full, complete engagement of me in the rich depth of my humanness. But full engagement with what?

In the case of theology, with *theos*, with "God." The Greek term need not imply a capital G, since a household deity or an idol may be a *theos*. But when Christians use the word "theology," no such diminished association is tolerable. Moreover, the one God whom Christians wish to study is no mere item of interest, however complex; no impersonal object, however alive or active. God, according to Christianity, is the supreme Subject, not just a person, but *the* Person, from whom all other persons—including the studier!—are derived. It may be that *logos* rightly applies itself to all sorts of objects to understand and appreciate them, but here human *logos* is summoned to its highest challenge, and it promises to be fully outstripped.

Does this work of theology sound like a simple quest to get the correct answers about a certain subject matter? Or like an effort to understand a thing in order to solve problems? Surely not. Persons are never problems to be solved (even if, in our weaker moments, we are tempted to treat them as if they were). A man wants to understand his wife not so that he can fix her, but so that he can love her. He wants to appreciate her more fully, to perceive intricate subtleties and beauties that are not readily evident to a superficial glance. Indeed, if his marriage needs "fixing," it is very likely to be because he has spent more time trying to fix his wife than trying to know and love her. If this is true of a relationship between human persons whose life and significance are on par with one another, how much more will it be when we as creatures approach the Person who is the living God, the source of all created personhood?

If theology is really to involve the fullest *logos* applied to the truest *theos*, then it begins to look as if "getting the right answers" or "solving the puzzles" cannot be the authentic task of the theologian. There will, of course, be "right answers." To abandon the distinction between truth and falsehood would be not to maximize *logos*, but to sacrifice it from the very outset. Yet the rightness of the answers will have to consist in something more than descriptive fidelity, since there will be no ordinary, created object to be simplistically described. God is not a puzzle, and to relate rightly to him is not to analyze or classify or master, but to worship. It is in this spirit that the Eastern Orthodox Christian tradition has always insisted that, while correct theological formulations are crucial to one's being a Christian, no amount of correct formulating can make one a theologian. A theologian, in the technical sense, is a person who has *seen the very face of God*. Following such a definition might quickly thin the ranks of "theologians" in our seminaries and colleges.

Even if we set aside such a technical designation, we are still aware that the goal of genuine theology is not to solve puzzles, but to know God. And if God is in fact the kind of reality that Christians have proclaimed him to be, then there can be no conflict between the pursuit of "theology" and the reality of "mystery." Indeed, it might start to surprise us that the two would ever have been separated in the first place. Mystery must always be reckoned with in theological reflection. Of course, there are different ways of "reckoning" with mystery, some more philosophically nuanced, others more popular or experiential. But whatever approach one adopts, the reason Christians want to understand the mystery of God is not merely that they may set the metaphysical record straight, but that they may live and worship well—and life and worship depend on a right relation to a divine person more than on a right analysis of cosmic metaphysics.

So, to repeat, the task of this book is to explicate the notion of mystery theologically. The goal is not merely that we should get our theological formulations right, but also and more significantly that we should get ourselves right; not that we should master theology, but that we should be mastered by the *theos* whom theology must approach. To borrow another image from C. S. Lewis, we may say that theology is like a map: its purpose lies not in itself but in where it can get us to.[3] In a word, the goal of theology is *worship*, and our contention is that no theology that is not ultimately oriented toward the living, obedient worship of God can be fully or finally satisfying.

Guiding Assumptions and Overall Plan

It might be wise here at the outset to spell out a few of the guiding assumptions that underlie this book. In the first place, as already noted and as will become clear as the work proceeds, we as authors and (prospective) theologians are committed to the distinction between truth and falsehood in matters theological. We are sensitive to the dangers of a mysticism that, as the old quip goes, begins in "mist," centers in "I," and ends in "schism." In particular, while there may be a certain "mist" in approaching any God worthy of the name, this cannot be a mist that confuses Creator with creature, or that undermines the distinction between orthodoxy and heresy, or that otherwise casts aside the "faith which was once for all delivered to the saints" (Jude 3 NKJV). We believe that there is a genuine, full-blooded truth to be articulated, and any approach to mystery that loses the truthfulness of theology has fundamentally missed the mark.

Second, we believe that the truth theology seeks is normatively displayed in the biblical texts that God himself has given to the people of God. No attempt will be made here to defend the divine inspiration of these texts, but we do take it for granted, and we seek an understanding of the mystery of God that grows out of and is faithful to God's revelation of himself in his Word.

Third, our approach to theological mystery attempts to take seriously not only what God has revealed in the biblical texts but also what God has

---

3. C. S. Lewis, *Mere Christianity* (1952; repr., New York: Simon & Schuster, 1980), 136.

explicated in the history and tradition of the church. Neither of us is prepared to say that Tradition (with a capital *T*) is infallible, and in this respect we show our roots in Protestant evangelicalism. Indeed, the book is addressed largely, though not exclusively, to fellow evangelicals. Yet we think it would be very, very surprising if some "self-evident" truth of Scripture, having been overlooked or distorted or obscured by millions of faithful, God-fearing, Bible-believing Christians for two millennia, should suddenly become plain to some solitary Christian who, after reading his or her Bible, is thereby endowed with the authority to correct the historic errors of Christendom. It is *possible* that such a thing could happen, but we think appeal to Scripture *against* the historic testimony of the church ought to be a last resort—and one that we have not been driven to here. Whether one thinks of tradition as a "source" of theology or not, it seems to us that it certainly should be regarded as a crucial "re-source" for theology.[4]

In this respect, our approach to theology is likely to be more irenic in spirit than some readers will appreciate. Convinced of the Spirit's ongoing guidance of God's people wherever and whenever they are located, we wish to take seriously the theological conclusions of *all* of God's people whenever the opportunity presents itself. Part of the reason a proper understanding of divine mystery seems to us to be so valuable is that it allows us to understand why different groups of Christians can see certain theological truths in such wildly different ways, or can even see different theological truths altogether—and it allows us to understand this phenomenon without always having to relegate one or the other of the competing views to the scrap heap, with a pious, "Ah, they must not have loved God as much as we do, or God would not have let them be deluded into such a heinous error." There is, of course, such a thing as "theological error" (see our first assumption above), and it is undoubtedly possible for Christians to fall into it. Indeed, which of us wishes to insist too confidently that he or she is entirely immune? Nevertheless, it is a grave matter to say of a long-standing, Christ-honoring, fruit-producing tradition that it is really just such-and-such a heresy. Perhaps it is so, but we think it important to ask whether there are other, more plausible explanations of theological diversity.

Partly for this reason, we hope that readers who would not describe themselves as evangelicals will still find the book to be instructive and enriching. Our aim, as we understand it, is not a narrowly evangelical one, but one common to all of orthodox Christianity for the last two millennia.

The overall plan of the book is simple, and it builds directly on the metaphor introduced above. God, according to Christianity of every stripe, is the supreme mystery, a blinding sun too bright to look at, but the source of

---

4. This formulation is that of Gabriel Fackre, *The Christian Story: A Narrative Interpretation of Basic Christian Doctrine* (Grand Rapids: Eerdmans, 1978), 20.

illumination that allows us to see everything else on the landscape. In part 1, we shall investigate this "blinding sun" and attempt to articulate an understanding of God that does justice to this central feature of the divine reality. In part 2, we shall turn our attention to the landscape that this sun illuminates. From a wide variety of possibilities, we have chosen several theological loci at which we think the nature of God as mystery influences theological conclusions deeply. Some of these loci are relatively standard points at which divine mystery is often invoked (e.g., the incarnation); others are more controversial (e.g., the nature of salvation).

All of part 2 is intended to be suggestive and provocative, to invite conversation and interaction, and in this sense part 2 is less definite or conclusive than part 1. This might seem odd, insofar as it is in part 1 that we deal with mystery itself, and one would expect this discussion to be the less definite one. But it is not so. The *reality* of mystery is very definite indeed. It is the precise *application* of mystery to our intellectual and practical lives that will prompt the real questions for most of us. These questions are made all the more pressing by the distressing fact that it is sinners who are asking them, and to be a sinner is inevitably to be more or less confused and more or less self-destructive. So our effort in part 2 is to examine, sometimes more theoretically and sometimes more practically, how the reality of mystery turns out to be relevant to the concrete ways we redeemed sinners do theology in our families, in our churches, in our academic institutions, and in our world. We hope that perceiving this relevance can lead all of us to a theological posture that is increasingly more humble and confident and reverent: more humble, because it gladly acknowledges that the God it approaches is past finding out; more confident, because it has finally ceased to rely on perfect dogmatic completion for its assurance; and more reverent, because it sees clearly that the aim of all theology is not that our answers may be correct, but that our hearts may be bowed in rightful worship.

Part 1

The
SUN

1

The MEANING
of MYSTERY

Mystery is the vital element of Dogmatics. . . . Dogmatics is concerned with
nothing but mystery, for it does not deal with finite creatures, but from beginning to end raises itself above every creature to the Eternal and Endless
One himself.

Herman Bavinck[1]

We are not now discussing possible ways of understanding the text. . . . It can
only be understood in ways beyond words; human words cannot suffice for
understanding the Word of God. What we are discussing and stating is why it
is not understood. I am not speaking in order that it may be understood but
telling you what prevents it being understood.

Augustine[2]

1. Herman Bavinck, *The Doctrine of God*, trans. and ed. William Hendriksen (1951; repr.,
Carlisle, PA: Banner of Truth Trust, 1977), 13.
2. Augustine, Sermon 117.3 (*WSA* 3 4:210), quoted in *Ancient Christian Commentary on
Scripture: John 1–10* (New Testament IVa), ed. Joel C. Elowsky (Downers Grove, IL: Inter-
Varsity, 2006), 10.

There are many ways to describe the sort of project that this book undertakes, and the word "mystery" would not necessarily appear in many of them. We have chosen the term both because it is commonly used in theology and also—perhaps even more so—because of its open-endedness. It definitely points to something, but to something that is not immediately clear, or rather to something that is clear precisely in a depth or an intensity or an immensity that makes even its clarity hard to pin down. In this way, "mystery" seems to open us up to . . . well . . . we do not quite know what it opens us up to. To something exciting and stimulating, no doubt, but also to something challenging and perhaps a bit frightening. We do not really know what is in store. And this is exactly where a fully Christian understanding of God should begin.

However, the term "mystery" has certain drawbacks, most notably the fact that it is used very flexibly in the English language. So we must begin by clarifying what we mean by it, so that we can then go on to describe (as best we can) the majestic God to whom it points.

Not Knowing and Knowing

We may distinguish no fewer than five significantly different senses in which the word "mystery" is used, and these different senses involve very different approaches to the mystery of the living God. All of these different meanings have something in common: they all refer to that which, in the language of Webster's dictionary, "resists or defies explanation." But things can resist or defy explanation in many ways, for many reasons, and with many responses expected.

First, and perhaps most obviously, a "mystery" might simply be *an intriguing puzzle*. We already noted this usage in our introduction. In this case, "mystery" refers to a state of affairs in which something is unknown and must be figured out, as expressed paradigmatically in detective fiction. This sort of mystery defies explanation in the sense that we do not yet have enough information to allow us to see the whole picture. We have certain clues, but they are not numerous or detailed enough to allow the sort of comprehensive explanation that would solve the puzzle, so that the true criminal can be arrested. To solve the puzzle, we (or the detectives) must do more investigating—and so we might refer to mystery in this sense as "investigative mystery." The whole goal is to investigate and thus to solve the puzzle, to know what happened. This sense of "mystery" is often at work even when strange or uncanny phenomena are involved, as when we speak of the Bermuda Triangle or of the origins of Stonehenge as "mysteries" (though there may be other factors at work here as well). These are things that we do not fully understand, but we are trying to understand. By means of available clues and creative thinking, we are trying to solve the puzzle.

Now some people who have a philosophical bent are interested in investigating the "mystery of God" in just this way. There is currently much discussion among philosophers of religion about the so-called hiddenness of God—that is, about the apparent lack of evidence for the existence of God. "Why is God hidden?" they ask. Some critics of Christianity argue that the hiddenness of God is a strong argument that God (in the traditional sense) does not exist at all; many Christians argue that the evidence for God's existence is available to those who are willing to see it, or that there are good reasons for the evidence to be as ambiguous as it seems to be.[3] Pretty clearly, thinkers on both sides of this debate are dealing with the hiddenness of God as a mystery in the investigative sense. There is something to be discovered, a question to be answered: Does God exist? We have certain bits of evidence, certain clues, that we must put together into a comprehensive explanation, and we are trying to show that one comprehensive explanation (say, the theistic one) is better than the others.

This philosophical discussion is a significant one for many people, both Christian and non-Christian, but we will not be pursuing it here. Our point is simply to note the *kind* of mystery that is involved, namely, an investigative mystery, in which the aim is to solve the puzzle. But let us consider a second and very different sense of "mystery."

According to the most common (though not the only) biblical usage, "mystery" denotes *a marvelous plan or purpose that God has revealed* for creation. The emphasis on revelation is particularly significant, for in Scripture a "mystery" is almost always something that has been made known. Even in cases where the investigative sense is still present, such as when the young prophet Daniel must interpret the mystery (*rāz*) of Nebuchadnezzar's dream (Dan. 2:18), the mystery ends up not being solved but being "revealed" (see Dan. 2:19, 30, 47; see also Rev. 1:20; 17:7). This connection to revelation is even more forceful in the New Testament, where, for instance, Jesus speaks of the apostles as those who have "been given the mystery [*mystērion*][4] of the kingdom of God" (Mark 4:11 NASB). Jesus is not saying that the apostles have been given a puzzle to solve or a question to answer. If anything, the mystery *is* the answer, so that the apostles are, so to speak, "in on the secret."

Yet oddly enough, the mystery remains a mystery as well, and so it is not just a "secret." This is both surprising and crucial. If the kingdom were simply a secret in the normal sense, then the apostles, having been "given" the secret, would be among the insiders—they would be "in the know." Therefore,

---

3. Recent discussion has been occasioned, or at least given fresh impetus, by J. L. Schellenberg's *Divine Hiddenness and Human Reason* (Ithaca, NY: Cornell University Press, 1993), which makes the case that the phenomenon of hiddenness itself provides compelling evidence that the Judeo-Christian God does not exist. For a fine sampling of the ongoing debate from many of its most significant participants, see Daniel Howard-Snyder and Paul K. Moser, eds., *Divine Hiddenness: New Essays* (Cambridge: Cambridge University Press, 2002).

4. Or "mysteries"—see the parallels in Matt. 13:11 and Luke 8:10 (NASB), where the plural, *mystēria*, is used.

although the mystery would still be mysterious *to others*, it would no longer be mysterious *to them*—it would no longer defy *their* reason. Yet this is clearly not what we find in the Gospels, for the apostles go through most of the gospel story utterly confused and befuddled by the mystery that they now supposedly know. True, part of their problem is no doubt that their conventional Jewish expectations about the kingdom continue to lead them astray. But note that even as the story continues, even after the resurrection and the coming of the Spirit at Pentecost, even after the apostles have begun to preach Christ with all boldness and authority, the mystery remains a mystery. The apostle Paul, who explicitly insists that to him "the mystery was made known . . . by revelation" (Eph. 3:3 NRSV) and whose whole commission is precisely to make known "the mystery that has been hidden throughout the ages and generations but has now been revealed" (Col. 1:26 NRSV)—even this apostle is happily ready to confess, "O the depth of the riches and wisdom and knowledge of God! How unsearchable are his judgments and how inscrutable his ways!" (Rom. 11:33 NRSV). For Paul, the marvelous plan of God is not an investigative mystery that is solved once it is communicated. Instead it is communicated precisely *as* a mystery.

This usage persists with some consistency all through the New Testament, as various aspects of mystery, or various related mysteries, are specified: the hardening of Israel is a mystery (Rom. 11:25); the final resurrection of the dead is a mystery (1 Cor. 15:51); the summing up of all things in Christ is a mystery (Eph. 1:9); the inclusion of the gentiles in the church is a mystery (Eph. 3:4, 9); the union of husband and wife as a picture of Christ and the church is a mystery (Eph. 5:32); "Christ in you, the hope of glory" is a mystery (Col. 1:27); "Christ himself, in whom are hidden all the treasures of wisdom and knowledge" is "God's mystery" (Col. 2:2–3 NRSV). In every one of these passages, mystery is linked decisively with its revelation, its being made known, and yet the mystery does not cease to be mysterious as a result. The mystery is in some sense established, not eliminated or solved, by its revelation. We shall refer to this somewhat paradoxical biblical usage as "revelational mystery." A revelational mystery is one that remains a mystery even after it has been revealed. It is precisely in its revelation that its distinctive character as mystery is displayed.

Now one is immediately struck by the contrast between this second sense of mystery and the first, for an investigative mystery revolves very intentionally around what is *unknown*, whereas a revelational mystery revolves around what is *known*. The whole fascination of a detective story lies in trying to solve the puzzle, and when one knows the solution the mystery is dissolved—it is no longer a mystery; it has lost its mainspring. But the fascination of many of the New Testament mysteries lies in their peculiar character even after they have been revealed. This unusual character explains why the response appropriate to revelational mysteries is so distinctive. A revelational mystery excites wonder, awe, amazement, astonishment. Think again about the mysteries that pertain to the gospel. We understand the good news, and yet it continues to overwhelm us by its elaborate intricacy, its unanticipated beauty, its stunningly benevolent glory. This is the way a revelational mystery works: we know, and yet the mystery remains.

Varieties of Revelational Mystery

It is not very hard to see how the mystery of God can be construed as a revelational mystery, since Scripture itself establishes the precedent. Yet we must now go a bit deeper, for it turns out that there are important differences among varying kinds of revelational mystery. Consider this question: What is it that would allow something that is known to remain a mystery nevertheless? The three possible answers to this question will introduce our three remaining senses of "mystery."

One possibility is that what is made known in the revelation is simply too extensive or too complicated to be drawn coherently together. Thus, we might speak, thirdly, of "extensive mystery" and use this phrase to refer to a *quantitative inexhaustibility*, a magnitude or an internal complexity that puts some proposed objects of knowledge out of reach. The marvelous elaborateness or beauty of the gospel seems to signal a kind of extensive mystery, but we also find this sense in much more prosaic contexts. "The workings of this DVD player are a mystery to me" means that the inner mechanisms of the contraption are so complicated and intricate that we cannot make sense of them. We can probably understand some aspects of the gadget; we might be able to understand any of its particular aspects if it is properly explained. But we find ourselves unable to hold these many particular aspects together in any way that would count as comprehensive "understanding."

We have referred to extensive mystery as "quantitative" in nature. Of course, an investigative mystery is quantitative too, but only in the sense that an *insufficient* quantity of information is available. This paucity of information is exactly why the mystery is not yet solved. With extensive mystery, however, we have an *excess* of information. It is all available; it has all been made known— but it is too much for us to grasp. Of course, this excess is often relative to the personal characteristics of the knower. The DVD player that is a mystery to an academic may not be too much for an electronics whiz kid. Yet every finite person, however brilliant or gifted, will reach a limit at some point, and it is at just this point that a mystery in this third sense materializes. An extensive mystery, therefore, defies explanation because of our limitation as knowers— because of what philosophers call our "epistemological" limitation (from the Greek word for "knowledge"). Unlike investigative mystery, the difficulty here results not from a lack of information, but from our inability to take it all in.

Now the mystery of God can easily be understood in this quantitative or extensive way too. Christianity insists that God has revealed himself—yet he nevertheless remains "too much to take in." There are always new and unforeseen facets to be explored, new elements to be considered. And of course, this is hardly surprising. God is, after all, infinite, and we are finite, and so it makes great sense to say that the mystery of God is an extensive mystery.

Yet one wonders whether the quantitative explanation is the whole story. Do we really want to say that knowledge of God is like other knowledge, except that God is bigger or more complex than other things? To put it crassly, do we call God a mystery for the same reason that we call the DVD player a mystery? It seems that something else must be going on. It is not only that there is *too much* of God for us to grasp. There is also something about the *nature* of God that seems ungraspable. Even when we say that God is "infinite," we seem to mean something more than quantitative extension, for one does not get to infinity by adding a little more and a little more. In this sense, infinity itself is *qualitatively* different from finitude. If this is so, then the thing that keeps us from exhausting the mystery of God cannot be only our epistemological limits. God is not just beyond our limits; God is *limitless*. An adequate account of the mystery of God, then, ought to be not just extensive or quantitative. It must also include qualitative elements.

So let us turn to a fourth sense, one that might be more attractive to many evangelicals. People sometimes use the term "mystery" to refer to a certain *nonrational opaqueness* in some experiences, a qualitative uniqueness that rules out rational explaining or "knowing" in the nature of the case. We might give to this kind of mystery the inelegant name of "facultative mystery," for its central feature is that it seems somehow to resist rational, analytical investigation and to call instead for some nonrational avenue of approach—that is, for approach by means of a different, nonrational human faculty.

Of course, such a careful, precise description of this sort of mystery already seems too analytical. The whole point is that a mystery like this does not lend itself to *thinking*. Consider, for example, what is sometimes described as the "mystery of suffering." Everyone "knows" (in the normal, rational sense) what it is to suffer, but "knowing" is not really the point. The mystery that is involved is not connected to a rational "knowing," but to the existential reality of the suffering itself. Or in the religious sphere, consider what is often referred to as "mystical" experience, what Rudolf Otto has taught us to call experience of the "numinous." We find ourselves confronted with a distinctive, inimitable, and somehow sacred phenomenon that cannot be mastered by a description or an analysis. Explanation is impossible not because of too little or too much information, not for any quantitative reason, but because the quality of the thing does not allow that kind of approach. The reality cannot be boiled down into neat, rational propositions—or even into words that have definite, clear-cut meanings. The attempt to "explain" the experience, or the thing experienced, leaves us with the feeling that we have missed its essence. We have not explained; we have explained away—and all of the sweetness has vanished as a result.

Now, this facultative understanding of the mystery of God seems to be very common among evangelicals, and for good reason. Even if we are suspicious of what sometimes passes for "mysticism," we all want Christians not merely to know facts or doctrines *about* God, but to know God himself, in some sort of personal experience. In this respect, lived experience trumps mere analytical understanding every time. Jesus offers Nicodemus not doctrinal instruction but new birth (John 3); Paul comes to the Corinthians not with intellectual achievements but with spiritual power (1 Cor. 2). Along these same lines, many of the more liturgical Christian traditions have emphasized the significance, for instance, of beauty as a religious category, such that medieval cathedrals or contemporary stained glass, Orthodox iconography or Wesleyan hymnody, all provide nonrational means through which God communicates with his people. All of this reminds us that God is not to be analyzed or explained but received and embraced. The facultative mystery of God is exactly that living, experiential embrace that transcends a dry intellectualism and that engages the whole person with existential depth instead.

Yet common as this approach is, it too has its limitations. For one thing, a facultative mystery, by its very definition, excludes approach by means of reason—and it thereby excludes theology in the traditional sense too, or at least sharply devalues it. Is this move really one that we want to make? Even if some evangelicals find themselves less than enthusiastic about theology as a polemical academic discipline, to question the legitimacy of the theological enterprise in this wholesale fashion would put us seriously out of step with the church throughout the ages. Many of the Christians throughout history who have gone deepest in the spiritual life have also been articulate exponents and ardent defenders of the doctrinal framework that supported their spirituality (one thinks of the apostle Paul, for instance). In other words, it is not as though rationally cogent doctrine were one thing and the mystery of God were another. The two seem to interpenetrate in ways that construing the mystery of God only in the facultative sense cannot account for.

Furthermore, there is an additional loss, and perhaps a surprising one, in understanding the mystery of God exclusively in the facultative sense. For if, in one respect, associating mystery exclusively with nonrational experience tends to devalue theology, yet in another it tends to devalue mystery itself. Consider: Nonrational opaqueness is really an aspect not just of certain extraordinary religious experiences but of *all* experience as such. We can think about what a rose is or about how our noses work when we smell a rose, but that is not at all the same as *experiencing* a rose, as actually smelling it. The concrete experience of smelling is an utterly irreducible, nonrational phenomenon, one that no amount of thinking and analyzing and understanding can ever provide. And in this sense it is a facultative mystery. Thus we come to the problem. While construing the mystery of God as facultative does allow God to be mysterious, all of our other experiences, even the most commonplace, turn out to be mysterious in just the same way. Strictly speaking, every time we catch the aroma of old sneakers or feel a splinter in our finger or hear the horn of an automobile on the highway, we have run up against what is by definition a facultative mystery, a unique, nonrational definiteness that cannot be reduced to mere logical propositions. But, to parallel a question asked a few paragraphs ago, do we really want to maintain that God is a mystery in the same sense that the smell of old sneakers is a mystery? It begins to look as if the facultative approach, by associating mystery simply with what is nonrational, makes the mystery of God something *outside* of reason, but not really something *beyond* reason.

There is yet another difficulty. By assuming that our encounter with God cannot be mediated by reason, this approach implies that the encounter must be mediated by some other human faculty—by some other aspect of our humanness *that is more adequate to the task*. But is there such an aspect? How could there be? What organ or capacity or element in us could possibly be adequate to perceive or to convey the living God in all his fullness? Feeling? Aesthetic awareness? Conscience? Sensation? Intuition? Some distinctive "religious faculty"? If reason is not adequate to the task, what human capacity is *more* adequate? This is a very important point, for in discussions of divine mystery, one often hears appeal to feeling over thinking, or to the rather indefinite "heart" over the all-too-definite "head"—as if emotional or intuitive or generally "heartfelt" commerce with God were not subject to the same frailness as intellectual commerce. But surely every human faculty that confronts the divine mystery will ultimately prove to be insufficient. The mystery of God, in its truest sense, will be great enough and terrible enough to surpass them all.

And so we come to our fifth sense of "mystery," one more radical and therefore more elusive and difficult to portray, but one that will be crucial for the remainder of this book. Let us begin with an analogy. Picture in your mind a simple, everyday circle. A circle is not, by ordinary geometrical standards, a very mysterious thing. It does not typically resist or defy explanation. On the contrary, with only a rather minimal knowledge of two-dimensional geometry, you could make all sorts of precise, even exhaustive mathematical statements about it, about its area or its circumference or whatever, and then there would not be much more to know about it. Reason (i.e., the logic of mathematics) clearly does apply here, and with its application mystery is largely eliminated.

But consider now another sense in which a particular circle might be a mystery. Suppose the circle in question is not just a circle; suppose it is one end of a cylinder. And suppose further that we called in an expert geometer who happened to be what Edwin Abbott used to call a "Flatlander," that is, a two-dimensional person who lives in and perceives only two dimensions (length and width but not depth). Now we are faced with a very different situation. The two-dimensional geometer can attend with all diligence to the figure before him. He can make all of the same calculations about this figure that we mentioned before. In principle he can know everything two-dimensional that there is to know about it. Yet for this Flatlander, there is still "more" about the figure that remains outside of his two-dimensional perception, namely, the third dimension, which makes this figure not just a circle but a cylinder.

Now this additional dimension constitutes a very peculiar kind of "more," one not easily susceptible of rational explanation for our two-dimensional friend, and hence a kind of mystery. Indeed, unless he took our word for it, it is hard to see how he could know what this odd thing called a "cylinder" with its additional dimension of "depth" even is. How should we try to explain it? There is here no quantitative excess in the normal two-dimensional sense: This is not the "more" that an additional circle or a nearby rectangle would provide. Neither does this "more" refer to some qualitative otherness that would make geometrical reasoning irrelevant. The "more" of the three-dimensional cylinder involves an unanticipated overthrow of all of the categories that a two-dimensional geometer has available. It is a radical transcendence not just of the individual circle but of two-dimensional geometry itself.

This analogy points us to our fifth and final sense of mystery, which we shall call "dimensional mystery." A dimensional mystery is characterized by *an unclassifiable superabundance* that transcends but does not invalidate rational exploration. Rational exploration is certainly possible, and yet it is pursued in light of a deeper or denser or more complex substantiality than reason is familiar with.

Clear or uncontroversial examples are harder to come by here than with our other kinds of mystery, for the very good reason that every instance can, in principle, be rejected as simple nonsense—just as a two-dimensional geometer might reject the whole apparently self-contradictory notion of cylinders. Thus the only really *clear* instances of dimensional mystery will be those hypothetical instances that show us how a lesser consciousness—one that lacks some perspective or capacity that normal human consciousness possesses—would be unable to see something that is perfectly obvious to us. The two-dimensional consciousness of a Flatlander is one such hypothetical example.

A similar example might be drawn from an imaginative consideration of the symbolism that gives many literary masterpieces their enduring power. Consider Shakespeare's *Hamlet*. One could understand the play simply as a sad story about an ill-fated Danish family—indeed, one could give a reasonable account of the entire story in those terms. But when one perceives as well the inexorable destruction that vengeance wreaks on all who are touched by it, one sees the story in a new light. The character Hamlet is now not just a man with whom to sympathize; he is also a living embodiment of vengeance, both as perpetrator and as victim. There is a greater significance or substantiality to Hamlet than the casual reader perceives. Thus the character is not just himself; he is also "more." Of course, careful readers can understand these larger implications; we might even hesitate to think of this symbolism as a kind of mystery. But that is because we are the ones who create or perceive the story's meaning. The characters in the story, by contrast, *are* the meaning, and that is a rather different thing. It seems likely that if Hamlet himself were ever to get a glimpse of the moral or even metaphysical "density" of his own character, he would find it very difficult to think through in any comprehensive way. For him, the term "mystery" might be a rather exact description.

What about actual, nonhypothetical instances of dimensional mystery? Even if they are likely to be disputed, we can recognize various cases where the word "mystery" is used in this fashion, especially in the sphere of religion. For example, the secretive cults of ancient Greece and Egypt known as "mystery religions" seem to have approached mystery in this way. Their mysteries were not just truths or propositions; they were in some sense powers, which granted the initiate access to higher worlds. Again, when Roman Catholics speak of the "mysteries of the rosary," they have in mind events in the career of Christ (such as the nativity or the crucifixion) that serve as the subject for meditative prayer precisely because they have a kind of inexplicable and inexhaustible depth or power. Or again, many Christian traditions readily refer to sacramental practices and rites (especially the Lord's Supper or Eucharist) as "mysteries," and they mean that these practices are bearers of a significance or a power or a depth that goes beyond their obvious rational content. What one makes of any of these claims is an open question that will depend on one's own theological leanings. But the kind of mystery that lies behind these claims is evidently dimensional.

With this last label in place, our proposed taxonomy of the various "kinds" of mystery is now complete, and it can be handily summarized in the following diagram.

Figure 1 – Kinds of Mystery

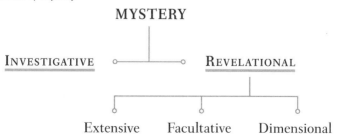

And now we are in a position (at last) to think with some degree of clarity about the subject of this book. When we speak of "mystery" from now on, we are speaking of a revelational mystery that is dimensional in character—that is, of a mystery that is impenetrable even after it is revealed, not by virtue of its quantitative magnitude, nor by virtue of its existential uniqueness, but by virtue of an unimaginable depth or density that transcends our rational capacities and all of our other capacities as well. And to speak of the "mystery *of God*" is to insist that, for finite creatures like ourselves, God the Creator, the living God of Christian faith, is just this kind of mystery.

A Hopeless Endeavor?

But wait. It seems that we have a problem. If God really is this sort of mystery, this "unclassifiable superabundance," then a book whose subject is this God looks to be a very precarious enterprise indeed. For we must admit from the outset that we have no capacity, no resource of any kind, for bridging the gulf between ourselves and that unimaginable "other" that we wish to know. In fact, it appears that our whole interest in "knowing" God has been utterly sabotaged by the nature of the God we must know. On this view, God turns out to be not just mysterious but sheerly and absolutely unknowable. If God is a mystery in this radical sense, must we not simply confess our ignorance and remain silent?

The answer is no. Human reason *can* and *should* be applied to God. If this sounds like an audacious claim in view of what we have discussed so far, then read on, for the next several chapters will investigate the claim more carefully. But even now, consider three points.

First, recall that the dimensional mystery of God is a species of revelational mystery. That is to say, our affirmation that God is a mystery depends not on what we do *not* know (this would be an investigative mystery), but on what we *do* know. The mystery of God has been revealed. It is true that it has been revealed *as* a mystery, but its ongoing character as mystery in no way undermines the efficacy of the revelation itself. We might find it difficult—indeed, we *shall* find it difficult—to understand exactly how "knowledge" and "mystery" relate to one another in the matter called "knowing the mystery of God," but the one thing we cannot do is to begin using "mystery" in a despairingly investigative sense, as describing our sheer, hopeless ignorance. In the nature of the case, a revelational mystery cannot be hopeless in this fashion. It carries within it the hint that mystery and rational knowledge are not opposed in quite the obvious, straightforward way we might initially expect.

Second, as we have noted above and will see in more detail in chapters 2 and 3, both Scripture and subsequent Christian history are chock-full of men and women whose zealous commitment to God involved exactly this juxtaposition of mystery and knowledge. From the books of Moses, from the Prophets, from the Gospels, from the Epistles, from the church fathers, from medieval theologians, from the Protestant Reformers, from contemporary evangelicals, the overwhelming picture one gets is of a faith that knows God and simultaneously confesses that God is beyond knowledge. Once again, it might be hard to pull these two elements together with unqualified consistency, but that they belong together the whole Christian witness seems to demand.

Third, perhaps surprisingly, Scripture and traditional Christian theology give us some important tools for understanding how the gulf between finite knowers and the infinite God can be faced with good hope. As we will see in chapter 4, the God who is beyond knowledge *intends* for us to know him and offers no little guidance in this provocative endeavor. To regard real knowledge of God as impossible would be to ignore much of what God has told us about ourselves and how we should live our lives.

All three of these considerations suggest that, while we have good grounds for expecting that reason will be unable to master God the Creator, we also have good grounds for believing that reason should not be abandoned as vain or worthless. No doubt one could say the same about emotion, or about intuition, or about sensation, or about any other human faculty. None will straightforwardly apply, yet none is straightforwardly ruled out. Or, to put the same thing in a more positive light, every faculty may approach God. But every faculty must approach God as God—and this means that every faculty should expect to be overwhelmed and undone by a supremacy that cannot be mastered. Since this is a book of theology, we focus on the rational faculty that engages in theological reflection. Reason, too, comes before the mystery legitimately, but she comes as a petitioner seeking her Lord's bounty, not as a judge demanding a satisfactory explanation.

This odd juxtaposition of legitimacy and humility challenges us to be on the lookout for two opposite theological errors as we proceed. We will need to avoid *both* an arrogant rationalism that denies the unspeakable greatness of God and thus loses mystery altogether, and an anti-intellectual irrational-ism that affirms mystery so quickly and uncritically that reason itself is un-dermined. Most of us probably judge one of these two errors to be the more pressing danger for contemporary believers, but it is worth noting that either one seriously cripples historic Christianity.

Furthermore, note that these two errors tend to feed upon each other in a perilously polarizing fashion. Some Christians, disenchanted with a lifeless dogmatics in which Scripture is taken as a divine fact-book that provides quick, final answers to every question, tend to be wary of "doctrine" and "theology" and to prefer the joyous life of the Spirit. Fearing the first error (rationalism), they have fallen into the second (irrationalism). Other Christians, perceiv-ing the volatility and creeping relativism that lie hidden in experience-driven "spirituality," tend to emphasize ever more vehemently the historic, doctrinal center of the faith and are hesitant about any kind of "vision" that goes deeper. Trying to avoid the second error (irrationalism), they have been ensnared by the first (rationalism). Each group sets out, quite rightly, to defend the real lifesaving gospel against the misreading perpetrated by the other side. They are like sailors battling to right a listing ship. The question is, to which side is the ship leaning? If to starboard, then those sailors who are shifting cargo to the port side of the deck are rescuing the ship. But if to port, then those same sailors moving the cargo to port are not the solution but the problem! In the same way, there are plenty of evangelicals in the twenty-first century on both sides of the theological ship, denouncing their counterparts on the other side. We tend to rush madly to our own side of the swaying deck, not perceiving that a ship can capsize in either of two directions.

Enlisting the Imagination

But what else is one to do? How can one apply reason appropriately without applying it idolatrously? How can one bow before the mystery of God without simply acquiescing to every bit of nonsense that happens to have a bowed head? The narrow path between these two errors will no doubt prove difficult to stick to, and we as authors of this book are not at all certain that we have stuck to it perfectly at every turn. But it might be helpful to have in mind an imaginative picture or two that can bring both sides of our dual affirmation together and that can therefore remind us of both errors by reminding us of both truths. Let us suggest two such images, one very ancient, the other more contemporary.

The ancient image, which has made very common reappearance throughout the history of Christian thought, is based upon the metaphor of "seeing." It is interesting to note that, while in principle every visible object can be seen (for that is what it means to be visible), it is another thing to say that *we can see* every visible object. In fact, there are some objects that we cannot see in any clear and prolonged sense, not because they are invisible, but because they are too bright for our gaze. The most common example is, of course, the bright noonday sun. The sun is visible, or at least it is not *in*visible in the common sense. Yet (as we noted in the introduction) this does not mean that we can readily see it, for its brightness dazzles our eyes, and if we do not turn away promptly we find ourselves unable to see anything whatsoever.

Now in every corner of Christian history, we find faithful Christians insisting that what the sun is to our eyes, God is to our reason. The living God is too bright for our minds to see. He dazzles us, and we are overcome. Does this make God "irrational" or "unintelligible"? Perhaps so, but only in the sense that the sun is "invisible." If we say that the sun is "invisible," we mean not that it is unavailable to our vision but that it overpowers our vision; not that

it cannot be seen but that it cannot steadfastly be looked at.[5] So also we might
say that God is "irrational," not in the sense of being below reason but in the
sense of being beyond it. God is "unintelligible" only by virtue of a supreme
intelligibility that is too great for our finite intellects to take in. The brilliance
of the divine light makes all of our knowing into a mysterious "unknowing,"
but it is an unknowing that is also a real knowing, just as having our eyes
blinded by the noonday sun is the *result* of seeing, not the *absence* of seeing.
Here is a metaphor that provides us with both of the elements that we need,
both real knowledge and real mystery. Bearing it in mind might remind us that
it is absolutely right for us to "look" rationally upon God, that God himself
intends for us to look—yet we will not be surprised when we quickly have to
look away as well.

The second imaginative picture is the metaphor of spatial dimensions referred to a few pages earlier, the image of two-dimensional persons trying to
understand a three-dimensional figure. As we saw before, Flatlanders have
none of the experiential machinery that would allow them to process sensibly
the notion of a cylinder or a sphere or a cube. For them, such oddities will
appear logically impossible—indeed, they *are* logically impossible so long
as one is considering only two dimensions. Of course, we who live in three
dimensions can easily understand these figures, but it is not hard for us to
see why Flatlanders cannot, and so we are not surprised when they reject our
three-dimensional "mysteries" as sheer nonsense.

But let us think now about a second group of Flatlanders who tend to be of
the less skeptical variety. Suppose they simply took our word for it that there
is a third dimension and that (say) six two-dimensional squares can come together to form a single three-dimensional figure called a "cube." They do not
understand how this is possible, but they are willing to recognize the limits
of their reasoning and to accept this "mystery." Might they not be tempted to
take this revelation in the wrong way? "Ah," they muse. "We always suspected
that something like this was going on. The problem with that other group
(silly rationalists!) is that they don't realize that reason applies only in two
dimensions. It is perfectly legitimate to combine and connect things in 'irrational' ways. Of course six squares can be combined into one figure! Or seven
squares can be, or ten squares, or two hundred squares! Reason just doesn't
apply in that higher dimension." Hearing a response like this, we might think
that this second group has rather missed the point. They have imagined that
three-dimensional space is a kind of irrational free-for-all in which "anything
goes" because the restraints of reason are cast aside. In actuality, of course,
this is not true. By strict rational necessity, six and only six squares can be
combined into a single three-dimensional figure. The problem with Flatlanders'

5. This contrast is derived from Louis Bouyer, *The Invisible Father: Approaches to the Mystery
of the Divinity*, trans. Hugh Gilbert (Petersham, MA: St. Bede's, 1999), 140.

attempts to understand three dimensions is not that reason does not apply but that they do not know how to apply it.

Let us return to the mystery of God. If God himself is the supreme or foundational instance of dimensional mystery, then it seems that we ought to expect God to be both reasonable and beyond reason in some way analogous to this. The problem we will face as we address the reality of God is not that reason does not apply but that we do not know how to apply it. The things of God are not internally self-contradictory, but what we say about God *would* be self-contradictory if we were speaking of the ordinary things of this world. Now this is an awkward position to be in. For it means, on the one hand, that we cannot simply dispense with reason: We should not blithely tolerate any and every bit of foolishness that happens to cloak itself in the mantle of mystery. Yet on the other hand, it means that we cannot uncritically rely on reason either, for "God's foolishness is wiser than human wisdom" (1 Cor. 1:25 NRSV), and we may very well encounter theological truths that are simply beyond reason, that appear to us as simply irrational.

Yet how can we tell the difference? There is no easy formula to answer that question. Certainly we shall have to consider the authority of any claim, how directly it is supported by God's own revelation. We shall have to consider as well how it might be related logically to other truths that involve mystery. Perhaps above all, we shall have to ask how any proposition that claims to be beyond reason helps to make sense of larger matters, allowing us to grasp more of the truth of God with depth and coherence. In other words, does it "fit"? Recall C. S. Lewis's observation that we know the bright noonday sun is in the sky not because we can see it but because by means of it we can see everything else. Does some purported theological mystery similarly allow us to "see everything else"? Would its being true shed light on other aspects of God and Scripture and the world and ourselves? When the answer is yes, we may (paradoxically) have good reason to say that we are dealing with something beyond reason.

Another way of saying the same thing, and of drawing this chapter to a close, is to say that while the mystery of God is by definition beyond rational comprehension, the *appeal* to mystery need not be. On the contrary, since God is not less than rational but more, our intention is never simply to jettison reason but to see—rationally—how God is exalted beyond it. If our argument is successful, we will often find ourselves saying, "Hmm. It seems that the acknowledgment of 'mystery' here really does make sense. If God is really God, then recognizing a limitation of reason at just this point is really the most rational thing we can do."

But before we make particular claims like these, about particular aspects of Christian doctrine, we need to consider more fully how a Christian framework invites—or even requires—us to think in ways that include mystery. Is mystery really necessary? We turn next to a biblical answer to that question.

2

The NECESSITY *of* MYSTERY

The knowledge of God given in this way through divine revelation is not from the known to the unknown, but from the hitherto unknown to the known. It is a mystery so utterly strange and so radically different that it cannot be apprehended and substantiated except out of itself, and even then it infinitely exceeds what we are ever able to conceive or spell out.

Thomas F. Torrance[1]

So soon as we become satisfied with any picture or image of God, we are in danger of idolatry: of mistaking the comprehensible image for the reality, of losing the numinousness, the mystery, the transcendent majesty of God. So soon as, consciously or unconsciously, we suppose we have grasped God, he must elude us, for he is always beyond the furthermost advance we make in knowledge about him.

Victor White[2]

---

1. Thomas F. Torrance, *The Christian Doctrine of God: One Being Three Persons* (Edinburgh: T&T Clark, 1996), 19.
2. Victor White, "God the Unknown," in *God the Unknown and Other Essays* (New York: Harper & Bros., 1956), 23–24.

W̲e have suggested in the previous chapter that there is a way of conceiving the mystery of God that stands midway between rationalism and irrationalism, a way that understands God to be both metaphysically self-consistent and also beyond the scope of any creaturely consistency, a way that both affirms the legitimacy and also undermines the autonomy of reason. We have also introduced some imaginative metaphors that can help us to see how this idea works. God is that brilliant sun that cannot be seen because of its brightness but that makes everything else visible by virtue of that same brightness. God is that extradimensional solid that relativizes our flat geometry but that does so precisely by establishing a higher geometry that includes and transcends the mathematical laws we grasp.

Perhaps this outline of divine mystery will strike some readers as self-evidently true, as exactly what the historic Christian vision of God requires. Those readers may want to consider moving on immediately to part 2, where we try to show very practically how this understanding of God affects the theological enterprise in valuable ways. This move will allow the already-convinced to begin to see how to make use of this doctrine of God without further preliminary efforts to persuade that it really *is* the Christian doctrine of God.

Other readers, however, may find themselves still in need of persuasion. They have seen (we hope) that dimensional mystery is a plausible notion, but they are rather suspicious of a new reading of God that is long on creative imagery and short on biblical substance. We think this is a very right and appropriate suspicion. So the remainder of part 1 is devoted to a more careful consideration of the biblical and historical grounds for this understanding of divine mystery. Ultimately, our contention is that, far from positing something new, we have simply taken the standard biblical view of God and spelled out its implications—and further, that we have spelled out these implications in a way that is completely consistent with the major currents of Christian theology and spirituality throughout the ages. The present chapter is devoted to sacred Scripture and the following one to the historical development of Christian thought.

The God of Creation

So what does Scripture tell us about God? An answer to this question could no doubt begin in many places, but we cannot be going far astray if we begin where the Bible itself begins, with the resounding claim that God is, quite simply, the Creator—"In the beginning God created the heavens and the earth" (Gen. 1:1). Note that, theologically speaking, God is "Creator" here with a capital C. Christians do not say merely that God is *a* creator, or that God was the first creator, or even that God is the greatest and most significant creator. God is *the Creator*, the source and origin of all things, "maker of heaven and earth and of all things visible and invisible" (as the Nicene Creed puts it). What is behind this forceful language? To answer that question, we turn to the first chapter of Genesis.

This is not, of course, the place for an exhaustive investigation of the Genesis creation narrative, or of the many and bitter controversies that continue to swirl around it. Suffice it here to say that, whatever value the text may have for historical or scientific purposes, it is plain that the theology of creation embodied in the opening chapter of Genesis reflects a vision of God and of God's world that is distinctive, departing in very decisive and provocative ways from the conventional outlook of other ancient Near Eastern cultures. One may note at least three significant emphases that are relevant for our purposes.

Divine Independence

First, Genesis 1 clearly pictures one absolute and independent God, who exists without any beginning or support, without any rivals or associates. The standard vision of the divine realm in Mesopotamian, Egyptian, and Canaanite cultures of the ancient world included a pantheon of deities, interacting and often conflicting with one another, and the standard vision of cosmic origins often included the origins of these deities themselves. By contrast, the Genesis account begins with God and God alone: It portrays no one alongside of God, and it gives no hint of any "origin" that is further back than the self-existent reality of God himself. This independent self-existence is highlighted by the fact that God creates in Genesis 1 with a simple word of command. There is no dramatic struggle between God and other forces that hinder the creative act; there are no complicated ritualized incantations by means of which the Creator taps into a power greater or more basic or other than himself. Instead, as the psalmist writes with a simplicity that reflects Genesis, "he spoke, and it came to be; he commanded, and it stood firm" (Ps. 33:9).

Divine Sovereignty

A second insight from Genesis 1 requires more development, but it is an extension of the first. Since God is absolutely independent, brooking no metaphysical rivals or associates of any sort, the narrative insists that the sovereign rule of God extends to all things and to all kinds of things, because everything that is depends upon God alone for its existence. In the beginning, God created not just a certain selection of items, but "the heavens and the earth"—that is, everything whatsoever.

This approach stands in sharp contrast to prevailing cultural expectations, where a god was likely to be associated with one isolated natural phenomenon (say, the sun) or with one specific geographical location (say, the Nile River). No such parochial limitations apply to God the Creator. In fact, even the barest association with them seems to be avoided in Genesis, as when the author

uses the unusual expression "two great lights" in Genesis 1:16 to describe the
sun and the moon that God creates. Why not simply say that God made the
sun and the moon? Perhaps because the common Hebrew names for sun and
moon (*shemesh* and *yareach*) would easily be linked to the sun god (Shamash)
and the moon god (Yarih).[3] Genesis knows nothing of localized deities like
these, for the one true God is Lord not just of sun or moon but of all creation.

We see this same universal divine rule in the biblical account of God's relationship to certain elemental powers in creation that the ancient world regarded
with reverence or dismay. For example, fertility was a ubiquitous sacred force
for all Canaanite religions. The gods might make use of this force, but it was
nevertheless an independent power that they did not create and could not
fully control. By contrast, fertility is portrayed in Genesis as a simple gift of
God, a contingent capacity that peacefully serves God's purpose by allowing
plants and animals to reproduce and fill the earth (vv. 11–12, 22). Or again,
note the reference in Genesis 1:21 to "the great sea monsters" (NASB), the
classic illustration in the ancient world of raging, destructive power. But here
in Genesis, these "monsters" are not rebellious enemies that God must subdue;
they are simply among the many creatures to which God gives life.[4] Created
by God, they are subject to his unqualified control.

Genesis goes on to show God's rule not only over every *creature* in the cosmos but also over *other kinds of rule* within the cosmos. Although the man
and the woman are portrayed as the crown of creation, and are thus granted a
much more noble position in the biblical economy than in ancient Near Eastern
alternatives (where human beings are generally presented as an irritation to or
as menial servants of the gods), it remains clear that human nobility is rooted
in humanity's subordination to God. All of the authority exercised by the man
and the woman is derived from their status as the "image" of God, and this
derivation is confirmed when God himself *commands* his image-bearers to
"subdue" the earth and "rule" over its other creatures (Gen. 1:28). Subduing
and ruling are not just the natural drive of one species to dominate another;
neither are they the autonomous effort of a particularly gifted creature to
unseat the Creator or compete with his universal reign. Instead, human rule
serves and reflects divine rule. It is part of the ordered plan of the Creator
whose uncontested will all of creation follows.

God's sovereign rule in Genesis 1 may even be said (somewhat paradoxically) to extend to the formless chaos that seems to stand opposed to it. The
first "Let there be . . ." in Genesis 1:3 is preceded in verse 2 by reference to
an "earth" and "waters" that are "formless and empty"—reference, in other
words, to an already-existing chaos that is not subject to God. This is part

3. Gordon J. Wenham, *Genesis 1–15*, Word Biblical Commentary 1 (Dallas: Word, 1987), 21.
4. Bruce K. Waltke and Cathi J. Fredricks, *Genesis: A Commentary* (Grand Rapids: Zondervan, 2001), 63. Cf. Ps. 104:24–26, where the fearful Leviathan is but one of the many creatures
God made to "frolic" in the seas.

of the reason that some biblical exegetes have objected to a formal doctrine of *creatio ex nihilo* ("creation out of nothing"): God apparently *does* create "out of something," namely, this pre-creation chaos. Yet the overall tenor of the Genesis narrative does not draw attention to this purportedly "preexisting" chaos. There is no hint that some already-established, uncreated reality sets conditions of some sort that God must simply accept. On the contrary, the narrative portrays all concrete, differentiated reality as the express result of God's creative work. The initial chaos, formlessness, and darkness are not "things" in any recognizable sense, but the *absence* of things. Only when God creates light and then separates this positive, recognizable reality from its absence (vv. 3–4) does the darkness gain some sort of definite identity, by virtue of its newly established contrast with the created light. In this sense, God "creates" the darkness (and therefore names it in v. 5) as fully as he creates the light. Similarly, though we might picture the chaotic "waters" of "the deep" in verse 2 as something like a stormy ocean, nothing recognizably like an ocean can exist until God has separated "water from water" by the creation of the dome called "sky" (vv. 6–8), and then further separated the water under the sky from the dry land (v. 9). Only then can the gathered waters be designated "seas" (v. 10), thus obtaining a definite identity by their contrast to the "earth." Prior to God's creative act, the "waters" are simply an oxymoronic embodiment of formlessness—and an embodiment that awaits and is utterly responsive to God's creative fiat.

Thus God is seen to be sovereign over the forces of chaos as completely as over anything else. Though the drama of the book of Genesis revolves in part around the horrible possibility of a return to pre-creation chaos (as, for instance, when the "floodgates of the heavens" are opened in Gen. 7:11 to unleash the great flood), even this possibility signals not an independent power of chaos against which God is constantly struggling but the freedom and independence of God, who can unmake his ordered world as easily as he made it in the first place. For all of these reasons, even if creation *ex nihilo* is not an explicit part of the narrative in Genesis 1, one can almost feel the doctrine lurking in the wings. The central thrust of creation *ex nihilo*—namely, that there is absolutely nothing that is independent of God or outside of his control—certainly is present. And so one is not at all surprised to find other biblical texts making this natural extension, so that even the primeval deep is seen to have its origin in God alone (e.g., Exod. 20:11; Neh. 9:6; Ps. 104; Heb. 11:3). The sovereign rule of God is over absolutely all that is.

Divine Glory

Growing out of the independence and sovereignty that set the biblical God apart from other ancient Near Eastern alternatives is a unique glory. This glory is mostly implicit in Genesis 1, hiding just below the surface in the consistent refrain that affirms the unqualified goodness of what God has made and that climaxes in verse 31, when God can examine the whole of creation and pronounce it all "very good." But the supreme goodness of what is made naturally reflects the glory of the Maker, and so we are hardly surprised to find throughout Scripture that reference to creation or to God as Creator is very commonly connected with the holy mandate to praise and glorify the Lord.

The praise that is associated with creation in the Bible has many emphases, flowing in and out of one another. But we may mention at least the following four elements.

1. Praise of God as Creator invariably rings with joy and merriment.

> Worship the LORD with *gladness*;
>   come before him with *joyful songs*.
> Know that the LORD is God.
>   *It is he who made us*, and we are his.
>
> Ps. 100:2–3

Or again,

> The heavens are yours, and yours also the earth;
>   *you founded* the world and all that is in it.
> *You created* the north and the south;
>   Tabor and Hermon *sing for joy* at your name.
>
> Ps. 89:11–12

2. Praise of God as Creator constantly marvels at God's glorious attributes. For instance, creation becomes the ground for celebrating God's faithfulness:

> Blessed are those whose help is the God of Jacob,
>   whose hope is in the LORD their God.
> He is the *Maker of heaven and earth*,
>   the sea, and everything in them—
> he remains *faithful* forever.
>
> Ps. 146:5–6

Creation causes us to wonder at God's wisdom:

> By *wisdom* the LORD *laid the earth's foundations*,
>   by understanding he set the heavens in place.
>
> Prov. 3:19; cf. 8:27–31

Creation prompts us to delight in God's providential care:

> How many are your works, LORD!
>   In wisdom *you made them all*;
>   the earth is full of your creatures. . . .

> All creatures look to you
>> to give them their food at the proper time.
> When you give it to them,
>> they gather it up;
> when you open your hand,
>> *they are satisfied with good things.*
>>> Ps. 104:24, 27–28

And above all, creation summons us to remember God's awesome power:

> Ah, Sovereign LORD, you have *made the heavens and the earth* by your *great power* and outstretched arm. Nothing is too hard for you!
>> Jer. 32:17

3. Praise of God as Creator unfailingly celebrates the confident security that God's people have, a security firmly grounded in God's unchallenged ability to accomplish his own purposes. Thus the prophets frequently point to God as Creator when they wish to stress the certainty of God's promises being realized, as when Isaiah introduces promises of the return from Babylon:

> This is what the LORD says—
>> your Redeemer, who formed you in the womb:
> I am the LORD,
>> the Maker of all things,
>> who stretches out the heavens,
>> who spreads out the earth by myself.
>>> Isa. 44:24

Again, those like Hezekiah who appeal to God for deliverance remember that he is Creator, and therefore that he *can* deliver:

> LORD, the God of Israel, enthroned between the cherubim, you alone are God over all the kingdoms of the earth. *You have made heaven and earth.*
>> 2 Kings 19:15; cf. Isa. 37:16

What greater security could there be than that possessed by those who can say,

> Our help is in the name of the LORD, *the Maker of heaven and earth.*
>> Ps. 124:8; cf. 121:2

4. Praise of God as Creator consistently delights in the finality or ultimacy of God himself, beyond whom there is simply nothing. When an angelic messenger in the book of Revelation needs to emphasize

the significance of a new revelation, he can do so no more forcefully than by invoking God as Creator:

> Then the angel . . . swore by him who lives for ever and ever, who created the heavens and all that is in them, the earth and all that is in it, and the sea and all that is in it, and said, "There will be no more delay."
>
> Rev. 10:5–6

When the elusive Melchizedek is ready to bestow upon Abraham (Abram) the supreme blessing, he returns to the same theme:

> Blessed be Abram by God Most High, *Creator of heaven and earth.*
>
> Gen. 14:19

When Paul describes the soaring greatness of the gospel of Christ, he, too, can soar no higher than to associate that gospel with the God who creates:

> This grace was given me: to peach to the Gentiles the boudnless riches of Christ, and to make plain to everyone the administration of this mystery, which for ages past was kept hidden in God, *who created all things.*
>
> Eph. 3:9

These references could very easily be multiplied, but they all tell the same tale. Knowing that God is the Creator of heaven and earth is never simply a matter of information. It is instead a summons—a summons to celebrate, to adore, to trust, to bow. When God is known as Creator, he is known with glad singing and with silent awe; as the loving protector and as the almighty judge; as the one who has done more than we know and who certainly will do more than we can imagine. To say that God is Creator is to say that he is utterly unique, for "all the gods of the nations are idols, but the Lord made the heavens" (1 Chron. 16:26; cf. Ps. 96:5). It is to say that there is nothing outside the scope of his rule, for "in his hand are the depths of the earth, and the mountain peaks belong to him. The sea is his, for he made it, and his hands formed the dry land" (Ps. 95:4–5). It is to say that worship belongs to him alone: "You are worthy, our Lord and God, to receive glory and honor and power, for you created all things, and by your will they were created and have their being" (Rev. 4:11).

God Exalted

Implicit in this entire picture is, of course, the conviction that God is not a creature. God is not even the biggest, strongest *possible* creature. He is the Creator. Some may think that God is like the idols of the nations, but "he who is the Portion of Jacob is not like these, for he is the Maker of all things" (Jer. 10:16; cf. 51:19). Some may associate God with the mere works of God's hands, but according to the psalmist, those works "will perish, but you remain; they will all wear out like a garment. . . . But you remain the same, and your years will never end" (Ps. 102:26–27). Some may confuse God with his prophets or messengers, but Paul and Barnabas declare, "We too are only human, like you. We are bringing you good news, telling you to turn from these worthless things to the living God, who made the heavens and the earth and the sea and everything in them" (Acts 14:15; cf. 17:24–25). Lofty angelic beings might overawe us, but still they proclaim, "I am a fellow servant with you and with your fellow prophets. . . . Worship God!" (Rev. 22:9; cf. 19:10).

Note that every created thing, however noble, however powerful, remains on the same side of the divide, with God and God alone on the other side. God is fundamentally different from any and every creature. This understanding is formulated most famously in the classic language of Isaiah's heavenly vision (which is echoed in the apocalyptic visions of Revelation) in which even the most exalted angels constantly call to one another around God's throne, "Holy, holy, holy is the LORD Almighty" (Isa. 6:3; cf. Rev. 4:8). To say that God is "holy" (Hebrew, *qadosh*; Greek, *hagios*) is to say that he is "set apart," "separate," "withdrawn," "other." It is to declare with Jeremiah, "No one is like you, LORD" (Jer. 10:6). All of God's people are called to be holy in a general sense, but in this deeper sense God stands utterly alone. "Who will not fear you, Lord, and bring glory to your name? For *you alone are holy*" (Rev. 15:4). The living God is separated by a great gulf from the frail, created things that populate our common experience.

Moreover, this gulf involves not only distance but also height. God is not just *different from* creation; he is *exalted over* creation. "The LORD is high above all nations," says the psalmist; "His glory is above the heavens" (Ps. 113:4 NASB). Divine exaltation is often explicitly related in Scripture to the concept of creation, as seen, for instance, when Isaiah describes God as follows:

> He sits enthroned above the circle of the earth,
>   and its people are like grasshoppers [exaltation].
> He stretches out the heavens like a canopy,
>   and spreads them out like a tent to live in [creation].
>
> Isa. 40:22

The same exaltation is also implicit in the common biblical awareness that God cannot be contained by created things. "Heaven is my throne, and the earth is my footstool. Where is the house you will build for me? Where will my resting place be? Has not my hand made all these things, and so they came into being?" (Isa. 66:1–2; cf. Acts 7:49–50). "But who is able to build a temple for him, since the heavens, even the highest heavens, cannot contain him?" (2 Chron. 2:6; cf. 1 Kings 8:27).

It is precisely because of this overflowing exaltation that the notion of God as Creator is so often coupled with a right and proper *fear* of the Lord. Note this linkage as God asks the rebellious house of Judah through Jeremiah, "Should you not fear me? . . . Should you not tremble in my presence? I made the sand a boundary for the sea, an everlasting barrier it cannot cross" (Jer. 5:22). Again, observe how Amos can punctuate his proclamation of appalling divine judgment with an ominous reminder about the nature of the God he represents: this is "he who forms the mountains, who creates the wind, and who reveals his thoughts to mankind, who turns dawn to darkness, and treads on the heights of the earth—the LORD God Almighty is his name" (Amos 4:13). The Creator, by virtue of being Creator, is highly exalted and ought to be feared.

God beyond Knowledge

This line of thinking comes to its climax, and to the point most relevant for our discussion, in the recurrent biblical affirmation that the Creator is not just different from creatures, not just exalted above creatures, but exalted so far above creatures that he is beyond their ken altogether. The link between God's work as Creator and this greatness that is unfathomable is found throughout the Bible. We have already noted it in Paul, who describes his apostolic task in terms of announcing the mystery that "for ages past was kept hidden in God, *who created all things*" (Eph. 3:9). When we are considering God's mystery, Paul seems to find it natural to think of God primarily as Creator. The same connection is found in Isaiah, where God invites the prophet to turn his eyes upward to the stars and then asks, "Who created all these?" The answer is quick to come: "The LORD is the everlasting God, the Creator of the ends of the earth. He will not grow tired or weary, and *his understanding no one can fathom*" (Isa. 40:26, 28). It is no surprise that God later announces through the same prophet, "My thoughts are not your thoughts, neither are your ways my ways," and then illustrates this teaching by appealing to the things that God has made, the heavens and the earth, the rain and the snow, provision of seed and of bread (Isa. 55:8–11).

But though this connection between God as Creator and God as incomprehensible mystery is found throughout Scripture, its classic expression is in the book of Job. One of the central themes of Job is, of course, humanity's inability to penetrate the divine mystery, but it is amazing how frequently this theme is conveyed by reference to God's work and rule as Creator. Job's friends make this connection (e.g., 5:9–10; 11:7–9); Job himself makes it (e.g., 9:4–10; 26:7–14); the young Elihu builds upon it repeatedly (e.g., 36:26–33; 37:5). But the chief spokesperson is God himself. Recall the stern challenge that God issues to Job at the climax of the book:

> Where were you when I laid the earth's foundation?
>   Tell me, if you understand.
> Who marked off its dimensions? Surely you know!
>   Who stretched a measuring line across it?
> On what were its footings set,
>   or who laid its cornerstone—
> while the morning stars sang together
>   and all the angels shouted for joy?
>
> Job 38:4–7

God's activity as Creator is here made to be the very foundation upon which the divine mystery is built, and also the point at which the mystery is most evident. How could Job possibly hope to understand the ways of the one who made heaven and earth? In the face of this fierce rebuke, Job finally bows in repentant worship:

> Surely I spoke of things I did not understand,
>   things too wonderful for me to know.
>
> Job 42:3

Job recognizes that to understand God the Creator aright is always to confess that he is exalted beyond our understanding.

The biblical doctrine of God, then, moves easily from speaking of God as Creator to speaking of God as beyond knowledge, until the fact that God surpasses human understanding becomes a staple of the biblical fare, even without any explicit link to his rule as Creator. We are following Scripture's own example when we say that God—or God's ways or God's understanding or God's nature—is "unsearchable" (Rom. 11:33 NIV), "inscrutable" (ESV), "undiscoverable" (Amplified), "untraceable" (HCSB), "unfathomable" (NASB). God is "beyond measure" (Ps. 147:5 NRSV), "inexhaustible" (Amplified), "infinite" (NKJV), "beyond comprehension" (NLT). God is "far beyond our reach" (Job 37:23 Message), "more than we imagine" (Job 36:26 CEV), "past finding out" (NIV), "exalted beyond our knowledge" (HCSB), "great, and we know him not" (KJV). The prophet asks, "Who has understood the mind of the Lord, or instructed him as his counselor?" and the implied answer is utterly clear, "No one!" (Isa. 40:13 NIV 1984). In opposite images, we learn that God dwells in "a dark cloud" (1 Kings 8:12) but also in "unapproachable light" (1 Tim. 6:16). Either way, no one has seen God at any time (John 1:18), for no one can see his face and live (Exod. 33:20).

Some of this biblical language no doubt reflects an inaccessibility that is rooted in human sin. God necessarily appears fierce, alien, hidden, and distant to fallen human persons, and the implication is that being cleansed from sin will eliminate this separation. After all, when the psalmist asks, "Who may ascend the mountain of the Lord? Who may stand in his holy place?" the answer is, "the one who has clean hands and a pure heart" (Ps. 24:3–4). Still, is it *only* sin that makes God unsearchable? The logic of God as Creator suggests not, for God is supremely exalted over *all* of creation, not just over *sinful* creation. Many of the texts we have been noting point in this direction. The fear of the Lord in Proverbs is commended not just to sinners but to all people who are wise. The dark cloud that drives worshipers from the temple in 1 Kings 8 is not a cloud of wrath but a cloud of glory. The reference to "unapproachable light" in 1 Timothy occurs in a context not of judgment but of eschatological glory and joy: This is why this text goes on to speak of God as the one "whom no one has seen *or can see*," that is, even in eschatological fulfillment (1 Tim. 6:16). It looks as if creatures will *always* perceive an overpowering "otherness" in the Creator—and perhaps will perceive it best when the blinding obfuscation introduced by sin is finally removed. Recall that even the sinless angels in Isaiah's vision must cover their faces and their feet in the presence of the thrice-holy God (Isa. 6).

Theological Terminology

Up to this point we have explored the biblical understanding of God using almost exclusively biblical categories and terms. It will now be useful, however, to introduce some technical theological terminology in order to make some connections with the previous chapter and also with the historical discussion that will come in the next chapter.

We may begin with "divine incomprehensibility," a phrase we have used rather sparingly up to this point, but one that does helpfully draw together many of the common biblical terms we have employed. For our purposes, "incomprehensibility" has two meanings that must be distinguished.[5] One meaning derives directly from the Latin etymology of the word: *prehendere* is literally to "grasp" or to "seize," and hence figuratively to "grasp mentally" or to "understand"; and *com-* is a prefix that indicates totality. So to "com-prehend" is to understand or grasp a thing in its totality—a sense still common in the adjectival use of the same word, namely, "comprehensive." In this sense, to say that God is incomprehensible is to say that God cannot be understood in his entirety: there is always something more to God than what we have grasped. Note the connection to what we were describing in the previous chapter as "extensive mystery," that is, to quantitative inexhaustibility: what we know of God we know precisely and clearly, but we do not know everything. Since "knowing everything" is exactly what "com-prehending" means, God is "in-comprehensible."

---

5. For a lucid account of this and related issues of terminology, see Phillip Cary, *Augustine's Invention of the Inner Self: The Legacy of a Christian Platonist* (Oxford: Oxford University Press, 2000), 57–58, and the relevant footnotes.

But as we noted in the last chapter, a merely quantitative mystery seems not to do justice to who God is, and we may now specify that it does not do justice to who God is *as the supremely exalted Creator*. God is not just bigger and stronger and wiser than we are: God the Creator is fundamentally different from what we creatures are. It is not simply that God has too many thoughts for us to manage: rather, his thoughts *are not* our thoughts, nor his ways our ways (Isa. 55:8).

And so we look to a second meaning of "incomprehensibility," one that is less etymological and more radical, for it refers not just to how much of God we can grasp but to the very possibility of grasping God at all. To be "incomprehensible" in this second sense is precisely to be ungraspable; it is to be unknowable, beyond all creaturely conception. Just as a three-dimensional object is inconceivable to a Flatlander not because of its size but because of its three-dimensional nature, so also the living God is not subject to creaturely understanding simply because God is not a creature. The parallel now is not with extensive mystery but with dimensional mystery, that unclassifiable superabundance that places the Creator beyond creaturely categories of intelligibility altogether. This does not mean that God is "unintelligible," like a logical contradiction, but it does mean that God is, in some sense, "supraintelligible," that he is outside the boundaries of what would otherwise count for intelligibility. God is *radically* incomprehensible.

A similar technical term, mentioned but not much discussed in the previous chapter, is divine "transcendence." Etymologically, "transcend" derives from the Latin *scandere*, to "climb," combined with the prefix *trans-*, which means "across" or "over" or "beyond." Hence, to say that God "transcends" the created order is to say that God "climbs beyond" creation: he does not, so to speak, stay within any of the creaturely categories we try to place him in. French evangelical Henri Blocher helpfully points out that though divine transcendence is conceptually linked to ideas like exaltation (as we have seen), its central and proper nuance is divine *otherness*, or what Blocher describes as "the absolute nonsymmetry between the Creator and everything that has come to be."[6] God is the Creator, not a creature, and therefore he cannot be classed with creatures. He is fundamentally different from anything else in reality.

Note that this way of describing "transcendence" makes it subtly different from "incomprehensibility," even from "incomprehensibility" in the second and more radical sense. When we say that God is incomprehensible we are speaking of our inability to know God fully; that is, we are speaking primarily about *us*. But to say that God is transcendent is to make a claim about the actual being of God and not merely about our knowledge, or lack of knowledge, of that being. To use philosophical terminology, transcendence describes God

---

6. Henri Blocher, "Immanence and Transcendence in Trinitarian Theology," in *The Trinity in a Pluralistic Age: Theological Essays on Culture and Religion*, ed. Kevin J. Vanhoozer (Grand Rapids: Eerdmans, 1997), 109.

not in terms of epistemology, what we know, but in terms of ontology, what a thing really is. Of course, the two are not unrelated: Christians insist that God is incomprehensible (epistemology) precisely because he is transcendently other (ontology). But the distinction is worth preserving, for understanding transcendence ontologically allows us to not just repeat that God is incomprehensible, but to give an account of *why* God is incomprehensible. Why is he? Because he is ontologically other, the Cause and not an effect, the Creator and not a creature. In this way, we are speaking about a reality not just beyond our knowing but beyond the created order entirely.

Radical Transcendence

Let's examine this notion of divine transcendence more closely by looking again at Blocher's very carefully worded description of it. Divine transcendence is "the absolute nonsymmetry between the Creator and everything that has come to be." What is "nonsymmetry"? Well, first of all what is "symmetry"? The word describes a certain balanced correspondence between the parts of a thing or in the relation between one thing and another. The letter O is symmetrical, for instance, because its right half exactly corresponds to its left half; the letter G, by contrast, is not symmetrical, for there is no such point-by-point correspondence.

Now this notion of symmetry, or balanced correspondence, can help us see what "otherness" commonly means. Suppose you took a break from reading this book to go and get a drink of water, and that some prank-pulling friend decided to slip his copy of *The Principles of Statistics* onto your chair in its place. What would you say when you returned? "Say, this isn't my book—someone gave me this *other* book instead!" Think about this statement. What is an "other" book? It is a replacement, a substitute, something that stands in for an original—and therefore something similar enough to be able to stand in. This is important. In this example, both of the items in question are books. They can be grouped together in a common category, and both of them fit into that category in the same way, namely, by *being* books. There must be a certain correspondence between them, a kind of parity or symmetry such that both items "exist" in the same sense, in order for one to be substituted for the other. The otherness in question here is what we might call a "symmetrical" otherness.

But the otherness that is at the root of transcendence involves a "*non*symmetry," says Blocher. Creator and creature are not just different from one another; they are different in a way that excludes the symmetry or correspondence that would let one stand in for the other. They are not just different things of the same kind; they are different *kinds* of things. This is a more significant, perhaps a more surprising, sort of "otherness." Indeed, even "different kinds of things" is misleading, for different kinds can still correspond to or be parallel to one another at a more basic level. Your friend might have taken your book and substituted for it not another book but a potted Bonsai tree or a chocolate-chip cookie. You would then have encountered a more basic otherness that is still symmetrical. You would not have had another *book*, and so a certain "nonsymmetry" would have obtained, but you would still have had another *thing*, and so no "*absolute* nonsymmetry" would yet have been involved.

In fact, any concrete thing whatsoever would seem to fall short of this "absolute nonsymmetry" simply by virtue of the fact that it is an "other thing." Even if we try to think of something *really* "other," something totally alien, not part of this universe at all, yet insofar as the book is one thing and the totally alien whatever-it-is is "an-other," the two can still be construed in a symmetrical way. And this symmetry is exactly what genuine transcendence excludes. To have an "absolute nonsymmetry," one would need something so "other" that even its otherness was not like other othernesses. One would need not just a different thing but a reality so different that it could not be thought of as a thing at all, something unimaginably incommensurable with any thing whatsoever, something whose otherness is abstrusely, elusively, *inconceivably* other. This would be an *absolute* nonsymmetry—hence, *real* transcendence.

Interestingly enough, Blocher thinks we find this very notion of transcendence in the Bible itself. He refers to the prophet Ezekiel, whose strange vision in Ezekiel 1 includes all sorts of things that resemble fire and wheels and living creatures and a throne and a man—note well that they *resemble* these things. But there is *only* resemblance, as the text makes clear with its constant, almost irritating repetition of *demuth* ("likeness") and *mareh* ("appearance"):

> And above the firmament that was over their heads was the *likeness* of a throne, as the *appearance* of a sapphire stone: and upon the *likeness* of the throne was the *likeness as the appearance* of a man above upon it. . . . I saw as it were the *appearance* of fire, and it had brightness round about. . . . This was the *appearance of the likeness* of the glory of the LORD.
>
> Ezek. 1:26–28 KJV

Such language seems designed to point enigmatically to the unimaginable, for we are confronted, says Blocher, with "the otherness, the unnatural character, of Ezekiel's complex machinery; [then with] the escalation up to super-superlative-superlativity; and then, . . . high above, seated on a hypercosmic throne, 'the likeness, as the appearance of a man'!"[7] Note well: Ezekiel does not see a man, nor even the *appearance* of a man. He sees the *likeness of an appearance* of a man, and then later on the *appearance of the likeness* of the glory of the Lord—a likeness in both cases that includes such deep unlikeness that the whole description must be hedged about with these qualifiers.

7. Ibid.

Blocher rightly comments that this vision reveals a Lord who "transcends even transcendence," who transcends "all our imaginings of transcendence."[8] This is radical transcendence indeed.

This provocative line of thinking shows us why a more common, user-friendly understanding of transcendence, as a kind of distance or aloofness that separates the transcendent from what it transcends, is too simple to describe God the Creator. According to this standard approach, divine transcendence refers to the fact that God is outside or far away from the created order, and it usually stands in contrast to divine immanence, which refers to God's presence within the created order. But Reformed theologian William Placher cogently argues that this common conception of transcendence involves a fundamental "domestication" of the notion, such that the God who is literally unthinkable is made to fit into the rationalistic categories of seventeenth-century philosophy.[9] Along the same lines, British evangelical Colin Gunton complains that this common view involves a hopeless attempt to conceive transcendence spatially (as if God were "above" the world or "outside" the world), with the result that we see God "as a thing-like or analogously thing-like entity in a relation of opposition to . . . the world."[10]

By contrast, the more radical notion of divine transcendence exalts the Creator beyond even the most exalted creature, by insisting that a different *kind* of exaltation is in order. God is other, but with an absolute nonsymmetry that makes even "other" too tame a category. God is not other than creatures in the same way that one creature is other than another. If we say that his otherness is like that of creatures, then we are unwittingly treating God as if he *were* a creature—which is, of course, the very essence of idolatry. No, divine transcendence is not the *opposite* of divine immanence; it is the *ground* of immanence. God can be present in all of creation as no creature can, precisely because God transcends creation as no creature does. We might say (though the language could be easily misunderstood) that God is so "other" that his otherness, unlike other othernesses, includes even sameness.

Now, all of this undoubtedly seems rather far from the simple biblical account of God. But our point is that the biblical account is not really quite so simple as we may be tempted to think. On the contrary, it is Scripture itself that pushes us in this direction, for it demands of us an almost impossible feat: the feat of avoiding idolatry. But how can we avoid thinking of God as if he were a created thing, when *all* of our thinking is conditioned by the things of creation? That is a difficult question indeed, and one that requires us to push our thinking to the very limit—and beyond. If this notion of a transcendence

---

8. Ibid.

9. William Placher, *The Domestication of Transcendence: How Modern Thinking about God Went Wrong* (Louisville: Westminster John Knox, 1996).

10. Colin Gunton, "Transcendence, Metaphor, and the Knowability of God," *Journal of Theological Studies* 31 (October 1980): 510.

radical enough to include immanence seems paradoxical or bewildering, then it may be just what we need. Any transcendence that is conceivable is shown by that very fact not to be genuinely transcendent. As Augustine famously said, "If you comprehend, He is not God."[11]

Transcendent Mystery Revealed

But what about Scripture then? If a careful study of biblical themes points us toward this notion of a God who is radically transcendent and utterly beyond human knowledge, then we might be inclined to wonder how reliable Scripture itself can be, insofar as it paints a fairly recognizable, understandable picture of the God of Israel and of the Triune God of Christian faith. How can this be? How can God be definitively known in Scripture, or in Christ, or in his revelation generally, and yet simultaneously be beyond knowledge?

Reformed theologian John Frame perceptively remarks that this tension between God being "knowable and known" on the one hand, and yet also "mysterious, wondrous, and incomprehensible" on the other, is not at all an issue for the biblical writers.[12] On the contrary, it seems that the more fully God is revealed in Scripture, the more readily the human authors of Scripture acknowledge his unfathomable greatness. Note, for instance, how Paul's great hymn to divine incomprehensibility in Romans 11:33–36 is immediately followed by his call for "reasonable worship" (*logikē latreia*) in Romans 12:1. And if the categories introduced in chapter 1 make sense, then this is just what we should expect. The "mystery of God" in which Paul exults is not an investigative mystery, not a puzzle we expect to solve or a haziness we want to dispel. Instead, the Creator is a revelational mystery, a marvel and a wonder that deepens precisely by being known. What else besides worship could possibly be appropriate?

Indeed, it is only because God is Creator in this robust, inexhaustible sense that he is truly worthy of worship. Only the absolutely nonsymmetrical polarity of Creator and creature can make worship a "reasonable" response. For here and here alone we are confronted not with a creature, however strong or noble, but with the Lord himself. Even the loftiest union of virtues in a creature remains but an instance of a principle of virtue that is beyond it. The highest archangel may conform to the standards of power and goodness with breathtaking perfection, yet it is conforming to something that is by very definition higher than itself—and with a different kind of height. The divine nature alone does not conform to the standard; it *is* the standard. This is what separates God from every other creator. Our parents may be said to have "created" us, St. Benedict to have "created" the Benedictines, Shakespeare

---

11. *Homilies on the Gospels*, Sermon 67 (117), 5, www.ccel.org/ccel/schaff/npnf106.vii.lxix.html.
12. John M. Frame, *The Doctrine of God* (Phillipsburg, NJ: P&R, 2002), 201.

to have "created" Hamlet—but in none of these instances do we expect the created thing to offer anything like worship to its creator. Why? Because in each case it is clear that the creator is not, so to speak, final; in each case the creator turns out to be dependent on some other Reality that is yet further back. By contrast, God is not just a creator, but *the Creator*—the ontological absolute that cannot be classified, upon which all depends, beyond which there is nothing. It is this incomparable supremacy, this unfathomable uniqueness and finality, that draws from us the recognition of inviolability and supreme worth—that compels us to worship with awe and reverence.

So it can be "reasonable," in the sense of "fitting," to worship God precisely because he is the transcendent Creator. But our worship can also be "reasonable" in another sense, insofar as it reflects our created character as rational, spiritual knowers of reality. And this also Scripture demands. Divine incomprehensibility in no way undercuts the unwavering biblical insistence that God really has made himself known to his people. Of course, we may wonder how a transcendent God *could* make himself known. But this is a problem only if we have unwittingly returned to a domesticated concept of transcendence that reduces to mere otherness, mere aloofness or distance. Once we have left that emasculated conception behind, we can see that the transcendent Lord is too exalted to be limited even by the category of transcendence. Hence, he is sovereignly free to make himself known.

And make himself known he has, as every Christian tradition declares. A lesser doctrine of revelation might leave us with frustrated silence, or with fragile human speculation about what is unimaginably beyond speculation. But the Christian doctrine of revelation, with its bold "Thus says the Lord," is not so paralyzed by human weakness. Indeed, both Old and New Testaments make consistent appeal to exactly this distinction, the distinction between the revealed wisdom of God and the frail, faulty "wisdom" of human speculation. "Let the prophet who has a dream recount the dream," declares the Lord, "but let the one who has my word speak it faithfully" (Jer. 23:28). "We did not follow cleverly devised stories when we told you about the coming of our Lord Jesus Christ in power, but we were eyewitnesses of his majesty" (2 Pet. 1:16). With the assurance of this revelation before us, we can gladly accept the Lord's invitation: "Come now, and let us reason together" (Isa. 1:18 NASB). We *do* know God, and not just in the nonrational experience of mystical ecstasy, but in the concrete categories of rational inquiry that his revelation unfolds.

A Double-Edged Sword

Yet the emphasis on revelation carries with it its own dangers. We are right to want to protect the truth of God from the errors and follies of those who ignore God's revelation, and so we are right to establish certain boundaries or to erect certain fences around orthodoxy, in order to keep out blatant error. But as Catholic theologian Hans Urs von Balthasar points out, every fence (or as he describes it in an astute metaphor, every "wire") that is laid down to protect God's truth "can only too easily and almost fatally become a snare to trap humans." How so? Von Balthasar says, "[The] impression may be created that it is *in the wire itself* that the mystery has been captured and tamed."[13] One thinks of the Israelites on Mount Sinai, receiving instructions from Moses to set up boundaries that will keep anyone from approaching or even touching the holy mountain of God (Exod. 19:12). Yet how quickly the Israelites forgot that the boundaries were established to keep impurity *out*, not to pen God *in*. Their idolatry right at the foot of the mountain seems to suggest that their knowledge of the boundary somehow made the God on the other side of the boundary seem more predictable, more controllable, less fierce, less "other." Even so, those who have understood the revealed truth of God may be in danger of subtly allowing the truth we know to annul or confine the holy mystery that is beyond knowledge. We should take warning.

Indeed, the dual affirmation to which we keep returning, the affirmation of a God unknown and yet known, of a mystery impenetrable and yet revealed, cries out to us unceasingly about the dangerous ground upon which all authentically Christian approaches to God necessarily stand. For to deny our knowledge of God is to fall into skepticism and to lose the gospel; and just as surely, to affirm knowledge of God in the wrong way is to fall into idolatry and to lose the biblical God. If we lack the knowledge of God, we are left in despair; yet if we think we "possess" the knowledge of God, we are left with a God of our own making—which is no real God at all. There is no safe path to walk.

But dangerous ground notwithstanding, we must be prepared to step forward boldly in proclaiming the mystery of the transcendent Lord. In doing so, we are following the example that we see everywhere in Scripture. No one knows better than Solomon that the Lord is too great to be circumscribed by any man-made house; and yet Solomon builds the Lord's temple, with the Lord's approval, because the Lord has promised to be there (1 Kings 8:12–13). Moses has heard from God himself that "no one may see me and live" (Exod. 33:20), but he heard it because God met with him "face to face," as one meets with a friend (Exod. 33:11). Christians can make bold to declare that we *do* know God, but that we know him *as* God, and therefore as the incomprehensible Lord of all. Divine transcendence means that, in a sense, God is always hidden from creaturely vision; yet his hiddenness is itself part of what God has revealed about himself. And therefore we can follow the

13. Hans Urs von Balthasar, "The Unknown God," in *The von Balthasar Reader*, ed. Medard Kehl and Werner Löser, trans. Robert J. Daly and Fred Lawrence (New York: Crossroad, 1997), 184 (italics added).

biblical example and allow this very hiddenness to lead not to despair but to doxology at the mystery of God: we worship reasonably, not just because of what we can grasp of the glory, but also because of the revealed mystery of a glory too deep for any grasping.

We turn next to the history of Christian theology to see whether it supports this portrayal of God.

3

The HISTORY
of MYSTERY

To tell of God is not possible . . . , but to know him is even less possible. For language may show the known if not adequately, at least faintly, to a person not totally deaf and dull of mind. But mentally to grasp so great a matter is utterly beyond real possibility.

Gregory of Nazianzus[1]

We are like him [God], he is like us, and we speak of him in terms of personal attributes, though we know if we reflect that such terms cannot properly describe him. And he is unlike us, and we take refuge in the impersonal language of ontology and call him being, cause, absolute and the like. But to those who have not the God-vision, and who take the words we use in their generally understood rational sense, both sets of terms will seem flat and empty. They mean something which they cannot properly say. They mean *ipsum esse*, the absolute, the numinous.

Herbert Hodges[2]

1. Gregory of Nazianzus, *On God and Christ: The Five Theological Orations and Two Letters to Cledonius* (Crestwood, NY: St. Vladimir's Seminary Press), 39.
2. Herbert Hodges, *God Beyond Knowledge*, ed. W. D. Hudson (New York: Harper & Row, 1979), 122.

We saw in the previous chapter that the whole tenor of Scripture, along with individual texts in both Old and New Testaments, draws us to the conclusion that the God whom the Bible reveals is radically, incomprehensibly transcendent. God is a mystery. Our next task is to ask what role divine mystery has played in the history of Christian thought. Of course, one could easily write many volumes on a subject like this one. Since we have no space for such thoroughness, we shall offer here, in a single brief chapter, a cursory survey of how Christians throughout history have tried to think about a God who is beyond thought.

For all of its limits, such a broad overview does accomplish at least one important thing. It invites us to see the "forest" as well as the individual "trees" in the Christian theological tradition. And that "forest" is marked by an overwhelming theological consensus that affirms both the integrity of reason and the reality of mystery. There have, of course, been exceptions to this general rule—for instance Tertullian (in the second century) who declared, "I believe because it is absurd," or at the opposite pole John Toland (in the seventeenth century) who wrote a book called *Christianity Not Mysterious*. But we will find that Christians as a whole have been consistently committed to a vision of God that is neither rationalistic nor antirational, but that happily draws together human reason and divine transcendence.

We will examine this historical consensus in four primary steps:

1. the era of the church fathers, with a bit of attention to contemporary Eastern Orthodox Christianity;
2. the medieval period, with a few comments regarding the continuing legacy of Roman Catholicism;
3. the Reformation era and its theological descendents; and
4. some important contemporary developments.

Of course, in a wide-ranging historical survey like this one, the significant diversity of these various theological traditions will inevitably surface. Christianity has never been a uniform, monolithic whole, and so such diversity should not surprise us. One of the crucial implications of the incarnation is that God does not mind the messiness of clothing his truth in scandalously particular forms of dress—and the particularities of theology have sometimes proven especially scandalous! Our contention in this chapter is not that all Christians everywhere have thought in exactly the same way about the mystery of God, nor is it that we should adopt every approach to divine mystery uncritically. Our contention is simply that through all Christian history divine incomprehensibility has been a regular, stable, productive feature of Christian reflection, and we think this consistency adds a measure of plausibility to the biblical case set forth in the preceding chapter. The notion that confident theology and transcendent mystery can paradoxically converge is not some radical, newfangled idea: it is simply historic Christianity.

The Two Emphases of the Church Fathers

When we look at the first thousand years or so of postbiblical Christian history, the age of the so-called fathers of the church (commonly designated the "patristic" period, from the Latin word for "father"), it is not hard to find explicit expressions of divine incomprehensibility. Right from the beginning, the biblical insistence on divine transcendence is plain. Second-century apologist Theophilus of Antioch declared, "The appearance of God is ineffable and indescribable, and cannot be seen by eyes of flesh. For in glory He is incomprehensible, in greatness unfathomable, in height inconceivable, in power incomparable, in wisdom unrivalled, in goodness inimitable, in kindness unutterable."[3] Similarly, Justin Martyr (ca. 100–165) notes that anyone who would try to attach a distinctive name to the ineffable God "raves with a hopeless madness."[4] Quotations like these would be easy to pile up.

But the character of the period can be seen more readily if we attend to two very different emphases that appear side by side, emphases that we might naturally be inclined to think of as conflicting with one another. In the first place, the age of the church fathers was a time of rampant theological disputation and debate. During the five centuries after Christianity became a legal religion (with the Edict of Milan in AD 313), no fewer than seven international ecumenical councils were convened, in which Christian leaders from all over the world were called together to hammer out crucial disputed points of Christian doctrine and practice. Near the time of the first of these councils, which was held in Nicaea (in modern-day Turkey) in AD 325, it was reported that you could start a fight in any barbershop or tavern simply by expressing a theological preference for *homoiousios* over *homoousios*—a difference of a single Greek letter![5] Clearly these were Christians who, for good or for ill, took their theology seriously—perhaps with a seriousness that some of us might envy in our day of theological inattention.

Yet simultaneously, the patristic period was characterized by a deep, abiding awareness of the transcendent mystery of God, of the fact that God would always, necessarily overflow the bounds of creaturely language and reflection. This emphasis can especially be seen in the dramatic mystical thrust of much patristic theology. For most of the church fathers, theology was not primarily

3. *To Autolycus* 1.3.
4. *First Apology* 61.
5. See the summary in Paul Tillich, *A History of Christian Thought: From Its Judaic and Hellenistic Origins to Existentialism*, ed. Carl Braaten (New York: Simon & Schuster, 1968), 75.

a speculative, theoretical matter. It was instead a matter of experience, of vision, of ecstatic encounter with the life-giving Trinity.

Note well this juxtaposition. We tend to think of "mysticism" as a phenomenon that is *opposed to* theological dispute, that clings to experience *in the place of* doctrinal reflection. By contrast, the mystical bent of the patristic age was clearly *rooted in* such reflection. Vigorous doctrinal theology fed and nourished a mystical outlook that gladly recognized the limitations of human reason.

Consider, for example, the work of Gregory of Nyssa (ca. 335–95). Gregory was one of the three so-called Cappadocian Fathers (along with his brother Basil the Great and their friend Gregory of Nazianzus), who together were instrumental in developing the doctrine of the Trinity in the fourth century and in overthrowing the ominous threat of Arianism with its diminished view of Christ. Gregory of Nyssa himself composed a forty-chapter *Great Catechism* to give a full, apologetical account of Christian doctrine to new converts, and he wrote many substantial theological treatises, on particular topics ranging from the nature of the Trinity to the fate of children who die in infancy to the nature of the soul. One of his best-known treatises is his three-hundred-page[6] work *Against Eunomius*, a very carefully argued piece of doctrinal theology, written to undermine the Arianizing theology of the mid-fourth-century heretic Eunomius, who argued passionately against the deity of Christ. In order to challenge Eunomius's line of thinking, Gregory marshals every dialectical weapon one can think of, appealing to biblical texts, to philosophical consistency, to the precise meanings of important terms, to the testimony of authorities, to analogy, to moral rectitude, and so on. Clearly Gregory is a theologian in the thick of formal, polemical debate.

But there is one element of his presentation that might surprise us. A major plank in Gregory's argument is to show, paradoxically, that God himself is beyond argument—that God is incomprehensible. Eunomius's case against the deity of Christ revolved around his contention that, whereas the Son of God was begotten or "generated" by the Father, God the Father was necessarily "ingenerate," having been begotten by no one. Since there was this essential difference between the Father and the Son, it was plain to Eunomius that the Son could not be God in the way that the Father was God—that is, the Son could not be really, fully divine. Of course, in order for this argument to work, one would have to understand the difference between the "ingenerateness" of the uncreated God and the "generation" of the (supposedly) created Son of God. In other words, only by a clear, unimpeded grasp of the ungenerated divine "essence"—that which makes God to be God—could one know that a generated being (such as Christ) could not possibly be divine. The details of

6. According to the online text available at www.ccel.org/ccel/schaff/npnf205.pdf. In the printed version of *The Nicene and Post-Nicene Fathers* (NPNF) the text of this treatise is 215 pages.

Eunomius's argument need not detain us. The point is that, for Eunomius, God had to be, and could be, fully and completely known by human reason.

Against this position, Gregory of Nyssa insists repeatedly that the divine essence is beyond knowledge. "Now if any one should ask for some interpretation, and description, and explanation of the Divine essence," Gregory remarks with more than a hint of sarcasm, "we are not going to deny that in this kind of wisdom we are unlearned." Gregory says that the conclusion of his "learning" amounts to "only so much as this, that it is not possible that that which is by nature infinite should be comprehended in any conception expressed by words." He proceeds (in prose that is difficult, but worth reading carefully):

> Since the Deity is too excellent and lofty to be expressed in words, we have learned to honor in silence what transcends speech and thought: and if he who "thinks more highly than he ought to think" tramples upon this cautious speech of ours, making a jest of our ignorance of things incomprehensible, . . . we shall follow the advice of the prophet, and not fear the reproach of fools, nor be led by their reviling to talk boldly of things unspeakable. . . . For this is what we understand that the Apostle wishes to signify, when he calls the ways that lead to the incomprehensible "past finding out," showing by the phrase that that knowledge is unattainable by human calculations, and that no one ever yet set his understanding on such a path of reasoning, or showed any trace or sign of an approach, by way of perception, to the things incomprehensible.[7]

Notice how readily Gregory appeals to the precedent set by apostles and prophets. He is convinced that Scripture allows, and even requires, this remarkable combination of a rational defense of the faith (which is the whole burden of his book) and a humble recognition that the object of faith is beyond rational comprehension ("too excellent and lofty to be expressed," "transcend[ing] speech and thought," "incomprehensible," "unspeakable," "unattainable by human calculations"). We might be troubled by the logical tension in these two commitments, but there is no sign that Gregory is.

In fact, for Gregory and the fathers generally, the explication of doctrinal truth never stands alone but exists precisely for the purpose of preparing the believer for a personal meeting with the ineffable God. Theology is not simply a set of truths to believe; it is a path to walk, or a living vision to pursue—and a vision always pursued in the awareness that God is unfathomably transcendent. Gregory, like many of his contemporaries, appealed frequently to the biblical account of Moses at Mount Sinai as a picture of humanity's approach to God. Moses ascends the holy mountain to meet with God, and Scripture explicitly describes this ascent as an entrance into the "thick darkness" of

7. *Against Eunomius* 3.5, www.ccel.org/ccel/schaff/npnf205.viii.i.v.v.html. We have slightly modified the translation.

God's presence (Exod. 20:21). So also, says Gregory, must every seeking soul approach the transcendent God:

> Leaving behind everything that is observed, not only what sense comprehends but also what the intelligence thinks it sees, it [the soul] keeps on penetrating deeper until by the intelligence's yearning for understanding it gains access to the invisible and the incomprehensible, and there it sees God. This is the true knowledge of what is sought; this is the seeing that consists in not seeing, because that which is sought transcends all knowledge, being separated on all sides by incomprehensibility as by a kind of darkness.[8]

Gregory elsewhere compares the believer's mystical knowledge of God to a hiker's experience of vertigo when peering over the edge of a sheer cliff with no handhold in sight.[9] When we approach the transcendent God, we find that every concept, every word, every "thing" we might try to hold onto is utterly inadequate. Every rational category by means of which we would be enlightened disintegrates into dust, and only the darkness of God himself remains. Gregory can go so far as to insist that "any man who entrusts to language the task of presenting the ineffable Light is really and truly a liar; not because of any hatred on his part of the truth, but because of the feebleness of his instrument for expressing the thing thought of."[10]

But what is left then? Only silent, despairing agnosticism? Certainly not. For Gregory, "The more reason shows the greatness of this thing which we are seeking, the higher we must lift our thoughts and excite them with the greatness of that object; and we must fear to lose our share in that transcendent Good."[11] Gregory knows that our words and thoughts cannot capture God, but then our goal is not to capture, but to worship. And we bow in deepest worship at just that point where we see most clearly that we cannot see clearly.

The Patristic Tradition, Then and Now

Now this pungent combination of zealous polemical theology and cautious, worshipful reticence about the object of theology is not a feature of the thought of Gregory of Nyssa alone. Similar expressions can be found everywhere in the patristic literature. (We will concentrate for the moment on the Eastern, or Greek-speaking, patristic tradition; the Western, or Latin-speaking, tradition will come in the next section.) For instance, another of the Cappadocians, Gregory of Nazianzus (the Theologian, ca. 330–90), who was also very active

8. *Life of Moses* 2.163. This quotation is taken from *Gregory of Nyssa: The Life of Moses*, trans. Abraham J. Malherbe and Everett Ferguson (New York: Paulist Press, 1978), 95.
9. *Homilies on Ecclesiastes* 7, quoted in Kallistos Ware, *The Orthodox Way* (Crestwood, NY: St. Vladimir's Seminary Press, 1995), 24.
10. *On Virginity* 10, www.ccel.org/ccel/schaff/npnf205.ix.ii.ii.xi.html.
11. Ibid.

in the formal articulation and defense of orthodox trinitarian doctrine, nevertheless composed a famous prayer that begins with the telling words:

> O all-transcendent God
>   (what other name describes you?)
> what words can sing your praises?
>   No word at all denotes you.
> What mind can probe your secret?
>   No mind at all can grasp you.
> Alone beyond the power of speech,
>   all we can speak of springs from you;
> alone beyond the power of thought,
>   all we can think of stems from you.[12]

Another well-known example is that of the popular preacher and bishop John Chrysostom (d. 407), who presented a famous series of twelve homilies on the subject of divine incomprehensibility, using careful reasoning to show precisely that God is beyond reason. Chrysostom refers, for instance, to 1 Timothy 6:15–16 (which says that God dwells in "unapproachable light") and notes that the light is not said to be "incomprehensible," which would mean that it cannot be fully or successfully *known*; no, the light is "unapproachable," and this suggests that we cannot draw near it in order even to *begin* to know it. Furthermore, says Chrysostom, the text declares not that *God* is unapproachable but that even the *light that surrounds* God is unapproachable. If we cannot approach even the light, how shall we begin to take in the supremely glorious God who dwells in that light?[13]

This decisive wedding of positive, definitive truths about God with a profound awareness of God's incomprehensible mystery leads throughout the patristic period to the employment of two related but paradoxically opposite theological methods. They are commonly referred to as the *via affirmativa*, the "way of affirmation," and the *via negativa*, the "way of negation or denial." The first is the so-called kataphatic method, which proceeds "according to" (Greek, *kata*) "assertions" (Greek, *phasis*): that is, it speaks in positive terms, affirming what is true about God. The second is the apophatic method, where we move "away from" assertions (Greek, *apo-phasis*), recognizing the intrinsic limitations of all positive speech about the transcendent.

A nice summary of this second method is provided by John of Damascus, the eighth-century systematizer of the patristic period, whose book *The Orthodox Faith* is regarded by some as the first historic instance of a "systematic theology." John carefully points out that "it is not within our capacity . . . to say anything about God or even to think of Him, beyond the things which

---

12. *Early Christian Prayers*, ed. A. Hamman, trans. Walter Mitchell (London: Longmans, Green, 1961), 162. We have slightly modified the translation.
13. *On the Incomprehensible Nature of God* 3.11–12.

have been divinely revealed to us,"[14] and for this reason, the things we say about God "do not indicate what He is, but what He is not."[15] Note the use of negation, the method of declaring what is *not* true about God in order to get at what *is* true. And why adopt this method? John explains that the living God

> does not belong to the class of existing things: not that He has no existence, but that He is above all existing things, nay even above existence itself. For if all forms of knowledge have to do with what exists, assuredly that which is above knowledge must certainly be also above essence: and, conversely, that which is above essence will also be above knowledge.[16]

This apophatic method unquestionably set the tone for much of the early history of our faith, and that branch of contemporary Christianity that draws its identity most intentionally from the patristic period, namely, the Eastern Orthodox tradition, still bears witness to the enormous significance of this method. Many Orthodox thinkers remain deeply suspicious even today of the Enlightenment-inspired ideals of what they perceive to be rationalistic Western theology. They prefer instead to emphasize apophatic "unknowing" over kataphatic "knowing." Twentieth-century Russian Orthodox theologian Vladimir Lossky says that apophaticism "constitutes the fundamental characteristic of the whole theological tradition of the Eastern Church."[17] This tradition strongly insists that logic cannot capture the transcendent God, that God himself will always remain an unknowable mystery. Yet Lossky quickly adds, "Unknowability does not mean agnosticism or refusal to know God." It means instead a more than merely rational knowledge. It means a paradoxical "knowledge [that] will only be attained in the way which leads not to knowledge but to union"—that is, union with God in Christ.[18]

Note how this contemporary Orthodox formulation maintains exactly the same dual commitment we have already detected in the church fathers. Positive and negative methods stand side by side, each supporting and enriching the other, sometimes even in bewildering ways. Consider the following remarkable passage from Pseudo-Dionysius, the immensely influential sixth-century author (known only by the pseudonym of "Dionysius the Areopagite"—i.e., the Greek convert of Paul mentioned in Acts 17:34) who first formulated the distinction between the two methods:

> God is known in all things and apart from all things; and God is known through Knowledge and through Unknowing, and on the one hand He is reached by

14. *The Orthodox Faith* 1.2, www.ccel.org/ccel/schaff/npnf209.iii.iv.i.ii.html.
15. Ibid., 1.4.
16. Ibid.
17. Vladimir Lossky, *The Mystical Theology of the Eastern Church* (Crestwood, NY: St. Vladimir's Seminary Press, 1976), 26.
18. Ibid., 43.

Intuition, Reason, Understanding, Apprehension, Perception, Conjecture, Appearance, Name, etc.; and yet, on the other hand, He cannot be grasped by Intuition, Language, or Name, and He is not anything in the world nor is He known in anything. He is All Things in all things and Nothing in any, and is known from all things to all persons, and is not known from any to any.[19]

If this sounds like self-contradictory gobbledygook to many of us, it may be because we want a clear and distinct answer to the question, "Can we know God?" The patristic answer is clear and distinct, but it is a clear and distinct "yes *and* no." Yes, we certainly *can* know God; Christians are not atheists or skeptics. And yet no, we obviously *cannot* know God with any of the rationalistic mastery that we associate with knowledge of created things. There is real knowledge of God, and there is real "unknowing" as well. There is a genuine revelation that makes known the mystery of God, and there is also a genuine mystery that no revelation can dilute. To lose either pole of this creative tension is to lose sight of the fullness of the Christian gospel.

One last word about Christianity's long, rich, and deeply apophatic patristic heritage. Given what we have already seen in the biblical testimony, perhaps we are not surprised to find that many patristic thinkers emphasized this mystical, apophatic method as strongly as they did. Still, it is possible that some emphasized it *too* strongly. There is debate in scholarly circles regarding just how faithfully "Christian" the influential theology of Pseudo-Dionysius really is,[20] and we need not resolve that question here. The point instead is to recognize the important place that Christians in the early centuries happily gave to divine mystery. Even if some made false steps in the way they affirmed mystery, it is clear that the denial of mystery was an equally dangerous false step. We who wish to be faithful to Christ should studiously avoid the errors in both directions.

The Western "Synthesis" and Its Roots

If Eastern Christianity looks for its inspiration to the undivided church of the patristic period, much of Western Christianity has looked to the so-called medieval synthesis of the High Middle Ages in a similar way. Even Protestants who are hesitant about the accretions and excesses that made their way into

---

19. *The Divine Names* 7, http://www.ccel.org/ccel/rolt/dionysius.pdf (p. 110). We have slightly modified the translation.

20. Some interpreters, like Jan Vanneste, insist that Pseudo-Dionysius succumbs to a merely philosophical apophaticism that abandons real Christian knowledge by construing even the Trinity as a limited manifestation of an ultimate reality that cannot be specified at all; others, like Vladimir Lossky, argue that Pseudo-Dionysius corrects a merely philosophical apophaticism and exalts the Trinity to the highest possible position in the divine darkness. See the helpful summary of the debate in John N. Jones, "The Status of the Trinity in Dionysian Thought," *Journal of Religion* 80, no. 4 (October 2000): 645–46.

medieval Catholic piety have found themselves appreciative of the thoroughness and elegance of Christian thought in that period, a period dominated by the universities and by various ecclesiastical schools and hence often referred to as the "scholastic" age. But this supremely ordered, rational vision of a cosmos with the Triune God at its head nevertheless consistently acknowledged that the God so positioned was a transcendent mystery who could never be "fit into" a large schema at all.

One could easily look back to the Latin-speaking sources from the patristic period, and especially to the famous North African bishop Augustine of Hippo (354–430), to find the roots of this emphasis in the medieval West. Augustine writes numerous volumes of carefully crafted and quite sophisticated theological argument, yet he frequently confesses that God is far beyond words, "ineffable" or "unspeakable," so that "we more easily say what He is not than what He is."[21] Of course, such ineffability gives rise to a logical problem, for "if the unspeakable is what cannot be spoken of, it is not unspeakable if it can be called unspeakable," and this is a dilemma "rather to be avoided by silence than to be explained away by speech."[22] Yet words do have a proper place, insofar as they "endeavor to reach the conception of a nature, than which nothing more excellent or more exalted exists."[23] We see here the same duality we saw in the Eastern fathers: God is past knowing, and yet we are invited to know him. Augustine thinks this is the most natural conclusion in the world:

> We are speaking of God; what marvel is it, if you do not comprehend? For if you comprehend, He is not God. Let there be a pious confession of ignorance, rather than a rash profession of knowledge. To reach to God in any measure by the mind, is a great blessedness, but to comprehend Him, is altogether impossible.[24]

This early Latin emphasis on mystery continues and expands as the Western tradition blossoms. For instance, Pope Gregory I (the Great, ca. 540–604), whose administrative skill and foresight set the stage for Christianity's survival of the so-called Dark Ages, commonly refers to God simply as "uncircumscribed Light," a light so devastating in its brilliance that extended contemplation is a dark and terrible thing, as it was for Job, who saw God's face and

---

21. *Expositions on Psalms* 86.11, www.ccel.org/ccel/schaff/npnf108.ii.LXXXVI.html.
22. *On Christian Doctrine* 1.6, www.ccel.org/ccel/augustine/doctrine.vi.html.
23. Ibid., 1.7.
24. *Homilies on the Gospels*, Sermon 67 (117), 5, www.ccel.org/ccel/schaff/npnf106.vii.lxix .html. We have slightly modified the translation. Phillip Cary argues convincingly that Augustine is a surprising exception in the Christian tradition insofar as his outlook does allow God to be "intelligible" in a strict Platonic sense (see "The Incomprehensibility of God and the Origin of the Thomistic Concept of the Supernatural," *Pro Ecclesia* 11, no. 3 [Summer 2002]: 340–55). But this difference does not affect the way Augustine's thought tended to influence the Western theological tradition as a whole.

was overwhelmed.[25] Ninth-century Irish philosopher-theologian John Scotus Erigena contributes to the same emphasis by translating all the works of Pseudo-Dionysius and some writings of the Cappadocian Fathers into Latin, and he draws upon their apophatic approach to ground his own speculative vision of God as the transcendent One who may therefore be described as "the non-being that transcends being."[26]

The Silence of Thomas Aquinas

There are many other points at which one could recognize the unswerving medieval quest for a real knowledge of the God who is beyond knowledge, but it is hard to give pride of place to anyone in the medieval Christian tradition except the great Dominican friar Thomas Aquinas (ca. 1225–74). Aquinas has for a long time been a foundational figure for much Christian theology, and especially for Roman Catholic theology, and he is often portrayed as the quintessential rationalist, a systematizer for whom God is just one more element in the system. Yet the last several decades have witnessed a remarkable spate of scholarly works that have called attention to Aquinas's deeper, more distinctive vision of God as the one who is graciously known as none other than an incomprehensibly unknowable mystery.

The best way to approach Aquinas, for our purposes, is to consider four crucial elements of his thought, for each one of which he is justifiably famous.

Reason

Let us begin with his straightforward commitment to orderly, systematic rational reflection. This commitment is obvious throughout Aquinas's work, perhaps most famously in his renowned "five ways" in the *Summa Theologica*, his five "proofs" for the existence of God.[27] The relevant passage is too long to quote here, but it can be read through in just a few minutes, and its cogency and elegance and systematic completeness have long captured the attention of admirers and critics alike. His basic contention is that we may be led to God by looking at five different aspects of our world, each of which fails to explain itself. The more we attend to any one of these aspects of our experience, the more we find ourselves intellectually puzzled and frustrated, looking for an explanation that the thing itself cannot provide. We need not evaluate here the specific line of reasoning Aquinas presents, for our point is simply to recognize that it *is* a "line of reasoning," one of the most famous lines of

---

25. Bernard McGinn, *The Presence of God: A History of Western Christian Mysticism*, vol. 2, *The Growth of Mysticism* (New York: Crossroad, 1994), 73.

26. *The Stanford Encyclopedia of Philosophy*, http://plato.stanford.edu/entries/scottus -eriugena/. See also McGinn, *Growth of Mysticism*, chap. 3.

27. *Summa Theologica* 1a.2.3, www.newadvent.org/summa/1002.htm#article3.

reasoning in the history of human reflection. If we learn nothing else from his approach here, we learn that Thomas Aquinas certainly is not a fellow who is ready to cast away logical reasoning as illegitimate or useless.

Indeed, the better we get to know him, the more we see this commitment at work. He always looked to the ancient Greek philosopher Aristotle for his intellectual inspiration, writing extensive commentaries on the works of Aristotle and employing Aristotelian terminology and argumentation repeatedly—hardly the method of one who mistrusts rational inquiry. Aquinas's own writings are a model of logical order and philosophical sophistication and rigor. He freely distinguishes between those aspects of Christian faith that we must simply accept on the basis of revelation and those aspects that are capable of rational demonstration, again giving clear evidence that revelation is trustworthy and that rational demonstration is a legitimate, even necessary part of human inquiry. Everywhere we look, Aquinas very clearly employs the tools and methods of reason with all of the care and vigor he can muster. In this respect, he sounds like (and is often portrayed as) a classic rationalist, as one who tries to follow the *via affirmativa* in a way that dispels every shadow of mystery from our knowledge of God.

The Divine Nature

A second element in Aquinas's thought, however, tends in an opposite direction, for if Aquinas is committed to systematic reflection about God, he is also deeply aware of the absolute uniqueness of the divine object being reflected upon. For instance, consider the central place that Aquinas's theology has for the notion that God is "simple."[28] Simplicity is the first point of discussion about God in the *Summa*, and most of us are tempted to see it as merely the first in a long list of sometimes obscure philosophical attributions—in this case referring to the idea that God cannot be broken down into pieces or parts. This claim that God is whole or entire, not "composite" or made up of smaller bits, may well be true, but it is hard for most of us to detect much deep significance in that admission.

Yet Aquinas has something more in mind. His point seems to be that absolutely all of the rest of our thinking, about everything in the universe without exception, *does* involve exactly this kind of "composition." Sometimes we consciously distinguish the different elements of something in order to understand it: we mentally take it apart and put it back together again. Other times we distinguish what a thing is made *of* from what it has been made *into* (in classical terms, this is the difference between "matter" and "form"); or we distinguish what a thing *is doing* from what it *can do* ("act" versus "potency"); or what is "essential" to the thing from what is nonessential or "accidental." Each of these methods of knowing involves recognizing a

28. *Summa Theologica* 1a.3.

kind of "composition" in the thing we are trying to know. But none of these methods applies to God, for God (as we have seen) is not a "thing." God is not "composite." God is a different sort of entity from any other, not really an "entity" at all in the way we typically use such language.

Thus we see that, for Aquinas, affirming divine simplicity is one way of insisting that God does not fit into any of the usual categories.[29] Simplicity is, we might say, a category that invalidates all categories, an affirmation that undermines all affirmations. We begin to understand why Aquinas begins his entire discussion of God's existence and nature with the rather surprising statement (though we have seen the like elsewhere in the Christian tradition!), "Now we cannot know what God is, but only what He is not; we must therefore consider the ways in which God does not exist rather than the ways in which He does."[30] Why would he say such a thing about the God who has revealed himself? Well, how could he say anything else about the God who is so unfathomably unique? God is the incomprehensible Creator; all supposed knowledge will inevitably fall short. Aquinas's words remind us of the *via negativa* that we have already noted in the church fathers and in the Christian East.

Analogical Predication

So Aquinas is not content with either the kataphatic or the apophatic method alone, and he goes on to give a very nuanced account of how the two are related—that is, of how positive theology is workable at all in the face of divine mystery. His account is rooted in his famous appeal to *analogy*, the third element in his thought that we must consider. Aquinas observes that different ways of using particular words convey meaning in different ways.[31] For example, when we describe both a ball and our planet as "round," the word "round" has the same meaning in both cases: as Aquinas puts it, the word is used *univocally* (from Latin roots that mean we are speaking with "one voice"). However, if we speak at one moment about a "bat" we might hit the ball with and at another moment about a "bat" that might fly out of a cave if we went in to explore, something very different is going on. Here, the words look and sound the same, but their meanings are utterly different and completely unrelated: we have used them *equivocally* (Latin for speaking with "equal voices," i.e., with two or more voices that lay equal claim to their own meaning).

Now Aquinas asks: How is the language we use about God like or unlike the language we use about creaturely things? When we speak of God, are we speaking univocally or equivocally? His answer is, neither one. We cannot be

---

29. See the excellent discussion in William Placher, *The Domestication of Transcendence: How Modern Thinking about God Went Wrong* (Louisville: Westminster John Knox, 1996), 22–23.
30. *Summa Theologica* 1a.3, preface.
31. *Summa Theologica* 1a.13.5.

speaking univocally, for we are speaking of the transcendent Creator, who is utterly different from all created things; yet we cannot be speaking equivocally, for then we would have no way of saying what our words mean when applied to God, and so we would be left with sheer skepticism. Aquinas suggests instead that when we speak of God we are speaking *analogically*: there is a similarity, a relation, an analogy, between what we say about God and what we say about creatures, but the meaning of the terms and concepts we use is not identical in the two cases.

We must be careful here. In most cases of analogical usage, since we ourselves invent the analogies, it is not hard to specify what the relation is that allows the different usages to be meaningfully related to one another. Aquinas notes, for instance, that we can call a person "healthy" and we can also call a climate "healthy," and these two meanings are obviously related to each other, since a healthy climate is one that causes health in a person. Thus we can say, and can say *univocally*, what that element is that allows the two usages to be related analogically. But our thinking and speech about God are never quite so manageable, since *all* of our creaturely concepts will be required to undergo a dramatic shift of meaning in order to allow them to point to the Creator. We are left with no univocal core of meaning to make appeal to.

Even in what seem the simplest statements, such as "God is here with us," we find that every word is affected by the fact that the sentence is about the mysterious Creator. For God is not "here"—that is, spatially present—in any way that we clearly understand; and he is not "with" us in the way that creatures are "with" each other. In fact, it is not even true that God "is" in the same way that a creature "is": as we saw a moment ago with respect to simplicity, God's "is-ness," God's being or existence, is not like that of creatures. At every point, the transcendence of God leaves us, in the words of Aquinas scholar Gregory Rocca, "hovering over the abyss" of meaninglessness.[32] Of course, for Aquinas, we never plunge into that abyss. Since God has made himself known in human language, we are absolutely right to speak *as if* God were "here with us" in the way that creatures can be, even though we know that God is not "here" in precisely that way. There is a real likeness, a real analogy, in language applied to God and to creatures, but in the final analysis we cannot specify in nonanalogical language what that likeness consists in.

Knowledge of God

But then how, it might be objected, does knowledge of God count as real *knowledge*, if we never know exactly what we mean when we apply human words and concepts to God? This brings us to the fourth element in Aquinas's thought. How can we be said to have real knowledge? Aquinas answers by

---

32. See Gregory P. Rocca, "Aquinas on God-Talk: Hovering Over the Abyss," *Theological Studies* 54 (1993): 641–61.

distinguishing between *what* we know and the particular *manner* in which
we know it, between what he calls the "thing signified" and the "mode of
signification." For instance, we can understand a material entity even though
our understanding itself (our mental activity, etc.) is immaterial and therefore
inappropriate to the entity. It is not, Aquinas says, that we understand *the entity*
to be immaterial; instead, we possess an immaterial *mode of understanding*.
So also, when we apply our minds to God the Creator, our understanding
is always creaturely, yet it is not that we understand the divine object to be
creaturely but that we possess a creaturely mode of understanding.[33] In this
way, Aquinas recognizes that the very way we think inevitably diminishes or
condenses the incomprehensible reality our thought is about. Yet this dimi-
nution is not simply equivocation or falsification; it is instead legitimate and
true thinking about a God who is beyond thought.

Roman Catholic Appropriation

Now, just as we noted with respect to the patristic era, the point here is not
to insist that every aspect of Aquinas's thought should be accepted without
qualification. Instead, the point is to recognize that, in the medieval tradition represented by Aquinas as fully as in the patristic period represented by
Pseudo-Dionysius or Gregory of Nyssa, unyielding commitment to doctrinal
truth and meaningfulness goes hand in hand with commitment to the unapproachable mystery of God. Aquinas is often thought of as a representative
of rationalistic philosophical theology at its worst, but he turns out to be
resistant to such rationalism at every turn: in his understanding of God's existence, of God's nature, of human knowledge of God, of everything. There
is a famous story according to which Aquinas received a mystical vision at the
end of his life that prompted him to give up writing entirely, confessing that
all of his writing seemed to him "like straw" when compared to the reality he
had now experienced. Josef Pieper shows, however, that this mystical embrace
of silence was hardly a new discovery for Aquinas; on the contrary, his whole
philosophical theology may be rightly summed up as a carefully articulated
embrace of silence.[34]

And in the last hundred years or so, this foundational mystical element
has become more and more appreciated by that Christian tradition that,
more than any other, has looked to Aquinas for theological direction, namely,
Roman Catholicism. Cardinal Walter Kasper (b. 1933) has noted that "the
outstanding event in the Catholic theology of [the twentieth] century" was

33. *Summa Theologica* 1a.13.12 ad 3, www.newadvent.org/summa/1013.htm#article12. See
also 1a.13.3.
34. Josef Pieper, *The Silence of St. Thomas: Three Essays*, trans. John Murray and Daniel
O'Connor (New York: Pantheon, 1957), 89.

the overthrow of the rationalistic brand of "neo-scholasticism" that had characterized some earlier Catholic thought[35]—an overthrow powered in part by the theological work of none other than Joseph Ratzinger, who is now Pope Benedict XVI. Once again, the result is not a mystical theology that is ready to abandon the truth as it has been given by God in Scripture and (for Catholics) in holy Tradition. On the contrary, Benedict was also the author of the Vatican declaration *Dominus Iesus*, published in 2000, a strong protest against the sort of wooly-minded religious pluralism that is founded upon "the elusiveness and inexpressibility of divine truth, even by Christian revelation."[36] Of course, the "divine truth" *is* elusive and inexpressible, even by Christian revelation! Yet the revelation can be relied on as authentic and normative nevertheless. Here is the same attempt we have seen elsewhere to insist that God is genuinely and truly known, and yet known precisely as a mystery who is beyond knowledge.

The Reformation Heritage

Important as patristic and medieval Christianity may be, Protestant evangelicalism traces its own lineage primarily through the Reformation of the sixteenth century, and so we need to attend with extra care to this period. In general, we find in the theology of the Reformation the same twofold commitment we have already noted in earlier Christian thought, but it is paired with sharp criticism of the ways in which both commitments had been or were being expressed in the life of the church.

In the first place, the Reformers were committed to the integrity of positive, doctrinal theology. Their dramatic call to return to Scripture and to the gospel of grace clearly implies that human persons can know the truth of God. Why else would the call be issued in the first place? If it was necessary to discriminate between the infallible Word of God and the many artfully contrived counterfeits that humanity has produced (and it certainly *was* necessary, in the Reformers' minds), then by all means it was *possible* to make that discrimination. In this sense, the Reformers could be said to affirm human reason. Yet they condemned in the very strongest terms the conventional way that reason was employed. They saw in medieval scholasticism not a legitimate effort to understand what God has revealed in Scripture but an arrogant attempt to set reason up as its own master apart from Scripture. For such foolishness as this the Reformers had no patience. On the contrary, they ridiculed the Schoolmen for a metaphysical hubris that was blind to the self-evident fact that God's

35. Walter Kasper, *Theology and Church* (London: SCM, 1989), 1, quoted in Fergus Kerr, *Twentieth-Century Catholic Theologians: From Neoscholasticism to Nuptial Mysticism* (Malden, MA: Blackwell, 2007), vii.
36. *Dominus Iesus* 4, available at www.vatican.va/roman_curia/congregations/cfaith /documents/rc_con_cfaith_doc_20000806_dominus-iesus_en.html.

thoughts are not our thoughts, and that even his foolishness is wiser than our most exalted wisdom.

So the Reformers were committed to rational knowledge even as they rejected the rationalism they thought had infected the tradition. But so also were they committed to divine mystery even while questioning its common medieval expression. They believed that the clear teaching of Scripture is that God was "past finding out," and in concrete Christian experience every person stood constantly in the presence of a God of unfathomable, overpowering majesty. But for this very reason, the Reformers were highly suspicious of the mystical thrust of much patristic and medieval Christianity. The mysticism of the tradition seemed to them to be not truly mysterious enough; it seemed to propose a path of nonrational penetration into the transcendence of God that Scripture did not clearly warrant.

Hence, we see an important parallel. Just as the biblical emphasis on the transcendent exaltation of God warred against an overconfident rationalism, so also it warred against an overconfident mysticism. In this respect, the Reformation understanding of divine incomprehensibility was distinctive. It was less speculative than that of the medieval West but also less ecstatic than the mysticism of East or West. It was more practical than both because more directly and concretely rooted in Scripture, and therefore more aware of our status neither as neutral reasoners nor as mystical seekers but as finite and sinful creatures who stand face-to-face with the Lord of heaven and earth. There is less a sense of the pleasures of rational investigation in the Reformers, less a sense of the joy of mystical assent, and more a sense of the holy fear of standing before transcendent majesty.

With these broad contours of Reformation thought in mind, let us consider in a bit more detail the two most influential of the Protestant Reformers as they think about divine incomprehensibility. We will find that a deep awareness of God's mystery significantly shapes both.

The Hidden God of Martin Luther

We begin with Martin Luther (1483–1546), the German monk whose theological questioning sparked the movement that quickly spread across Europe. Luther was scandalized by scholastic endeavors to prove the existence of God, and he famously ridiculed autonomous human reason as "the Devil's whore."[37] We should not regard this as a wholesale rejection of reason; Luther's own extensive exegetical and theological efforts forbid that move. But he was profoundly aware of the limitations of reason, of the sense in which it could be

37. Martin Luther, "Last Sermon in Wittenberg, Second Sunday in Epiphany, 17 January 1546," in *Dr. Martin Luther's Werke: Kritische Gesamtausgabe* (Weimar, Germany: Herman Boehlaus Nachfolger, 1914), 51:126, quoted in John Haas, "Christ, the Redeemer of Culture," in *On Wings of Faith and Reason: The Christian Difference in Culture and Science*, ed. Craig Steven Titus (Arlington, VA: Institute for the Psychological Sciences Press, 2008), 131.

used either to instruct or to deceive. And this inherent duality in reason became
all the more perplexing when one remembered that every person is naturally a
sinner, with an inborn propensity toward deception. So reason was useful (and
Luther sometimes explicitly commended its use[38]), but it could not be trusted
as it moved away from concrete living or from the plain meaning of Scripture
and attempted instead to decipher and then master the higher things of God.
Hence in much of Luther's work there is a deep mystical impulse (as seen,
for instance, in his lifelong attraction to the anonymous fourteenth-century
mystical treatise *The Theologia Germanica*), and he was never particularly
fond of what we might call systematic theology. Theology, he thought, did
not exist so that saints could make elegant rational systems but so that sinners
could understand the promises of God and respond to them in faith.

Yet it was not just the sinfulness of humanity that made reason inadequate;
it was also the transcendence of God. For Luther, God is the uncreated Creator
of all, "a supernatural, inscrutable being who exists at the same time in every
little seed, whole and entire, and yet also in all and above all and outside all
created things."[39] God cannot be limited or confined in any way, and his power
"is uncircumscribed and immeasurable, beyond and above all that is or may
be."[40] The very magnitude of God's awesome, uncreated reality places him
outside the bounds of human comprehension. Luther frequently appeals to
1 Timothy 6:16 (God "dwells in unapproachable light") to show that "God in
his essence is incomprehensible and dwells in a light which we cannot approach
even with our thoughts. [Therefore,] to want to inquire into his judgments
is truly to strive for things that are impossible."[41] Luther thinks that, for any
mere creature, and especially for a sinful creature, approach to this kind of
God would be positively dangerous, for "as God is in his own nature unmea-
surable, incomprehensible, and infinite, so is he to man's nature intolerable."[42]

The fact that the naked majesty of God would be "intolerable" to creatures
like ourselves has far-reaching implications for Luther as he thinks about how
God makes himself accessible—and does *not* make himself accessible—to
humanity. If human beings were wise, they would hesitate to approach the
transcendent God, lest they find themselves facing their own destruction. But
human beings are not particularly wise, and so God himself in mercy takes
up their cause. For their own protection, God hides himself from sinners.
This theme of divine hiddenness becomes a distinctive feature of Luther's
theology, with strong connections to his understanding of faith. For God

38. For example, in commenting on Gal. 1:3 and 3:15. See the discussion and illustrative
quotations in John Warwick Montgomery, "The Incarnate Christ: The Apologetic Thrust of
Lutheran Theology," *Modern Reformation* 7, no. 1 (January/February 1998): 8–9.
39. "Confession Concerning Christ's Supper," quoted in Dale A. Johnson, "Luther's Understanding of God," *Lutheran Quarterly* 16 (1964): 62.
40. "This Is My Body," quoted in Johnson, "Luther's Understanding," 62.
41. Comment on Gen. 17:10–11, quoted in Johnson, "Luther's Understanding," 63.
42. *Commentary on Galatians*, 43, quoted in Johnson, "Luther's Understanding," 63.

delights to hide himself in those places that will most fully and extravagantly
call for faith in the believer, and he therefore commonly clothes his attributes
in phenomena that are their exact opposite. This hiding in "contraries," as
it is often called, means that much of our knowledge of God will grow not
out of rational reflection but out of the wholehearted embrace in faith of the
paradoxes of the gospel. Luther writes:

> Faith is concerned with "things not seen" [Heb. 11:1]. So that there may be
> room for faith, all the things that are believed need therefore to be hidden. But
> they are not more remotely hidden than under the contrary object, perception,
> experience. So, when God makes alive, he does it by putting to death; when he
> justifies, he does it by making guilty; when he transports to heaven, he does it
> by bringing to hell. As the Scripture says in 1 Kings 2 [1 Sam. 2:6]: "The Lord
> slays and makes alive; he brings down to hell and raises up again." . . . So,
> God hides his eternal mercy and kindness beneath eternal anger, righteousness
> beneath injustice.[43]

This emphasis on God hiding himself comes to full expression in Luther's
theologia crucis, his "theology of the cross." In this teaching, Luther insists
that humanity's vision of God must grow exclusively out of the preaching of
Christ crucified—that is, the preaching of foolishness, defeat, and weakness.
This preaching constitutes the only mode in which the gospel can be known
to sinners in this life. We have no access, for Luther, to any *theologia gloriae*,
"theology of glory," that can give final, nonparadoxical description to the
supreme reality of God as it is in itself. The day when we see and know that
glory will come, but it is not here yet. And so the believer now glories exclusively in the cross.

Note the rather dramatic difference here between Luther and much of the
earlier mystical tradition. That tradition had generally tended to follow Pseudo-
Dionysius in his apophatic theology, and Luther in his very early work had
appreciated this emphasis in contrast to the analytical, rationalistic approach
of the Schoolmen. Yet appreciation gave way before long to sharp criticism
of Pseudo-Dionysius for a mystical speculation that, for all its bluster about
not knowing, employed the language of "unknowing" precisely to give an
exalted account of the heights of divine mystery. An approach like this may
boast a certain modesty and humility, but for Luther it is rooted too much in
its author's supposed insight into the glory, too little in his experience of the
suffering and humiliation of the cross.

By contrast, Luther's own experience was constantly punctuated with existential weakness. He spoke often of his *Anfechtungen*, his "attacks" or "as-
saults," wherein he encountered doubt and despair that drove him to the brink

---

43. *On the Bondage of the Will*, quoted in Brian Gerrish, "'To the Unknown God': Luther
and Calvin on the Hiddenness of God," *Journal of Religion* 53, no. 3 (July 1973): 270–71.

of suicide. These deep anxieties and uncertainties were the exact opposite of
Dionysius's ascent to God in a "dazzling darkness." Instead, Luther found
the hiddenness of God to be a sheer absence, an abandonment, reminiscent of
Christ's cry of dereliction on the cross (in Matt. 27:46: "My God, my God, why
have you forsaken me?"). This hiddenness was never something to be enjoyed;
it could only be embraced in faith, in the assurance that the incomprehensible
God would be found right in the midst of his paradoxical disguise.

Or perhaps even without the assurance. Luther speaks also of an even
deeper, even less welcome form of incomprehensible hiddenness, in which
the absence of God is replaced by a terrifying presence, the presence of the
absolute, inscrutable sovereignty that irrevocably ordains calamity as readily
as blessing, death as readily as life—even eternal death as readily as eternal
life. Here, says Luther, we confront that

> concealed and dreadful will of God, who, by his own design, ordains whom he
> wills to receive and partake of the mercy preached and offered, and what sort of
> persons they shall be. This will is not to be enquired into, but reverently adored
> as *far the most awesome secret* of the divine majesty, reserved to himself alone
> and forbidden to us.[44]

"Far the most awesome secret." This is indeed a hidden God, the appalling
Lord who is *behind* Christ, whose will is deeper and more efficacious than
Christ's, whose unfathomable intentions may be fundamentally different from
those made known in Christ. This deeper, hidden God is no friend of human
persons, no merciful savior or beneficent comforter. He is simply *God*, and God
utterly mysterious. It is no wonder that Luther insists that we "must discuss
God [as he is] preached, revealed, offered to us, and worshiped by us, in one
way, and God not preached, or revealed, nor offered to us, nor worshiped by
us, in another way." Where God is preached and revealed, there we speak of
glory and gladness and salvation. But "wherever God hides himself, and wills
to be unknown to us, there we have no concern. Here that sentiment, 'What is
above us does not concern us,' really holds good." Luther solemnly concludes,
"God in his own nature and majesty is to be left alone; in this regard we have
nothing to do with him, nor does he wish us to deal with him."[45]

These are sober words. In response to them, Luther advises simply and
candidly that we flee from this hidden God of majesty and take refuge in
the revealed God of mercy. He offers no careful, systematic resolution of a
merely academic dilemma, for in dealing with the incomprehensible God
we are confronted with unresolved and unresolvable realities that inevitably
leave us stunned and breathless, perhaps even at the edge of despair. And for
just this reason Luther insists that God is often found not in joyous mystical

44. Quoted in Gerrish, "To the Unknown God," 272 (italics added).
45. Quoted in Johnson, "Luther's Understanding," 63.

vision, which glimpses the theology of glory, but in grim, obedient suffering, a faithful living out of the theology of the cross. For Luther, this is what comes from knowing the God who is beyond knowledge.

Calvin's Thought

Now, if we are tempted to think that this dramatic account of divine mystery springs primarily from Luther's passionate Germanic temperament, we might be eager to turn to the other best-known Protestant reformer, John Calvin (1509–1564). Most of Calvin's work is a model of disciplined, orderly, systematic argument, and one suspects that here we have a logical mind that will have less patience with the paradoxes of mystery. Indeed, in popular lore, Calvin is often regarded as the supreme exemplar of relentless theological logic-chopping, the architect of an all-inclusive intellectual system ("Calvinism") that has a ready answer for any and every question, with chapter and verse in support.

Well, Calvin does have a far-reaching theological vision, and he does take the biblical testimony seriously, often down to particular chapters and verses. But in actual fact most of his theological work is conducted in a deeply pastoral spirit that emphasizes experiential knowledge in Christian theology and that intentionally eschews what he often calls "frigid speculation" as vain, unproductive, and dangerous. As a result, Calvin is profoundly aware of the worshipful humility that divine incomprehensibility calls for, and some of his most substantial themes grow out of just this awareness.

Consider his treatment of the ambiguous value of human reason. Like Luther before him, Calvin holds that human reason is a gift of God that remains functional even after the fall of humanity and that facilitates and promotes real knowledge. Indeed, Calvin can wax quite eloquent over the excellences of various "profane authors" in fields of law, philosophy (including "natural philosophy," which we would call "science"), rhetoric, medicine, mathematics: "Nay, we cannot read the writings of the ancients on these subjects without the highest admiration; an admiration which their excellence will not allow us to withhold."[46] Calvin even goes so far as to say that "every distinguished act" of intellectual or scientific achievement involves some "special inspiration" from God.[47] Yet also like Luther, Calvin finds that the knowledge fallen humans have regarding the things of God is much less reliable: he says that people "otherwise the most ingenious are blinder than moles" here.[48] What is the problem?

At least part of it is that God is simply too great for us to apply our limited reason to. Calvin is surprised that anyone would imagine that "the human

---

46. *Institutes* 2.2.15. All quotations are taken from John Calvin, *Institutes of the Christian Religion*, trans. Henry Beveridge, 2 vols. (Grand Rapids: Eerdmans, 1972).
47. *Institutes* 2.2.17.
48. *Institutes* 2.2.17.

mind [could] bring down the boundless essence of God to its little measure."[49] Of course, we want to fill up our "little measure" as fully as we can, and so Calvin goes to considerable lengths to explain and defend, for example, the revealed doctrine of the Trinity. Yet he clearly does not expect that we can comprehend the God who has revealed himself to be triune. On the contrary, he provocatively suggests that we should "willingly leave to God the knowledge of himself."[50] What? Should we not seek to know God? Of course we should. But the knowledge God intends for us is not a rationally acceptable and systematically complete account of reality. Instead, God gives us the practical counsel we need to live faithful lives in the presence of an overpowering mystery that will never submit to our rationalistic cross-examination. "The brightness of the Divine countenance, which even an apostle declares to be inaccessible (1 Tim. vi. 16), is a kind of labyrinth," says Calvin.[51] The revealed Word of God guides us safely through it, but its unfathomable, labyrinthine character remains.

Of course, God has made provision for our creaturely weakness in at least two ways. In the first place, since the divine being itself "is incomprehensible, utterly transcending all human thought," God allows us the indirect knowledge of himself that comes through the works of creation, where "his glory is engraven in characters so bright, so distinct, and so illustrious, that none, however dull and illiterate, can plead ignorance."[52] By this means, we really do know God, albeit in a way that fits the inherent limitations of human nature. Second, God addresses us in our weakness by "accommodating" himself to our condition and capacity. In what has become a classic image of God's loving condescension, Calvin pictures God as a kindly nurse who murmurs baby talk to an infant, "lisping" in order to communicate in the only way the infant knows. Thus, we get a true account of the things of God, yet an account clothed in images and metaphors and conceptualities that fall short of the full truth as God alone knows it. Says Calvin, "Such modes of expression . . . do not so much express what kind of being God is, as accommodate the knowledge of him to our feebleness. In doing so, he must of course stoop far below his proper height."[53]

But Calvin's overriding awareness that God's "proper height" is far above us never wavers, and therefore he is unwilling to allow any doctrine to exercise absolute logical control over his theology. This is true even of the doctrine of predestination—despite the typical Calvin mythology, which portrays predestination and "eternal decrees" and so on as the decisive fulcrum that governs every thought that ever entered into Calvin's head. It simply is not

49. *Institutes* 1.13.21.
50. *Institutes* 1.13.21.
51. *Institutes* 1.6.3.
52. *Institutes* 1.5.1.
53. *Institutes* 1.13.1.

so. As William Placher shows in some detail,[54] Calvin handles the doctrine of predestination with a deeply practical touch, moving from that revealed truth to different and apparently contradictory truths with the deft assurance that the God who is past finding out is trustworthy, our logical concerns notwithstanding. Similarly, in his discussion of the Trinity, Calvin warns that "we should speculate soberly and with great moderation, cautiously guarding against allowing either our mind or our tongue to go a step beyond the confines of God's word." The folly of others who are not so cautious "should be a warning to us to bring more docility than acumen to the discussion."[55] More "docility" than "acumen"—why? Not because intellectual acumen is worthless (it is not) but because the chief danger, especially for sinful creatures, is that we will unwittingly whittle down the incomprehensible mystery of God to a more manageable size. Any such retreat from the transcendent fullness of God cannot but undermine our worshipful approach to God from the very outset.

And worshipful approach to God is, of course, what theology is all about for Calvin. He is certainly interested in the knowledge of God, but never in arid, intellectual demonstration. True knowledge of God is always knowledge rooted in faith, and in a faith that both grows out of and also leads to a life of worship. When we speak of this kind of authentic knowledge of God, says Calvin, "we do not mean comprehension, such as that which we have of things falling under human sense," for knowledge of God "is so much superior, that the human mind must far surpass and go beyond itself in order to reach it." Certainly followers of Christ do know God, "but rather as confirmed by a belief of the divine veracity than [as] taught by any demonstration of reason."[56] This is what Calvin calls the "knowledge of faith," and it signals not that we have rationally discerned the secrets of God but that we are boldly confident of truths given by God himself that are far beyond what reason alone can grasp. We joyously contemplate God in his works and in his Word, but we do not attempt "with presumptuous curiosity to pry into his essence." God desires that we should know him, but such knowledge should always have a practical edge, since the essence of God "is rather to be adored than minutely discussed."[57]

Later Calvinism

The Reformed tradition that has followed Calvin has occasionally been tempted by the pleasures of "minute discussion," but it has also been instructively consistent in its stress on the uniqueness and mystery of the transcendent God. For instance, the late seventeenth century witnessed the introduction of

54. Placher, *Domestication of Transcendence*, 60–64.
55. *Institutes* 1.13.21.
56. *Institutes* 3.2.14.
57. *Institutes* 1.5.9.

a careful distinction, technically formulated by Franciscus Junius (1545–1602), between "archetypal" and "ectypal" theology to underline the significance of divine mystery in the way we think about theology. Archetypal theology is theology that comes from the *archē* (Greek for "beginning" or "origin"), that is, from God himself: it is that uncreated knowledge that God has of himself and that therefore belongs to God alone, not to any creature. By contrast, ectypal (or sometimes "ectypical") theology is what comes "out of" (Greek, *ek*) the divine archetype and into the realm of human comprehension. Ectypal theology is the true expression in a creaturely mode of that archetypal theology that utterly transcends it.

In other words, here is a technical terminology in the Reformed tradition that establishes both the concrete difference and the necessary link between the truth of God as it is in itself and the truth of God as known by creatures. The difference is obvious: it is the difference between God and world, Creator and creature, Lord and servant, Original and derivative. But the linkage is also noteworthy, for God makes precisely *himself* (archetype) known precisely *to us* (ectype). Thus, as Willem van Asselt observes, a distinction that initially might strike us as colossally abstract and speculative turns out to make the supremely practical point that "Christian theology is fundamentally a relational enterprise, determined by and determinative of the divine-human relationship."[58]

Divine incomprehensibility became the focus of attention in Reformed theology in a rather different—and less peaceable—form in the middle of the twentieth century, and in a context that helpfully illustrates complexities that still arise. In 1944, Reformed philosopher and theologian Gordon H. Clark was accepted as an ordained minister in the conservative Orthodox Presbyterian Church, and his acceptance occasioned a formal objection by other theologians in the denomination, who expressed concern that Clark's theology was inappropriately rationalistic and did not sufficiently allow for the mystery and incomprehensibility of God.[59] Clark's critics, led by Cornelius Van Til of Westminster Theological Seminary, complained that Clark failed to account for what they called a "qualitative" difference between human knowledge and divine knowledge and advocated instead a merely "quantitative" difference between the two. This amounted, the critics claimed, to denying divine incomprehensibility, which was in effect to deny that God was really God. Clark and his supporters, however, maintained that the real question had to do not with whether God could be comprehended (they agreed that he could not) but with whether human knowledge is real knowledge. In their view, to

58. Willem J. van Asselt, "The Fundamental Meaning of Theology: Archetypal and Ectypal Theology in Seventeenth-Century Reformed Thought," *Westminster Journal of Theology* 64 (2002): 324.
59. For the most thorough account of the whole affair, see Fred H. Klooster, *The Incomprehensibility of God in the Orthodox Presbyterian Conflict* (Amsterdam: T. Wever, 1951).

assert some "qualitative difference" between what human beings mean when they say that $2 + 2 = 4$ and what God means by the same statement is to deny that human "knowledge" is genuine knowledge at all. They argued that, while we doubtless know *less* than God, what we do know must be known *as God knows it*, or else we do not really know it at all.

There are plenty of complex, technical issues involved in this debate, and we cannot enter into them here. But the foundational intentions on each side are very enlightening. Clark's critics wanted to protect Christian faith from a proud *rationalism* by affirming a strong version of divine incomprehensibility; Clark's defenders wanted to protect Christian faith from a skeptical *irrationalism*, not by denying incomprehensibility but by affirming that God can be genuinely known. Contemporary Reformed theologian John Frame is surely right to acknowledge that both sides had valid concerns. When Frame's own even-handed discussion of the relationship between divine knowledge and human knowledge takes the form of a long series of "discontinuities," "continuities," and ambiguous or unresolved "problem areas,"[60] it is hard to think that either Calvin himself or the broader Christian tradition would substantially disagree. There certainly are "discontinuities," for God is the transcendent Creator, whose blinding reality eclipses the vision of every created thing; yet there are also "continuities," for God has graciously made himself known in Christ and in his Word. And there undoubtedly remain "problem areas" too, for we must continue to insist that just as the mystery of God does not invalidate the revelation, so also the revelation does not dispel the mystery.

Contemporary Interest

We could look in a multitude of other places throughout Christian history to see more ways in which theologically articulate Christians have affirmed and rejoiced in divine mystery. But perhaps we would do better to conclude this chapter by considering how very relevant divine incomprehensibility is to today's "postmodern" theological scene.

Contemporary postmodernism is a wide-ranging movement that grows out of a profound dissatisfaction with the approach to knowledge that dominated the so-called modern period, roughly the seventeenth to the mid-twentieth centuries. Philosophers and theologians of this period, paradigmatically represented by French mathematician and philosopher René Descartes (1596–1650), sought to build all intellectual endeavor on a foundation that was certain beyond doubt, and so they relied on a method of critical investigation that rejected anything that *could* be doubted, so that only what was *beyond* doubt

60. John M. Frame, *The Doctrine of the Knowledge of God* (Phillipsburg, NJ: P&R, 1987), 21–40.

would remain. In this way, they thought that rational certainty could take the place of mere speculation or probability.[61] But in the 1960s and 1970s, several observers began to question this approach because of a growing awareness of the way that our thinking is inevitably influenced by various nonrational factors (such as personal history, culture, or language). As a result, the Western world in the late twentieth century grew more and more skeptical about any method of knowing that claimed to achieve rational certainty. Since it was moving beyond the optimism of the "modern" period, this new mood quickly became known as "postmodern."

It is not hard to see why postmodernism would come to be regarded by many Christians as detrimental to traditional faith, for its overall effect on Western culture has been to undermine not just claims to absolute certainty but claims to truth of any kind. A "postmodern" climate is one in which truth itself seems to have been excluded from the conversation: every opinion is equally good, since it is impossible in the nature of the case for anyone to discover what is finally and ultimately true. Yet some Christians think that there is another side to postmodernism, a side that we should consider carefully before rejecting the whole phenomenon.

Many of the more sophisticated proponents of postmodernism seem to be very explicitly *not* advocating a wholesale abandonment of truth, a kind of "anything-goes" intellectual free-for-all. Instead, they are inviting us to recognize that our knowledge of the truth is always influenced by who we are as finite, fallen creatures. The truth that we know is never "absolute" because we ourselves are not absolute. For human persons who are both finite and fallen, no single truth claim, no set of truth claims, can ever capture the *whole* truth, completely undistorted and undiluted, with nothing whatsoever falling through the cracks. Our knowledge is always partial, always in need of correction or refinement. Yet postmodernism looks around at the world and sees people who think they really *do* know with absolute certainty, people who are not aware that their knowledge, true though it may be, is still flawed and incomplete. If they are religious people, the danger is all the greater, for they think that their *theology* is flawless and complete: they believe, or act as if they believe, that their *logos*, their logic, has fully understood *theos*, the transcendent God. In the face of such hubris, postmodernism loudly objects. No, we have not captured God in our theological formulas. The truth that we know is never the full and absolute Truth that God himself is.

Well now, if *this* is the insight that postmodernism is built on, then it does not seem nearly so hostile to Christian orthodoxy. Indeed, from this angle

61. Descartes is almost always cited as the prime illustration of modern rationalism, but some commentators note that this portrayal may be somewhat oversimplified. Descartes was certainly aware of the transcendence of God and the limitations of human reason. See, for instance, the discussion in Richard R. La Croix, "Descartes on God's Ability to Do the Logically Impossible," *Canadian Journal of Philosophy* 14, no. 3 (September 1984): 455–75.

it begins to look as if the entire postmodern revolution is really a deeply Christian protest against a modernistic rationalism that has taken hold of our culture, a protest whose main intention is to affirm once again the utter incomprehensibility, the final, unspeakable mystery of God the Creator. Many observers think that it is this concern for the legitimacy of mystery that has driven postmodernism to its center-stage position in contemporary discussion.

This sympathetic reading of the postmodern agenda is not undisputed, but it has been plausibly maintained, even in some surprising cases. Consider, for instance, one of the archvillains in the philosophical lineage of postmodernism, the nineteenth-century German philosopher and theologian Friedrich Nietzsche, whose provocative cry "God is dead!" has become so infamous in theological circles. Nietzsche's work is a bitter and relentless attack against Christianity in any and every form, an attack that Christians have had to fight against for almost two centuries. But it is interesting to note the surprising similarities between the attack leveled by this atheist and the one that originated in the acutely Christian sensibilities of the nineteenth-century Danish thinker Søren Kierkegaard, who was angered by the lifeless, rationalistic religion of the state church of his day and whose withering assault against this kind of "Christianity" was every bit as devastating as Nietzsche's own. Could it be that Nietzsche also was rejecting a "Christianity" that fully merited rejection? Purdue philosopher Calvin Schrag thinks so.[62] He describes Nietzsche's system as a "reactive atheism," an atheism that is reacting against a portrayal of God that is genuinely false. In Neitzsche's experience, "God" was simply the specious name given by ecclesiastical paper pushers to a philosophical super-being to whom they could appeal to support their own benighted church customs and cultural prejudices. Nietzsche rejected such a feeble and easily manipulated deity—and he was *right* to do so.

Of course, this may be an overly optimistic, perhaps even an idiosyncratic, reading of Nietzsche. But suppose it is on target. Suppose Nietzsche really was reacting against the "Christianity" that he knew rather than rejecting the one true God. How would this shift in focus affect our thinking about his philosophical project? This may be a difficult question to answer for many Christians, who have always thought of Nietzsche as the paradigmatic philosophical "bad guy." When Nietzsche denies the existence of a being called "God," we are tempted to retort, "There *is* a being called God; the Bible says so!" But wait. Does the Bible really say that there is a "being" called God, that is, that God is a "being," a thing that "be's," a thing that "is" or "exists" just like every other thing, except that this one happens to be bigger and stronger than most? We have already seen the Christian answer to this question. The living God is *not* a "being" in the normal sense of the word: God is *Creator*

62. See Calvin O. Schrag, *God as Otherwise Than Being: Toward a Semantics of the Gift* (Evanston, IL: Northwestern University Press, 2002), esp. 45–56.

of all beings, of everything that "be's," of every "thing" whatsoever. In this sense, God utterly transcends "being" or "existence."

If Nietzsche's rejection of God is really a rejection of the notion that God is a "being" (and a being of a particularly spineless and feeble kind), then historic Christianity actually gives us grounds to *agree*. Of course, we probably would not want to go along with Nietzsche very far, for we want to maintain that, while the "God" that he rejects does not exist, still the God of Scripture—the one true and living God, the incomprehensible God who is Father, Son, and Holy Spirit—this God is indeed a reality, even if we cannot say what kind of "reality" he is. In this respect, we must certainly insist that Nietzsche's uncompromising atheism is wrong. But the point is that we do not have to accept his full-blown atheism in order to reject the particular kind of "theism" that he also rejected. We can respond sympathetically, "Yes, Nietzsche was right to reject the kind of God he initially rejected; we Christians reject that kind of God too. How sad that Nietzsche didn't take the next step and ask whether there is a *real* God, far greater than that one." This approach puts us in a position to respect and correct Nietzsche and his modern-day disciples rather than simply disagreeing with them.

Now, whether this way of understanding Nietzsche's philosophy is correct is for scholars to decide. But unquestionably, a great deal of the contemporary phenomena of postmodernism has roots that go back to Nietzsche and to concerns like these. Here is a brief sampling of the approaches taken by several of the "founding fathers" of postmodernism:

- Michel Foucault (1926–84) tries to show that all human reasoning is inevitably influenced by unconscious forces, both individual and social, that keep it from being the pure, objective investigation that modern philosophy would have us think. The self-serving interest in "power" (not unlike what Christians have always called "original sin") is a force constantly to be reckoned with.
- Emmanuel Levinas (1906–95) meditates on what might be called "the otherness of the other," pointing to our fatal tendency to take what is different from ourselves and construe it in ways that make it more like us, more conventional, easier to digest, easier to control. Against this tendency, we need to allow the "other" to be fully, authentically "other," to challenge our neat, tidy categories, to push us toward a reality that is utterly beyond us.
- Jean-François Lyotard (1924–98) maintains that every grand story, every "metanarrative," is told to provide us with a fully rational, self-justified account of our universe. But such stories cannot justify their own starting points, and therefore they are unable to give a *fully* rational account. We need to acknowledge this limitation, thus making room for what Christians have called "faith" in a reality that will not submit to our rational probing and questioning.

- Jacques Derrida (1930–2004) believes that human finitude makes all of our knowledge only partial and imperfect. We take the limited insights available to us, and we do our best to "construct" a comprehensive philosophy or worldview, but it is still a human "construction," and we discover what it has unwittingly obscured or left out only as we "de-construct" our knowledge.
- Jean-Luc Marion (b. 1946) argues that Western philosophy's historic preoccupation with "being" has led Christian theology into a kind of conceptual idolatry, in which only "beings" that can be rationally understood and categorized are taken seriously. To avoid this idolatry, we need to move "beyond being"—we need an approach to reality that is centered in what is "beyond" rather than in what already is.

Please note the common, central intuition of each of these representatives of postmodernism. Every one of them insists in one way or another that our thinking about life goes wrong when we fail to acknowledge our own limitations. In other words, every one of them—even when reputed to be "post-Christian" or "anti-Christian"—contends that we must come to terms with the reality of ultimate mystery. And this is the very reality that Christians have affirmed and delighted in for two thousand years! It begins to look as if the starting point of much contemporary postmodernism may be—of all things!—a deeply Christian truth.

This is the reason that some evangelicals are arguing that evangelicalism itself needs to appropriate the insights of postmodernism in order to guard against a dangerously rationalistic and "modernized" version of the faith. For instance, Carl Raschke calls for a new "Reformation" on this ground, in order to protect the historic Reformation from being taken hostage by the alien philosophical presuppositions of the Enlightenment.[63] Or again, James K. A. Smith argues at length that postmodernism is actually an affirmation of the deeply faith-based character of all intellectual endeavor, an affirmation that invites us to embrace revelation in a way that reinforces rather than obscures the mystery of God.[64]

There is still a fair amount of resistance among evangelicals to this positive reading of postmodernism, and the in-house debate will no doubt continue for some years to come. It would probably be a great disaster if all evangelicals were suddenly and uncritically to accept postmodernism. Still, we need to think long and hard about those elements in current evangelical piety that are prompting some evangelicals to regard postmodernism as a sensible, or even a helpful, response. Evangelical philosopher Merold Westphal suggests

63. Carl Raschke, *The Next Reformation: Why Evangelicals Must Embrace Postmodernity* (Grand Rapids: Baker Academic, 2004).
64. James K. A. Smith, *Who's Afraid of Postmodernism? Taking Derrida, Lyotard, and Foucault to Church* (Grand Rapids: Baker Academic, 2006).

that one way to approach the issue is to acknowledge that the gurus of secular postmodernism really do make good *Lenten* reading for evangelical Christians.[65] In other words, they remind us of how foolish and presumptuous we are when we act as if we have mastered the God of the universe by means of our theology, and they rightly prompt us to repent of such folly. So far, so good. Yet we eventually want to get beyond Lent to Easter: we want to insist not just that we do *not* know but also that we *do* know. This is where evangelical debate over postmodernism becomes so tricky.

Fortunately, we need not resolve this debate here. But one cannot even understand it, much less enter into it, without careful, nuanced attention to the mystery of God. Such attention seems to be part of our contemporary task as thoughtful Christians, and, if so, it is reassuring to see that the Christian tradition in its entirety has pondered these same questions. No single outlook on divine mystery has captured the allegiance of all Christians, but the joyful acknowledgment of mystery is all but universal. If God is really God, then we must draw near to him with the delight and circumspection that come from knowing genuinely what can never be penetrated fully.

Next, we must turn our attention to how the genuineness of our knowing can be supported theologically and practically. How is it possible to know the God who is beyond knowledge? That is the subject of our next chapter.

---

65. Merold Westphal, "Onto-theology, Metanarrative, Perspectivism, and the Gospel," in *Christianity and the Postmodern Turn: Six Views*, ed. Myron B. Penner (Grand Rapids: Brazos, 2005), 143.

4

The KNOWLEDGE
of MYSTERY

The eye cannot see God, although he is spiritually visible. He is incomprehensible, though he is manifested by grace. He is beyond our utmost thought, though our human faculties conceive of him. . . . He is beyond our conception, but the very fact that we cannot grasp him gives us some idea of what he really is. He is presented to our minds in his transcendent greatness, at once both known and unknown.

Tertullian[1]

Let us then call him the ineffable, unintelligible God, invisible, incomprehensible, surpassing the power of human language [to express], exceeding the comprehension of mortal mind, unexaminable by angels, invisible to the seraphim, unintelligible to the cherubim, undetectable by principalities, dominions and powers—in a word, by the whole creation—known only by the Son and the Holy Spirit.

John Chrysostom[2]

1. Tertullian, *Apology* 17, quoted in *Ancient Christian Doctrine*, vol. 1, *We Believe in One God*, ed. Gerald L. Bray (Downers Grove, IL: IVP Academic, 2009), 8.
2. John Chrysostom, *On the Incomprehensible Nature of God* 3.1, quoted in Bray, ed., *We Believe in One God*, 41.

U p to this point, we have seen how the incomprehensibility of God is taught in Scripture and also how it has been included in the theological reflection of various Christian traditions. Yet we might still be inclined to ask, quite simply, how can it be so? If God really is beyond knowledge, then how can it be that the whole Christian church talks so readily about "knowing" God?

Note that this question is not quite the same as the more skeptical, *can we know God?* Given the discussion of the last two chapters, we can rule out the notion that real knowledge of God is simply impossible. The united testimony of Scripture and tradition combines with the concrete experience of the people of God throughout the ages to insist that knowledge of God certainly is possible, for it actually does happen. We really do know God. So our question is not "whether" but "how."

Yet this "how" question is still real and extremely significant. We evangelicals might sometimes overlook its force, because the question seems to be so easily answered by a straightforward appeal to God's revelation, and especially to his revelation in Scripture, where the mystery has been revealed. We can know the incomprehensible God because, to put it simply, he has told us about himself. This answer is right in so many ways that one is hesitant to quarrel with it, but we must pause to remember just what we mean—and what we do *not* mean—when we speak about knowing the *incomprehensible* God.

To say that God is "incomprehensible" is not to say merely that he *is* not comprehended; it is to say that he *cannot be* comprehended by finite, creaturely minds. God is not an investigative mystery that could, in principle, be resolved if only we consulted the right sources (say, an inerrant Bible). No, God is a revelational mystery, who has made himself known precisely *as* a mystery, precisely *as* a transcendent reality that does not fit neatly into the logical or linguistic categories of creaturely reflection. Remember our analogy from Flatland. It might, of course, be a very good thing for Flatlanders to have an inerrant revelation about the mysterious object called a cylinder rather than merely relying on their own flawed perceptions and speculations. Such a revelation might allow the Flatlander to say, "Yes, I am convinced: there are objects that are both round and square at the same time." But what the revelation *cannot* do is to show him how that roundness and that squareness concretely fit together in a single figure. In this sense, he still does not *know* what a cylinder is. He believes that there is such a thing on the basis of the revelation given to him, but he still does not *comprehend* it, and he has little idea how to live with his new knowledge in day-to-day, practical terms.

So also, Scripture can give us true propositions about the transcendent Creator, spoken to us in a creaturely idiom that we can readily understand. And we can certainly expect that God knows how best to use that idiom: his revelation is fully trustworthy. But for us really to *know* the reality of which the revelation speaks requires something more. The Flatlander, if he is to engage a three-dimensional world, does not need simply a set of incontrovertible propositions: he needs to be drawn out of Flatland altogether. Similarly, the creature who would know God needs—somehow—to move beyond mere creatureliness. To know the God who surpasses knowledge requires not just having the right sources of information. It requires being the right kind of knower.

How, then, is this seemingly impossible task to be accomplished? How can we approach the one who dwells in unapproachable light? How are mere creatures to gain and to live in the knowledge of a truly incomprehensible God? The answer is bound to be complex, but its basis can be easily stated. The fundamental premise for true knowledge of God is this: God desires for us to know him, and he has acted, in creation and redemption, to make just such knowledge a reality. The basic assertions here rest squarely on the Christian understanding of who God is, and so we must start our investigation at that point—the nature of God.

The Intensely Personal Creator

It is customary in Christian circles to speak of God as "personal." It might not be easy to define the term very rigorously, but there is something about God's status as "person" rather than "thing," as a "Thou" rather than an "It," that is unavoidable for Christians. This is clear from even the most cursory reading of the Bible, for we very quickly find in Scripture the God who creates, speaks, acts, loves, hates, wills, intends, chooses, remembers, grows angry. An impersonal thing does none of these, for they are not in its nature. In this respect, the God praised by Jews and Christians has revealed himself as a personal being to be encountered rather than as an object we can place on a microscope slide to study at our convenience and according to our timetable. Each moment that we are studying this God, he is studying us too, in a deeper, more penetrating fashion than we can imagine. When we gaze upon this "object," we are very likely to find a pair of knowing eyes looking back at us.

It is important, however, for us to go further than the basic intuition that God is personal. God is not merely personal rather than impersonal. God is also supremely, intensely, incomparably personal, personal in a manner or to a degree that exactly corresponds to the incomprehensible transcendence of Creator over creature. There is no more personal being in the entire universe than the living God.

We can explore this intensely personal character in a variety of ways. For instance, we might consider how God supremely and perfectly instantiates everything that he is. Just as Christians have often said that God is not merely good but also "Goodness itself," not just pure but also "Purity itself," so also he is not merely personal but also "Personalness itself." Personalness is not just a quality that God has; it is what God *is*, and for this very reason he is the source and fount and ground of all that we otherwise call personal. God's intense personalness is essential to his nature: his personal being is eternal and necessary and self-existent. God does not first exist and then develop attributes of personality, as a human person does. There is no time when God is "growing into" his personhood. God is personal from the beginning—or even from before the beginning, when there exists nothing (that is, no *thing*) whatsoever, but only the eternal, personal "I AM." All of creation—and most significantly, all personality in creation—flows from this abundant spring. "In the beginning, God created" (Gen. 1:1), and thus the personal God through a personal act of creating gets all of reality as we know it started.

All of this is good, as far as it goes. Yet we can go further, for "personalness" in God involves not just being personal, not even being the most personal of all persons. The living God, according to Christians, is a *communion* of persons—God in *three* Persons, blessed Trinity. If we go back to the beginning of all things from this vantage point, we discover a rather more subtle foundation: not simply "In the beginning, God created," but "In the beginning was the Word, and the Word was with God and the Word was God" (John 1:1). Even before the world existed, God was a plurality as well as a singularity, a threeness ("trinity") as well as a oneness ("unity"). There was never a time when God was merely an "I," alone, inert, unrelated. No, God was always—*is* always—a "We." This is why Scripture can affirm so boldly that, in his own deepest nature, "God is love" (1 John 4:8). Note well: God is not just *loving*, not just kind and compassionate to everyone he comes into contact with. God is *love*. In his own self-contained being, he is the full, rich reality of lover and beloved, of giving and receiving, of union in distinction. God is not simply a self but also an ecstatic mutuality of delighted interpersonal communion.

Details of the doctrine of the Trinity can wait till our next chapter, but note the priority that this doctrine grants to the intensely personal character of God. According to historic Christianity, the essence of God is not an impersonal *genus*, some kind of divine "stuff" that the Father, Son, and Spirit share. Rather, the Father and the essence of God are numerically one and the same. There is no abstract nature called "God" that the person of the Father happens to have. No, the person of the Father *is* that "God," and everything that "God" means, is fully and personally existent in the Father. There simply is no "divinity" except the Father's own personal reality. The Son and the Spirit are likewise numerically one with the essence of God, eternally receiving from the Father (who begets the Son and who breathes forth the Spirit) the fullness of the divine being, so that they also are fully and personally divine. The only God there is, is this personal-times-personal-times-personal, this *exponentially* personal, Trinity.

Observe, further, that the intensely personal character of God as Father, Son, and Spirit entails an unqualifiedly *mutual* or *relational* component in the divine life. The three divine persons are distinct, but they are not, by any stretch of the imagination, independent of one another. On the contrary, they are so dependent, so interdependent, that though *each* is the one God, they also *together* constitute the one God. Christian tradition has sometimes referred to this startling feature of the divine life using the Greek word *perichoresis*, a term whose root has to do with dancing (as in our English word "choreography"). The idea is that the divine persons flow in and out of one another like participants in an intricate dance, but more so: they *fully and totally* interpenetrate or indwell one another—as Jesus himself intimated when he prayed to his Father and said, "You are in me and I am in you" (John 17:21).

This profound interpenetration tells us a lot about God's intensely personal character. There is within God's nature no tiniest potential for loving relationship or mutual glory or any such thing that has not been fully, personally, and interpersonally actualized from all eternity. Before the world was created, the love of the Father for the Son in the Spirit (John 17:24) and the reciprocal glory of Father and Son and Spirit (John 17:5; 16:14–15) were already permanent, living, joyous realities. At the core of all being, there was, and there is, fully actualized mutual love, an indescribably rich, inimitably relational, intensely personal plenitude.

Creation by the Personal God

What does this trinitarian way of thinking about God do for our understanding of creation? The answer is twofold, for through the beauty of the Trinity we perceive both the utterly gratuitous character of creation and also the amazingly personal intention that stands behind it.

On the one hand, the gratuitous character of creation. On Christian grounds, we cannot begin to think of the created world as satisfying some internal need in God. The Holy Trinity has never been lonely, has never found itself lacking in companionship. God did not create the universe, angels, or human beings to fill a relational vacuum in his own life, a divine "felt need" of sorts. Instead, creation is a fundamentally contingent reality. It did not have to exist at all; it is solely the result of God's freely chosen act of unconditional, unconstrained giving. In this respect, it *reflects* the interpersonal self-giving of Father, Son, and Spirit from all eternity, but it is not *essential* to it, as though the mutual love within the Trinity needed somehow to be supplemented. No, God's decision to create was utterly free, since deepest self-giving was already present in God's own inner life to an infinite extent. Hence, creation is strictly unnecessary, a sheer, unaccountable act of generosity, a gracious gift from beginning to end. When the richness of God's own trinitarian life fills our vision, we might almost forget that creation exists at all. God owes us nothing and needs nothing from us. Certainly creation can make no "claim" of any kind whatsoever on God, for his attention, his interest, his love.

On the other hand, when the act of creation takes place, it is none other than the intensely personal God who does the creating. Though he has no need to create, still the act of creation truly does reflect the infinite, eternal love that God himself is, a love whose very nature is to share, to give, to relate, to move toward the other. The creating God *is* this love, and this means not only that love is foundational to all created things (as we shall see in the next chapter) but also that the act of creation itself cannot be thought of merely as a work of detached, inhospitable "production," nor can the created world be thought of merely as an objective, external "product." If relationally rich, infinitely personal love graciously speaks the universe into existence and then joyously maintains its existence, we will hardly be surprised if creation also is somehow intended to share in that very same eternal communion. The intensely personal nature of God invites us to expect that the relationship between God and creation will never be merely a static business of maker and made, source and product. It will instead involve real personal engagement, real mutuality, real self-giving, real interpersonal knowledge and exchange.

Scripture confirms this expectation. When we come to the opening chapters of Genesis, we find in the sequential days of creation just what we might have anticipated, that is, a steady movement of increasing diversity and complexity both in the creatures themselves and in their relationships. The story culminates in the appearance on the sixth day of a remarkable creature that is different from all the others and that completes all the others. With the appearance of the man and the woman, the whole narrative is drawn to a very intentional, because deeply personal, climax.

We know that this climax is intentional because the text of Genesis 1 goes out of its way to make the point. We find no fewer than five significant indications that something unprecedented is taking place with the creation of the human pair on the sixth day.

1. There is a *linguistic change*, from language of God's sovereign fiat ("Let there be . . . ," etc.) in verses 3, 6, 9, and so on, to language of tender fashioning ("Let us make . . .") in verse 26.

2. There is a *stylistic change*—very significant in ancient, usually illiterate cultures—from prose to poetry in verse 27.

3. There is a *change in the nature of the created thing* in verse 26, as God decides to make this last creature, and this creature alone, in his very own image—a point to which we shall return in a moment.

4. There is a *relational change* in verses 26 and 28, as God bestows upon the man and the woman an authoritative dominion over every other creature.

5. Finally, there is a *change in God's evaluation* of the whole of creation, advancing from "good" in verses 4, 10, 12, and so on, to "very good" in verse 31.

Each of these features of the narrative provides an unmistakable hint that with the introduction of this last, best, unique creature, the work of creation is completed, and the created world is now prepared to be all that its intensely personal Creator intends.

The Climactic Image-Bearers

The climactic position of the man and the woman in this account is intimately connected with the enigmatic capacity or status or responsibility that they have received as the "image of God" (Latin, *imago Dei*). In all the rest of the narrative, though every creature is created directly by God and no doubt reflects God's glory in some fashion, though every creature is pronounced unequivocally "good" by God himself, yet no creature is said to have (or to be) anything like God's own image, God's own likeness. Evidently we have come upon a feature of the biblical account of humanity that is significant in the highest degree.

It is therefore somewhat surprising that we are given no explanation whatsoever of what the image of God means or refers to, either here in Genesis or elsewhere in Scripture (except the significant note in the New Testament that Jesus Christ images God perfectly—see below). As a result, this furtive reference in Genesis 1:26–27 to a notion that is clearly important to the narrative, and hence to our whole understanding of what it is to be a human person, has opened the door for Christians throughout the ages to attach a variety of specific meanings to the "image of God," each one an attempt to see what it is that gives to the human creature its distinctive nature and task. We might think of the *imago Dei* as consisting primarily in

- *rationality*—that is, the human capacity to reason and to speak, just as human "logic" derives from the divine *logos* (Greek for "reason" and "word"), the "Word" who was with God in the beginning and who enlightens everyone (John 1:1, 9);
- *morality*—humanity's ability to tell right from wrong, since the law of God is "written on their hearts" (Rom. 2:15);
- *aesthetic awareness*—our power to appreciate and even to create things of beauty and meaning, our own artistry and craftsmanship reflecting God's orderly creative work (see Gen. 1:28; 2:15);
- *volition*—the gift of free will, which allows men and women not merely to be determined by other factors but also to exercise conscious self-determination (see Ps. 32:9), once again reflecting the God who creates freely and without constraint;
- *religious capacity*—that elusive aspect of men and women (perhaps the human "soul" or "spirit") that allows us to worship in spirit and truth the God who is himself Spirit (John 4:24);

- *relational mutuality*—that is, humanity's interpersonal nature, as expressed both in sexual union (Gen. 1:27; 2:18) and in familial and social contexts (Gen. 4:9; Gal. 6:10), all of which sounds strikingly similar to God's own nature as unity in diversity (see Eph. 3:15); or, finally,
- *function*—that is, the peculiar "dominion" granted to humanity, the Godlike authority to rule over creation on behalf of God himself (Gen. 1:26; Ps. 8:5–8).

It may not be necessary to hitch our exegetical wagons to any one of these readings in isolation from the others. The point here is to see that the image of God, however it is understood, is a remarkable reality that sets the man and the woman at the apex of creation, above all other creatures—in a certain sense, even above creation itself. Talk about the *imago* moves us very quickly to a vision of humanity that is shockingly high. Our culture may teach us to think of human beings as simply another species of animal, and not a particularly distinguished species at that. But the astonished psalmist sees things differently, as he declares to God about the divine image-bearers, "You have made them a little lower than God, and crowned them with glory and honor. You have given them dominion over the works of your hands; you have put all things under their feet" (Ps. 8:5–6 NRSV). These human creatures, the psalmist seems to say, are like God in ways no created thing should be! Who would have thought that such a God-endowed, God-reflecting creature could exist?

The implications of this portrayal of humanity are immense. How can mere creatures know the incomprehensible God? One of those creatures is made for exactly that purpose! Humanity is uniquely endowed with capacities and tasks that make direct relationship with God possible, and even natural. To be a human person is to be nothing less than a great highway in which each lane converges upon the great destination that is God himself. Each aspect of created personhood serves as a path along which to approach the transcendent mystery that stands behind and in the midst of all of creation. Of course, as transcendent mystery, God cannot be confined to any created path: he will always overflow these boundaries and overload our capacities. Yet the paths themselves are designed with genuine interpersonal knowledge in mind. All humans are created with an invitation to know God stamped on their very nature, for the trinitarian God who is beyond knowledge desires to be known.

Trouble in Paradise

Ah, if only the God who desires to be known and the creature made for just such knowledge were the whole story! Unfortunately, they are not. As everyone knows, the story of creation in Genesis 1 and 2 moves quickly forward to a scene not so picturesque and tranquil. Genesis 3 tells of an enemy in God's good world, and of a temptation, and of a horrible and self-chosen "fall" into disobedience. Thus sin enters into the world, and nothing is left untouched.

Christians understand the details of Genesis 3 in many different ways, but the devastating results of humanity's defection from obedience to God are plain for all to see. While we humans still bear the divine image after the fall (Gen. 9:6), we presently do so in a tarnished, defaced, crippled manner. We have gone bad, like rotted wood; we are corrupt, twisted, splintered. The corruption manifests itself in a thousand ways: *physically*, as from the moment of our birth, we begin to die; *intellectually*, for we think and reason, but our thoughts are often dark, hurtful, confused, and self-serving; *relationally*, for we love, but we anxiously demand to be loved in return, and we often love what we should hate and hate what we should love; *volitionally*, for we can still discern right from wrong, yet our moral awareness is hazy and unreliable, and our will is vitiated. In biblical terms, we suppress the knowledge God graciously gives us (Rom. 1:18–21), so that outrageous behaviors ensue; we hate the light and love the darkness instead (John 3:19–21), and the world is filled with the havoc that results.

This is a dreadful situation, not least because, while all of our knowing and loving and willing is affected by sin, our knowledge of and love for and obedience to God himself is affected most directly. Though created to know God, we find ourselves now alienated from him, as the corrosiveness of sin turns even our ordinary finitude into an intolerable burden.

Yet there is still a wonder at work, for the tragedy of Genesis 3 leads to the glories of the rest of the biblical story. Despite the corruptive bacterium now infecting us, we remain God's personal image-bearers (cracked and distorted though the image may be), and so God has not left us to ourselves, slowly and inevitably rotting away. Instead, he has acted—and has acted repeatedly—in order to undo the effects of sin, in order to mold us back into what we were created to be.

The Old Testament is filled with this news. God has given the law to his people, that they may learn to live and to love in a way that reflects his own holiness. He has inspired wisdom, both in Israel and beyond, that all people may catch glimpses of a reasoned, practical truth that leads to life rather than death. He has sent prophets to provide concrete guidance in constructing a society rooted in justice and obedience. In all of this, God has marvelously revealed himself, drawing us back into relationship with him. He invites sinners to give up boasting of their wisdom or strength or riches, and instead to "boast about this: that they have the understanding to *know me*, that I am the Lord, who exercises kindness, justice and righteousness on earth, for in these I delight" (Jer. 9:24).

Then in the New Testament, something even greater takes place. "In the past God spoke to our ancestors through the prophets at many times and in various ways, but *in these last days he has spoken to us by his Son,* whom he appointed heir of all things, and through whom also he made the universe" (Heb. 1:1–2). In the fullness of time, God sent his own Son, the wonder of wonders, the culmination of his redemptive presence and activity in the world. This had been the plan all along. Even as far back as Genesis 3, God had offered prophetic hints that evil, sin, and death would not speak the last word to the human race. Eventually someone would come to crush Satan's head completely and irrevocably, though in the crushing he himself would also be wounded (Gen. 3:15). Through this wounding, the eternal Word speaks the final, lasting, triumphant, redemptive word. The story that has gone wrong in every human life is now made right as God the Son becomes the incarnate image of God, entering our world as one of us to rescue, redeem, and re-create his corrupted image-bearers.

Renewing the Image by Being the Image

We noted a few pages back that "image of God" is a phrase that is given maddeningly little formal definition in Scripture. This is true—except that when we examine the New Testament testimony, the christological and incarnational focus of the *imago* is striking. Paul preaches to the Corinthian Christians about "the glory of Christ, who is the image of God" (2 Cor. 4:4), and he tells the Colossians that it is Christ who "is the image of the invisible God, the firstborn over all creation" (Col. 1:15). Christ, the image of God, is the Word made flesh (John 1:14), "the only begotten God who is in the bosom of the Father" (John 1:18 NASB), the eternal Son who has created all things (Col. 1:16). The Letter to the Hebrews states that the Son "is the radiance of God's glory and the exact representation of his being, sustaining all things by his powerful word" (Heb. 1:3). We may want to know what the obscure language of *imago Dei* really refers to, but the New Testament does not define it. Instead, it points to where we can see the *imago* in action: we must turn our eyes to Jesus Christ. To look closely at Christ is to see at last what a real human being looks like.

This untarnished image of God, who represents God so perfectly that whoever sees him "has seen the Father" (John 14:9), has come into the world to redeem us. And how has this redemption been accomplished? In chapter 6, on the nature of Christ, we will address this question at some length, and we will appeal there to the approach taken by the great fourth-century defender of Christian orthodoxy Athanasius of Alexandria. As a preview, let us note here one famous analogy that Athanasius uses to explain the redeeming work of Christ:

> You know what happens when a portrait that has been painted on a panel becomes obliterated through external stains. The artist does not throw away the panel, but the subject of the portrait has to come and sit for it again, and then

the likeness is re-drawn on the same material. Even so was it with the All-holy Son of God. He, the Image of the Father, came and dwelt in our midst, in order that He might renew mankind made after Himself.[3]

It is a beautiful metaphor. If the seriousness of sin forbids a solution that is merely external and therefore superficial, here is a powerful account of the eternal Word taking on human nature precisely in order to make it new *from the inside out*. Later thinkers of the patristic era would formulate this idea pithily in terms of the famous principle, "Whatever is not assumed is not healed"[4]—in other words, our diseased human nature is "healed" only when every aspect of it is taken on ("assumed") by God the Son and is thereby united with the intensely personal Godhead itself. Then, when our lifeless nature is connected to the Source of infinite life, it is regenerated, raised, re-created, renewed, restored. It becomes again what it was meant to be, a genuine, authentic image of the living God, ready once again to know God himself.

Of course, this account of the saving work of Christ is only one part of a much larger story (again, see chapter 6 for details), but the emphasis here reminds us of the comprehensiveness of Christ's achievement. *Whatever* was broken in the created image of God has now been restored by the incarnation of the eternal image of God. Human nature is remade, as God the Son unites it to himself in order to make it new from the inside out (2 Cor. 5:17); our ignorance is overcome, as he lives a perfect life in order to show us what real humanity is (Heb. 4:15); our guilt is atoned for, as he dies a sinner's death in order to cancel forever the charge that is against us (Col. 2:13–14); our corruption is healed, as he rises to life again in order to inaugurate a new humanity with a new nature for a new age, that all who are in Christ may walk in newness of life (Rom. 6:4). As if all this achievement of Christ were not enough, God the Spirit also is given, to inscribe the law on believers' hearts (Heb. 10:15–16), to work inside us to draw us into the newness, the fullness, that is ours in Christ (John 16:13–15). Salvation is nothing less than full entrance into the life of Christ by the Spirit.

And when we are in Christ, we possess the Spirit-formed mind of Christ (1 Cor. 2:16)—that is, the mind of the Son, who knows the Father fully. We thus find that we have come full circle. Having been created for the knowledge of God, we are now re-created in Christ for that same knowledge of God. Do we doubt that Christ possesses real knowledge of God? Jesus himself tells us, "No one knows the Father *except the Son*" (Matt. 11:27). Do we doubt that we ourselves can possess such knowledge of God? Jesus goes on to say even

---

3. Athanasius, *On the Incarnation: The Treatise De Incarnatione Verbi Dei*, trans. and ed. A Religious of C.S.M.V., with an introduction by C. S. Lewis (Crestwood, NY: St. Vladimir's Seminary Press, 1982), 3.14, pp. 41–42.
4. See Gregory of Nazianzus, *Epistle 101, To Cledonius the Priest Against Apollinarius*, in *The Nicene and Post-Nicene Fathers*, series 2 (NPNF²), ed. Philip Schaff and Henry Wace (Peabody: Hendrickson, 1994), 7:440.

more: "No one knows the Father except the Son *and those to whom the Son chooses to reveal him*" (Matt. 11:27). As we enter into Christ, as we begin to have the mind of Christ, we once again are positioned for the unimaginable gift and task of knowing what is beyond knowledge, even the transcendent Lord of heaven and earth.

As we noted earlier in the chapter, the fundamental premise for human knowledge of God is fairly straightforward. God desires for us to know him, and he has acted to make such knowledge possible. The intensely personal God has created human beings in his image and in love has revealed himself to them; even after their self-destructive rebellion, he has chosen to speak rather than to remain silent, to instruct rather than to abandon; ultimately, in Christ and by the Spirit, he has extended to us the fullness of that unfathomably personal love that was always present within the Holy Trinity, stooping to envelop us in his own incomparable glory.

The Practice of Entering In

If God has done so much to make it possible for us authentically to know him, then we can surely maintain a good hope that that goal can be ever-increasingly realized. But along with hope, there is also disciplined, practical labor, and it is time now to consider this element in our knowledge of God. How can we *intentionally* enter into knowledge of the incomprehensible One? How can we nurture our relationship with the Father, Son, and Holy Spirit so that our knowledge and love of God continually deepen in response to the infinite love offered to us in Christ?

One answer is ready at hand: the Bible. "How can a young person stay on the path of purity? By living according to your word" (Ps. 119:9). The fundamental means God uses to teach us and to mold us into Christlikeness is the Bible. Of all Christians, evangelicals are probably the ones who least need to be reminded that our approach to God must be informed by and rooted in Scripture. This is one of the great strengths of evangelicalism.

Yet the Bible can so easily be treated as if it were merely God's answer book for all of our theological questions—as though life in Christ consisted in nothing more than having right answers! If the transcendent Lord really is a mystery, then no set of "answers"—not even the most thoroughly biblical set—will suffice to give us the deepest knowledge of God. On the contrary, "knowledge" of an anemic, rationalistic sort may do more harm than good, for "knowledge puffs up while love builds up" (1 Cor. 8:1). Knowing God is a matter not merely of analyzing data about him but of entering into him. Hence, we need more than accomplished exegetical skills and an awareness of the history of Christian thought. We need to become holy people, sons and daughters increasingly sanctified for our Father's use.

But how does this happen? How can mere "knowledge" be steadfastly transformed into authentic *knowledge of God*? It is a very large question, but any satisfying answer will include at least two important elements.

First, it will include *honest, humble repentance*. As we approach the God who has freely and lovingly given himself to us, we do well to draw near with great humility, much like Moses approaching the burning bush in the wilderness (Exod. 3). For like Moses, we tread on holy ground, where every form of duplicity, posturing, and self-reliance is struck down. Before the holiness of God, we can openly acknowledge who we are as human beings: our capabilities, our glories, our opportunities, but also our limitations, our frailties, and yes, our sins. We are created for the knowledge of God, but presently we are bent and wounded—skewed by our disproportionate desire for lesser goods and our twisted craving for a multitude of evils. Comprehending the incomprehensible God is no longer natural to us. Instead, it demands the regeneration of our dead nature and the radical reorientation of our minds and hearts.

Second, entrance into the knowledge of God will include *bold, faith-filled hope*. As troubled as our condition is, God's merciful invitation to draw near is still extended, even to us. "I, by your great love, can come into your house; in reverence I bow down toward your holy temple" (Ps. 5:7). The marvel of the gospel for those who welcome it is this: through the wonder of the person and work of Jesus Christ, God heals, redeems, and restores his image-bearers. Lifeless hearts begin beating. Hardened eardrums become supple, resonating to the tonal qualities of divine speech. Long-blind eyes regain their sight. Confused minds begin to comprehend. As redeemed, restored image-bearers, we can follow Christ to the Father through the Spirit, hopeful and confident as we embrace the grace bestowed upon us in the cross and resurrection. For now we are not only consulting the right sources of knowledge; we are also being formed into the right kind of knowers, the kind made for knowledge of the mystery of God above all else.

Knowledge and Doxology

More concretely, this whole process may be described as an increasing embrace of the *doxological* character of the knowledge of God. "Doxology" is an old-fashioned term that literally means a "word" (*logos*) of "glory" (*doxa*). To give a "doxology" is to speak a word or to sing a song that gives glory, that glorifies, and so the doxological character of the knowledge of God is its tendency to move from doctrine to *worship* of the living God in humility and faith.

Picture the scene on the Mount of Transfiguration in Matthew 17. It was just a few days after Peter's famous acknowledgment of Jesus's true identity as not just an articulate teacher or a miracle worker but as "the Messiah, the

Son of the living God" (Matt. 16:16). Peter had finally understood who Jesus was—an understanding that had come, Jesus says, not by mere human insight but by revelation from God (v. 17). Of course, Peter had not understood fully, for when Jesus went on to explain that he, as the Christ and the Son of God, would go to Jerusalem to suffer and die, it was Peter who rebuked him for this highly un-Jewish view of the Messiah's work on earth. Nevertheless, we might say that Peter's doctrinal knowledge was moving in the right direction through the guidance and discipline of the Spirit.

Then it was time for the next lesson. So Jesus invited Peter, James, and John to come with him up onto a nearby mountain to pray. Time alone with Jesus was always a special gift, and so we can imagine these disciples gladly accepting the invitation—never guessing what they would encounter at the mountaintop. The text gives a brief but astonishing description of what occurred as Jesus prayed:

> There he was transfigured before them. His face shone like the sun, and his clothes became as white as the light. Just then there appeared before them Moses and Elijah, talking with Jesus. . . . A bright cloud covered them, and a voice from the cloud said, "This is my Son, whom I love; with him I am well pleased. Listen to him!"
>
> Matt. 17:2–3, 5

A memorable experience to say the least! Perhaps we are not surprised that when the disciples saw all of this and heard God's own voice from heaven, "they fell facedown to the ground, terrified" (Matt. 17:6). Here was a stunning, overpowering revelation of an unparalleled glory, "the glory [*doxa*]," John tells us, "of the one and only Son, who came from the Father, full of grace and truth" (John 1:14). It was so much more than Peter had bargained for. He had already acknowledged publicly—and understood partially—that Jesus was the Son of God: his doctrine was technically correct. But on the mountain, he suddenly found himself *inside* the doctrine, not just believing that it was true as a propositional claim but encountering its truth and living in its majesty as well. The encounter on the mountain produced awe and terror in Peter and his companions, for they knew that the transcendent Lord of all was actively present.

The pattern of the transfiguration fits the overarching revelatory rhythm of much of Scripture. Mystery is straightforwardly revealed—that is, it is disclosed—and in that sense certain doctrines are made "known." But then the orthodox doctrine moves to a new level as the divine revelation generates spiritual life and power. No doubt it is still graciously accommodated to our capacity and need, yet now it strikes us as so beautiful, so awe-inspiring, so breathtakingly pure and perfect, that (at our best, most attentive moments) we are drawn out of ourselves to the holy self-forgetfulness of worship.

To worship is to wrap the mind and heart around the beauty of God, to discern and adore the unfathomable glory that we were created to experience and whose depths we long to explore. Worship encompasses gratitude for God's gifts, but it then moves beyond thanksgiving to fix its gaze on the magnificently transcendent otherness of the great Giver. This holy Lord invites us into his own presence in the power of his Spirit, for he has given his Son for our salvation, that we may believe in him, listen to him, feed on him, eat his body, drink his blood. In so doing, our knowledge of the incomprehensible God blossoms, as he himself comes to us in the Son and in the Spirit.

Christians have long recognized this doxological thrust that lies at the heart of authentic biblical doctrine. For example, Cyril of Jerusalem (AD 318–86), an ancient Christian leader responsible for teaching catechumens (young believers who were soon to be baptized), asks his pupils a telling question: "If the divine nature is incomprehensible, why bother even talking about these things?" Indeed! It is a question many Christians still struggle with. How can we seriously attempt "theo-logy" if the God (*theos*) we are talking about is past finding out? The answer that Cyril gives is very revealing. We think and speak in these orthodox theological ways because they lead us to worship. They allow us, he says, to

> praise and glorify him who made us, for it is a divine command that says, "Let everything that has breath praise the Lord!" (Ps. 150:6). I am endeavoring now to *glorify* the Lord, not to *describe* him.[5]

Cyril's obedience to the psalmist's command to "praise and glorify" the Lord moves him past mere *description*—and for that very reason it justifies the work of theology, for worship increases his comprehension of the mystery and moves him deeper into its depths.[6]

In this way we see that just as biblical truth inevitably draws us to worship, so also worship prepares us for biblical truth. The concrete rhythms of worship—its words, practices, disciplines, structures—center our attention on the heart of the matter: God's work in Christ, ongoing in the power of the Spirit, with the lived reality of God the glad result. The language and forms of worship support our wandering minds as we attempt to live in ways that reflect the centrality of Christ in all things. Thus, participation in worship functions as a kind of scaffolding for our knowledge of God. It establishes a consistent and remarkably tangible environment in which our redeemed life as God's image-bearers can flourish.

Worship's language is often quite earthy and physical. It is the language of eating, drinking, seeing, hearing, singing, praising, following—a language of active participation more than of objective description. We do, of course,

---

5. Cyril of Jerusalem, *Catechetical Lectures* 6.5 (NPNF² 7:34; italics added; we have slightly modified the translation).

6. Ibid.

praise God for who he is and what he has done for us; objective doctrine is
found throughout our praise. But, as Robert Webber and others have reminded
us, worship is a *verb*. In worship we engage more than our minds. We also
employ our bodies in specific acts: our throats as we sing and speak, our eyes
as we look upon stained glass or icons, our knees as we kneel, our arms as we
lift our hands in praise, our stomachs as we fast, our mouths as we taste the
Eucharist. In all of these movements, our doing sustains our knowing, even
as doing also grows out of knowing.

Spiritual Life and Discipline

Hence, the deepest theological insights are almost always birthed in conjunction with definite activities, the language and practices of disciplined, regular
worship, which are concrete means of grace given to us by the Holy Trinity to
provide a doxological pathway to the knowledge of God. Note our emphasis
on *discipline*. Knowledge comes by hearing God's voice, and we must learn
to be quiet if we are to hear. Knowledge comes as we are nourished by God's
own light and life, but this means we must avoid filling ourselves with the
spiritual junk food that "Christian" culture so readily provides. In a broken
world like ours, the habitual practice of classical spiritual disciplines can become the linguistic and practical substructure for greater blessings and deeper
knowledge than we would ordinarily think possible.

There is a great deal to be said about these practical disciplines of the spiritual life, though a book like this is not the place to say it.[7] The biblically rooted
experience of God's people throughout the ages very strongly suggests that
certain specially graced practices, reflections, habits, and dispositions, certain
specific ways of thinking, speaking, loving, and acting, tend to empower our
response to God's invitation to know him, so that we are led ever more fully
into his incomprehensible mystery.

7. We recommend Richard J. Foster, *Prayer: Finding the Heart's True Home* (San Francisco:
HarperSanFrancisco, 1992); Foster, *Celebration of Discipline* (San Francisco: Harper & Row,
1988); Richard J. Foster and James Bryan Smith, *Devotional Classics: Selected Readings for
Individuals and Groups* (San Francisco: HarperSanFrancisco, 2005); Dallas Willard, *The Spirit
of the Disciplines* (San Francisco: Harper & Row, 1988); John Ortberg, *The Life You've Always
Wanted: Spiritual Disciplines for Ordinary People* (Grand Rapids: Zondervan, 2002); Jan Johnson,
Spiritual Disciplines Companion: Bible Studies and Practices to Transform Your Soul (Downers
Grove, IL: InterVarsity, 2009); Adele Ahlberg Calhoun, *Spiritual Disciplines Handbook: Practices
That Transform Us* (Downers Grove, IL: InterVarsity, 2005); Susan S. Phillips, *Candlelight: Il-
luminating the Art of Spiritual Direction* (Harrisburg, PA: Morehouse, 2008); Michael Casey,
Sacred Reading: The Ancient Art of Lectio Divina (Liguori, MO: Liguori, 1996); M. Robert
Mulholland Jr., *Shaped by the Word: The Power of Scripture in Spiritual Formation* (Nashville:
Upper Room Books, 2000); Gerald L. Sittser, *Water from a Deep Well: Christian Spirituality from
Early Martyrs to Modern Missionaries* (Downers Grove, IL: InterVarsity, 2007); Richard J. Foster
and Gayle D. Beebe, *Longing for God: Seven Paths of Christian Devotion* (Downers Grove, IL:
InterVarsity, 2009); Dallas Willard, *The Divine Conspiracy: Rediscovering Our Hidden Life in
God* (San Francisco: HarperSanFrancisco, 1998).

This is not, of course, to suggest that these practices have some sort of magical power. On the contrary, the value of spiritual disciplines grows out of the ordinary, uncomplicated fact that our minds and bodies have been deeply, regularly influenced by all kinds of errors, illusions, fanaticisms, and entice-ments that are utterly antithetical to the values of Christ's kingdom. We, like our brothers and sisters throughout Christian history, are prone to distraction from Christ's call, drawn to the allurements of sin as surely as iron filings are drawn to a magnet. We often find ourselves responsive to the pull of spiritual and natural forces over which we appear to have little control. If we are not *vigilant*—a significant term, as we shall see in a moment—a radical disjunc-tion can occur between our theoretical beliefs and our concrete behaviors. We slip into spiritual schizophrenia, affirming key ideas and practices one minute and then violating them the next, advocating the truthfulness of one reality but habitually living in another.

So, although God invites us to enter freely into his abundance, entering in wisely, fruitfully, safely, and sanely is anything but easy in the brokenness of our culture and our lives. It is a craft to be learned, a skill to be honed, through the power of the Spirit and through the coaching of believers who have walked this path before us. One trustworthy group of believers to heed consists of the so-called desert fathers and mothers, Christians of the patristic age who practiced obedience to Christ in a monastic fashion in the desert and wilderness areas of Egypt, Syria, and Palestine. These desert dwellers invested long years developing exactly the "vigilance" that is necessary for persistent, diligent, focused pursuit of God in the midst of the brokenness that fallen humanity constantly faces.

The experience of these ancient believers consistently tells us that it is im-possible to stay spiritually healthy, attuned to the movement of God's Spirit, engaged with Scripture, and grounded in worship, without adopting and practicing some form of *ascesis* (pronounced "as-KEE-sis") or "exercise." *Ascesis* is an ancient term from which we get our English word "asceticism," and this connection may be jarring for some Protestant readers, for whom asceticism is associated primarily with certain medieval practices that seemed to emphasize works rather than faith and grace. But the idea itself is not far from biblical usage, for the apostle Paul commonly refers to Christian living in terms of the metaphor of an athletic competition and the kind of "strict training" (1 Cor. 9:25) that such competition requires. What sort of strict training might contemporary discipleship require? In order to answer this question, let us unpack the biblical metaphor a bit more.

All athletes in ancient Greece maintained a strict *ascesis* or training regimen, that included a specific diet, certain precise exercises (depending on the athlete's particular sport), hours of training on a daily basis, and so on. *Ascesis* was difficult, demanding, even grueling; it was usually repetitive, and often boring, occurring as it did behind the scenes, apart from the public's gaze. Yet if an athlete was lazy or unmotivated, neglecting the prescribed regimen, it would be naive to expect to succeed in the stadium or the arena. For each regimen was designed to develop the specific skills needed for excellence in a particular sport. Long-distance runners engaged in one type of *ascesis*. Wrestlers practiced another. Occasionally, the connection between a certain part of the training and the sport itself might not be immediately apparent; then the athletes had to trust that their trainers knew the sport well enough to select exercises that were appropriate. But everyone agreed that a well-designed *ascesis*, under the eyes of an expert coach, was the key to honing the athlete's innate abilities and enabling performance at peak levels throughout the competition.

This athletic metaphor sheds light on the practices of many of the great pastors, teachers, and theologians of the ancient church, wise believers who habitually engaged in some specific *ascesis*, some spiritual regimen designed to enhance, enliven, and deepen their relationship with God. This regular training frequently included both secular and spiritual practices (since spiritual growth never occurs in isolation from intellectual, emotional, and cultural factors), but its heart was the practice of key spiritual disciplines, such as prayer, fasting, study, meditation, confession, simplicity, and service. Such practices—then and now—promote the healing and shaping of the human personality ever more fully into the image of Christ, so that Christ's disciples can think about and live in the mystery of God with increasing clarity, insight, and power.

Counsel from the Desert

For the purposes of this book, we cannot investigate these various spiritual disciplines with much thoroughness. However, we can attend to four basic bits of counsel from the ancient world that will be an important part of almost any thoughtful, intentional, spiritual *ascesis*. What must contemporary Christians do if we want to follow the path of disciplined pursuit of the knowledge of God?

We Must Cultivate Sacred Space in the Midst of Our Busy World

That the world is busy no one will probably dispute, and its busyness is frequently of a kind that sucks us in and leaves us breathless. In our globalized, technologized world, we are inundated with noise, news, crowds, information, and entertainment. Distractions bombard us daily, all too frequently diverting our attention from the most important things. Perhaps this is just the accidental character of our age—or perhaps something more spiritually alarming is going on. Richard Foster writes, "Our Adversary the devil majors in three things: noise, hurry, and crowds. If he can keep us engaged in 'muchness' and 'manyness,' he will rest satisfied."[8] In any case, in such a hectic, fragmented, unruly environment, we ourselves also become deeply, deplorably fragmented.

How, then, can believers in the one true God regain their center, their grounding, the integration of the mind with the heart? How can followers of Christ consistently, habitually set their internal compass toward "true north," toward Christ himself? Our ancient brothers and sisters suggest that we can succeed only by finding "space" that is calm enough, settled enough, free enough from distractions and competing voices, that we can once again discern the quiet, insistent voice of God calling us into his mystery.

Note that the "space" that is sought here is not merely open fields and starry skies (though it may include both). Instead, it refers to any free, unrestricted, unhurried setting that can nurture health and growth and life. It includes what we might call "interior space," that is, spaciousness in our mental and emotional inner life, where we so frequently need freedom from the demands and urges and anxieties that seem to fill us. It includes the "spaces" of our concrete ecclesial world, so that intentional locations and times and attitudes can challenge and transform the tedious business of everyday life. It includes the "spaces" of our physical environment, what we regularly see and hear and touch, for our surroundings will inevitably have a subtle but decisive influence upon our spiritual equilibrium, either supporting or preventing our development as lovers of what is good and true and beautiful.

Consider for a moment how early Christians found exactly this kind of multifaceted "space" in the beautiful and harsh desert geography that many of them inhabited day and night. The desert offered intense, unremitting solitude and silence, so that Christians could learn to listen intently to Scripture, to hear the voice of God in prayer, to enter into the liturgy of the church, to confront their own habitual thoughts, and to rejoice in the unique sounds and silences presented by this particular part of God's creation, so stark, silent, and demanding. Here there were no distractions, but only the immediate, unavoidable reality of oneself (one's deepest dispositions, one's strongest loves—good and bad) and the living God. Here, "space" of the productive, fruitful kind was at a maximum.

The sacred openness of the desert is a live option for very few modern Christians (though monastic communities still flourish in some desert locales), and in our modern context similar "learning spaces"[9] are difficult to find. Yet find them—or create them—we must, for the knowledge of God will rarely be available without them. If we are to enter deeply into Christ, we need a consistent space in which prayerful, worshipful reflection can occur, in which steady, measured meditation and immersion in the Scriptures is supported and

8. Foster, *Celebration of Discipline*, 15.
9. The phrase is Parker Palmer's, and we are indebted to Palmer's thoughts on learning in the space of the desert. See Parker Palmer, *To Know as We Are Known: Education as a Spiritual Journey* (San Francisco: HarperOne, 1993), 69–76.

sustained, in which we are forced to deal with the issues, distractions, and habits that squelch worship rather than nurture it. For us today such space might be found in a chapel, a private study, a bench by a lake, a closet illuminated by a candle, a daily walk, a soup kitchen, a hospital ward, a prison, a hospice. The list of possibilities seems endless. But we should consider what specific, strategic steps we can take to introduce a deeper, receptive silence into our inner lives, into our communities, into our physical environment.

We Must Develop Self-Awareness through Discipline

Many of the classical spiritual disciplines (prayer, confession, simplicity, and the like) strike contemporary Christians as good, wholesome spiritual habits, and so they are. But there is also more going on. Encountering God in disciplined, life-giving worship ignites a fundamental movement in the believer from self-deception to self-awareness, a movement aimed at developing a deep knowledge of both who we are and who we are called to be in Christ. This is why most of the disciplines have a not entirely pleasant "edge" to them.

Take, for instance, the discipline of fasting. We may like to believe that we are patient, long-suffering people. Yet what do we frequently see when we fast? Along with our hunger, a variety of hidden issues bubble to the surface: we chafe at inconvenience, we snap at those around us, we crave specific sensations, we demand satisfaction. The temporary deprivations involved in fasting crack us open like nuts, revealing some of the hidden realities that lie within us, truths hidden from our direct consciousness by our dependence upon food, distractions, amusements, and so on. After a few hours of fasting, our whole consciousness echoes the scream of our bodies: "I want to eat, and I want to eat *now!*"—though in fact we could refrain from eating for hours or even days with little physical harm. In this way the discipline of fasting serves as a means of grace that God lovingly employs to expand our self-knowledge and deflate our self-deception, to help us to discern who we actually are and who we ought to be.

It is not only in their traditional forms that these disciplines can be helpful. For instance, some people have discovered the challenges and benefits of the classical discipline of fasting not by giving up food periodically but by giving up entertainment media for a season. In a recent semester at Eastern University (where both authors of this book teach), some forty students agreed to take part in a "media fast." They agreed to fast from all forms of media over a seven-week time span—no music, no films, no radio, no television, no texting, no Facebook, no YouTube, no internet, no video games, no CDs, no DVDs, and extremely limited use of cell phones and email (no more than fifteen minutes a day). Some participants initially reported that they felt quite anxious. Others struggled with boredom. Many found that other, nonmedia temptations increased. There was initially much distress on every side.

Yet for almost all participants, after a week or so these initial difficulties subsided as deeper things began to happen. Many students reported that God, the world, and they themselves began to look different. Their media fast created time to read the Bible in a much more concentrated manner. Conversations with others became more frequent and generally deepened. Students' awareness of the effect of their environment upon them heightened. They became more attuned to what had shaped their thinking, speech, and behaviors. Many found themselves more sensitive to the Holy Spirit. With the absence of almost all distractions and diversions, they could not hide from themselves. Behavior and thought patterns that had been ignored or unrecognized for years suddenly rose to the surface of their consciousness. Areas that needed the healing and transformation of the Holy Spirit clarified. Concrete change began to occur in students' thinking, speaking, and behavior as the Spirit spoke into the silence of these new learning spaces. Many participants said at the end that this fast had sometimes been deeply painful, but also redemptive and restorative. Their hunger for God deepened as other, lesser hungers were reined in.

The experience of this group of students is by no means exceptional. The challenge of disciplined spiritual living very frequently draws practitioners closer to God precisely by unveiling to them the truth about themselves—a truth that, painful as it is, we must face honestly if we are to enter into the knowledge of God. It is too easy to move unthinkingly through our more-or-less comfortable lives in a state of vast self-deception. A sizeable body of empirical research demonstrates the deep resistance humans have toward facing unpleasant truths about themselves, truths regarding everything from practical failure at some simple assigned task to profound moral transgression.[10] We very commonly lie to ourselves and to others about the true state of affairs in our lives. We imagine ourselves generous yet rarely give anything away; we think we are fairly pure in our thinking despite being addicted to a weekly jaunt through the Web's darkest corridors; we thoughtlessly attack someone's character one minute, and the next minute we are humming a praise chorus or sitting in a worship service—or even writing a paragraph on the mystery of God!

To admit the truth about ourselves is always a harrowing, and sometimes a horrifying, experience. Yet if we persist in lying to ourselves and to others and even to God about our own character, as it is shown through our habitual patterns of thinking and behavior, our spiritual growth and ultimately our knowledge of God cannot but be stunted. Our dispositions and behaviors,

---

10. See William M. Bernstein, Walter G. Stephan, and Mark H. Davis, "Explaining Attributions for Achievement: A Path Analytic Approach," *Journal of Personality and Social Psychology* 37, no. 10 (October 1979): 1810–21. See also Gifford W. Bradley, "Self-Serving Biases in the Attribution Process: A Reexamination of the Fact or Fiction Question," *Journal of Personality and Social Psychology* 36, no. 1 (January 1978): 56–71.

our habituated affections and thoughts and actions, profoundly affect what
we can "see," understand, and discern theologically. The very worst, most
destructive theology is produced by those who desire to write about God
without allowing themselves to be changed by God.

We Must Foster the Conscious Imitation of Praiseworthy Models

The relation between teacher and students, or between master and disciples,
was precious in the ancient world. Entering into healthy, life-giving knowledge
of God was closely linked to following the right teacher or teachers. But "following" was a full and rich concept, rooted in part in the classical discipline
of intensely purposeful *imitation* of the teacher. Many Greek students, for
example, were instructed to "install Demosthenes in their souls."[11] How did
such "installation" work?

Students would spend years studying and memorizing the works of the one
they wanted to follow, perhaps a classical author such as Homer or Virgil.
Most educated Greeks had memorized the entire *Iliad* by the time they were
eighteen years old. This memory work took time and effort; it was clearly an
ascesis of sorts. Sentences, paragraphs, pages, and entire texts were studied
and vocalized, then restudied and revocalized, and then restudied and revocalized again. Gradually, through this disciplined *ascesis*, the thoughts of Homer
settled firmly and lastingly into a student's memory. The student's consciousness changed through this intense immersion, as he or she began to see the
world through the eyes and mind of the ancient Greek poet. In a manner of
speaking, the mind of the student and the mind of Homer merged.

So much for Homer; what about Christ? Early Christians took this same
focused regimen of imitation and skillfully adapted it to a life of Christian
discipleship. Desiring to be shaped into the image of Christ, who is himself
the image of God (Col. 1:15), and knowing that in Christ were hidden all the
treasures of wisdom and knowledge (Col. 2:3), followers of Christ took very
seriously the call to imitation. Consider the apostle Paul's constant exhor-
tations to imitation—the imitation of Christ, of God, of himself, of other
faithful disciples, and of the church:

- "*Follow God's example*, therefore, as dearly loved children and walk
  in the way of love, just as Christ loved us and gave himself up for us
  as a fragrant offering and sacrifice to God" (Eph. 5:1–2).
- "Even if you had ten thousand guardians in Christ, you do not have
  many fathers, for in Christ Jesus I became your father through the
  gospel. Therefore I urge you to *imitate* me" (1 Cor. 4:15–16).

11. Margaret M. Mitchell, *The Heavenly Trumpet: John Chrysostom and the Art of Pauline
Interpretation* (Louisville: Westminster John Knox, 2002), 43.

- "Join together in *following my example*, brothers and sisters, and just as you have us as a model, keep your eyes on those who live as we do" (Phil. 3:17).
- "Whatever you have *learned or received or heard from me, or seen in me*—put it into practice" (Phil. 4:9).
- "You know how we lived among you for your sake. You became *imitators* of us and of the Lord. . . . And so you became a *model* to all the believers in Macedonia and Achaia" (1 Thess. 1:5–7).
- "For you, brothers and sisters, became *imitators* of God's churches in Judea" (1 Thess. 2:14).

In all these texts the central theme is the same: there is a pattern of thinking and living that Christ's followers are called to imitate. This pattern is displayed most exactly in Christ himself, but it is also displayed in apostles like Paul and in faithful Christians everywhere. As we follow it by imitating them, we learn to think what they thought, to live as they lived, to love what they loved.

John Chrysostom, late fourth-century archbishop of Constantinople, exemplifies this pattern well. Rather than installing Demosthenes or Homer in his soul, Chrysostom substituted Paul and Christ. During two years spent in solitude in a cave above Antioch, a "learning space" for immersion in Paul's letters, Chrysostom memorized most, if not all, of the New Testament. As Margaret Mitchell notes, "Chrysostom inscribed on his brain a lot of Paul, and, at that, a lot of Paul speaking in the first person, now vocalized through [Chrysostom's] own mouth. Not only did constant rereading and memorization of these texts serve to lay the foundation for a life of Scriptural exposition, but it also oriented Chrysostom's own consciousness in a Pauline direction."[12]

During the years in the cave, Chrysostom developed key habit patterns he would later encourage his own congregation to develop. "The inexperienced reader when taking up a letter will consider it to be papyrus and ink; the experienced reader will both hear a voice, and converse with one, the one who is absent. . . . The things their writings said, they manifested to all in their actions. . . . You have a most excellent portrait [of the apostle Paul]. *Proportion yourself to it*."[13] In Chrysostom's thinking, to *proportion* oneself to Paul—through the use of a highly developed memory soaked in the Scripture and through concrete imitation of key aspects of Paul's life—is by definition to proportion one's mind and life to Christ.

All of us probably have individual teachers and mentors whom we want to emulate. If they are still living, we want to spend time with them whenever possible; if they have died, we want to read their works and find out more about

---

12. Ibid., 67.
13. Ibid., 48–50 (*NPNF*² 12:35; 13:240); cf. Christopher A. Hall, "Chrysostom," in *The Blackwell Companion to Paul*, ed. Stephen Westerholm (Oxford: Blackwell, 2011), 331–32.

their lives. In the case of Christ himself and of his apostles and prophets, one can hardly go wrong by entering into the Holy Scriptures, as Chrysostom did, with careful, gracious imitation always in mind. To imitate Christ is to regard his words and deeds as precious treasures, to contemplate them, memorize them, meditate upon them, to chew on them as a cow chews its cud. To imitate Paul is to ask how he conducted himself from day to day, and what were the practices that nourished and sustained his own life in Christ.

Of course, this call to attend carefully to the biblical witness regarding Christ and Paul is not merely *in order* to imitate; we are also attending to *an instance* of imitating, since both our Savior and his apostle were (like all good Jews) steeped in the Scriptures. If we are to follow them in the knowledge of God, our thinking, too, must be profoundly shaped by the steady, paced memorization of the Word of God. This need not, and should not, signal slavishly rote memorization, but creative practical application as well. The aim of memorization is not to pass some cosmic Bible quiz but to have our intellectual and imaginative consciousness shaped by God himself. We need not have a biblical phrase to toss into every conversation, but we do want to speak and to live in the world in the way that Scripture itself illustrates. As theologian Kevin Vanhoozer has suggested, the whole goal of theology, when it is faithful to the Bible, "is to train the Christian imagination . . . to see, feel, think about, and act in the world in ways similar to those of the biblical authors, the commissioned witnesses to the event of Jesus Christ."[14]

This sort of thoughtful, committed, creative imitation of the exemplary lives we see in Scripture (and elsewhere) prepares us for deeper entrance into the knowledge of God that such lives embody. As we noted above, thinking and behavior, behavior and thinking, are all one piece, one whole. On this matter, Athanasius of Alexandria gave counsel in the early fourth century that is still worth our attention today:

> One cannot possibly understand the teaching of the saints unless one has a pure mind and is trying to imitate their life. . . . Anyone who wants to look at sunlight naturally wipes his eye clear first, in order to make, at any rate, some approximation to the purity of that on which he looks. . . . Similarly, anyone who wishes to understand the mind of the sacred writers must first cleanse his own life, and approach the saints by copying their deeds.[15]

We Must Grow in Humility and Other Virtues That Support Theological Insight

This last recommendation is especially relevant to those whose professional work involves explicit theological reflection. Pastors and other teachers of

14. Kevin J. Vanhoozer, *The Drama of Doctrine: A Canonical Linguistic Approach to Christian Theology* (Louisville: Westminster John Knox, 2005), 377.
15. Athanasius, *On the Incarnation* 9.57, p. 96.

theology are in no wise immune from the wide variety of vices that grow like weeds in the personalities of the self-deceived. Some seem to find their own grasp of God's truth to be so firm and complete that it is virtually indistinguishable from the revealed Word of God. Others are tempted to view theology as a competitive sport in which the most important outcome is victory over one's opponent. Still others so tightly identify their distinctive theological outlook with their sense of self that admitting weaknesses in their position becomes a threat to their personal identity. The doctrine of one's own personal, deeply deceitful sinfulness is often that part of a systematic theology that is most difficult for "the professionals" in theology to bear steadfastly in mind as they do their work.

This difficulty is concretely expressed in at least two different ways. First, theologians often struggle—perhaps more than most other believers—with the devastating malady of *theological pride*, that is, with an overblown, exaggerated estimation of their own theological capabilities, insights, and positions. Should we be surprised by this? If pride, to a greater or lesser degree, manifests itself in all human personalities, it will also appear in the self-estimation of theologians and in the theology they produce.

Pride is deeply opposed to limitations of any kind on the self, and this resistance often shows up as an insatiable thirst for "completeness" in our understanding, an unwillingness to admit any significant limitations on our own theological insight. Think of the Eunomian theologians whom we met in chapter 3, who were a thorn in the side of many orthodox Christians of the fourth century. These theologians mistakenly believed they had thoroughly plumbed the depths of the divine essence through what they considered foolproof, fail-safe logical syllogisms. They had figured God out, both his actions and even his very essence.

Writing against this movement, fourth-century bishop Gregory of Nazianzus suggested that the Eunomians had forgotten who they were and who God was—and is. They had irreverently overstepped their bounds. In particular, Gregory discerned a haughtiness and a flippancy in the Eunomians' attitude toward their theological vocation, a tone of mind and heart that was more appropriate for a discussion of the chariot races or the most recent play or concert.[16] He describes their attitude and ideas as undisciplined, frivolous, and immodest.[17] There is a wise way and a foolish way to theologize, Gregory exhorts. Wise theologians exercise their reason reverently, thinking and writing while they are kneeling, so to speak. Reverent humility—the gracious fruit of the Holy Spirit, who is at work within us—is an indispensable disposition if we are to ponder the beauty of God with doxological integrity. "Holy things," Gregory coaches, must be approached in a "holy manner." We do

16. See Gregory of Nazianzus, *The First Theological Oration* 3 (NPNF² 7:285).
17. Gregory of Nazianzus, *The First Theological Oration* 3 (NPNF² 7:287).

well to whisper God's mysteries "under our breath" rather than trumpet our knowledge from the housetops.[18]

These are wise words not just for ancient Eunomians but for any forgiven sinner who regularly stands in public in order to proclaim the truth of God. "Not many of you should become teachers," the apostle James warns, "because you know that we who teach will be judged more strictly" (James 3:1). Scripture gives us no indication whatsoever that we will always be able to answer with confidence every question we wish to ask, or every question we are asked by others. Words like "The Bible clearly teaches . . ." do have their place in any authentic account of the gospel, but words like "It's not entirely clear . . ." or "Faithful Christians have disagreed . . ." or even the good, old-fashioned "I don't know . . ." surely also have a place. Proud, unbridled reason, Gregory says, is much like a wild, untrained stallion that refuses to submit to the bridle in its mouth—and that therefore cannot go where it is intended to go. Empty, hollow, and brittle speech about God must be rinsed out of our theological vocabulary, to be replaced by a more quietly humble, more wholesomely discerning theology.[19]

There is a second, related danger for "the professionals." Theologians can often manifest all too easily a *polemical spirit*, a spirit that delights in pointing out the faults in others' theologies, that readily brands controversial ideas as "heresies" and their promulgators as "heretics," and that smugly separates from anything and anyone that does not measure up to "the truth."

This is a profoundly difficult matter, in which God's people need the "wisdom that is from above" (James 3:17 KJV) to an unparalleled degree. There certainly is a time to refute heresies and to rebuke heretics; there certainly is a time to expel sinners or to separate from them. In certain contexts, the refusal to refute or to rebuke, to expel or to separate, may itself be a sign, not of humility, but of a terrible spiritual malaise. Those who do not love the Lord deeply will never be much concerned with the details of his truth.

Yet this very fact makes it easy for us to conclude that we *do* love the Lord deeply so long as we are scrupulously, tirelessly, ruthlessly committed to every detail of what we perceive to be a biblical theological system. But this conclusion simply does not follow. A whole host of other explanations for doctrinal fussiness is available, explanations related variously to greed, vanity, malice, impatience, fear, envy, and every other deadly vice. It is the crassest naïveté to believe that all doctrinal arguments are merely, or even primarily, about doctrine. In the highly competitive climate of professional theology, where large ministries and international reputations and prestigious appointments and lucrative book contracts are all at stake, we cannot be too careful to guard ourselves against the sort of destructive pride that cloaks itself in the mantle of "Guardian of the Faith."

18. Gregory of Nazianzus, *The First Theological Oration* 3 (NPNF[2] 7:286).
19. See ibid.

This danger suggests that those of us whose vocation really *is* to guard the faith should exercise every caution to ensure that our work is rooted in the all-embracing beauty of Christ, where every virtue is made perfect. As much as any other Christians on earth, we must be prepared to heed Paul's wise counsel to the church at Colossae:

> As God's chosen people, holy and dearly loved, clothe yourselves with compassion, kindness, humility, gentleness and patience. Bear with each other and forgive one another if any of you has a grievance against someone. Forgive as the Lord forgave you. *And over all these virtues put on love, which binds them all together in perfect unity.*
>
> Col. 3:12–14

Without this crucial grounding in love, our unanswerable defense of orthodoxy may turn out to be only a resounding gong or a clanging cymbal (1 Cor. 13:1).

Probably every reader has his or her own view of where to draw the line that separates a legitimate commitment to doctrinal purity from an illegitimate polemicism. This is not the place to resolve that issue (if it is even *possible* to resolve it: recall that Scripture often commends godly wisdom more than punctilious casuistry in such matters; see Prov. 26:4–5), but we do want to insist that the theologian who fails to recognize the danger here is easily the one most likely to fall into it. Discerning the line and living wisely according to it are not simply a matter of academic training and intellectual astuteness and polemical skill. They are a matter first and foremost of virtue—that is, of personal and communal holiness. Without holiness, no one—not even a hyperorthodox theologian—will see the Lord (Heb. 12:14).

A deep rooting in the spiritual practices and the doxological context of the church throughout the ages can help to protect us from our internal propensity toward theological hubris and polemical immoderation. It is protection that we all sorely need. It is not uncommon for a well-trained pastor or theologian to give an authoritative lecture on a theological hot-spot, to pray an eloquent public prayer, to identify the flaws in a competitor's argument, to lead a sinner to follow the Lord, and to grant an interview to the public media, all in a morning's work. This is heady stuff, all of it—and all part of our God-given duty as orthodox teachers and leaders of the faithful. Yet the danger of a Pharisaic blindness to our own theological shortcomings and waywardness remains real. May God in his great mercy protect us from it.

Conclusion

It is time to draw this lengthy chapter, and also this first part of our study, to a close. First, the chapter. We have seen that, if human beings are ever to know the God who is beyond knowledge, it will be because they were marvelously created for such knowledge in the first place; because they have been lovingly re-created and spiritually empowered to enter into the mind of Christ; and because they have followed the disciplined, practical wisdom of the church in order to shape their lives in a manner that consistently supports their lofty aim. In this entire endeavor, the interpenetration of doctrine and life is evident. Plain and simple, we dare not attempt to speak and think about God in a doxological vacuum. If worship and its accompanying habits have not formed our appetites, how can we expect to relish the meal God sets before us in Christ? Rather than eating, we will be tempted merely to think about our supper, to analyze it, to discuss it, all the while keeping our distance lest our neat, tidy shirts be stained. But knowledge of the mystery comes in the tasting.

This is why, as important as particular words are in theological discourse, they are not what ultimately matters. The aim of theology is always to move *through* the words to the authentic, everlasting glory of the transcendent God himself, a glory that no words will ever be able to contain. Here in part 1, we have looked biblically, historically, and practically at just how central this incomprehensible glory is for Christian faith and life. We have found that it is . . . well . . . *everything*. The idea that we should know the God who is beyond knowledge is at the heart of the biblical portrayal of God; it is a decisive feature of every brand of authentic Christianity that history has produced; and it is foundational to the church's experience of what it is to be human and to live a holy life of love and beauty before God. The incomprehensible God is the dazzlingly bright sun that dominates the sky every day of our lives, that all the world depends upon and revolves around.

Now as we move into part 2, we will focus more explicitly on particular matters of faith and life, as we try to see how divine incomprehensibility helps to make sense of all sorts of lesser matters. In other words, once the bright sun is high in the sky, what does the landscape now look like? Where do we find ourselves able to see more clearly precisely because our vision is strengthened by something that is too bright to see at all?

Part 2

The
LANDSCAPE

5

The MYSTERY
of the TRINITY

He is insane who dreams that he may learn
   by mortal reasoning the boundless orbit
   Three Persons in One Substance fill and turn.
Be satisfied with the quia of cause unknown
   O humankind! For could you have seen All,
   Mary need not have suffered to bear a son.

Dante[1]

The Trinity is understood and worshiped by faith—by faith, not by inquiry or investigation or demonstration. The harder you look, the less you will find; the more you seek, the more it will be hidden. God ought therefore to be worshiped by believers with an incurious mind. Believe that God exists in three hypostases [persons], but how this can be is beyond our understanding, because God is incomprehensible.

John of Damascus[2]

---

1. Dante, *Purgatorio* 3.34–39, in *The Divine Comedy*, trans. John Ciardi (New York: W. W. Norton, 1977).
2. John of Damascus, *On Heresies, Epilogue*, quoted in *Ancient Christian Doctrine*, vol. 1, *We Believe in One God*, ed. Gerald L. Bray (Downers Grove, IL: IVP Academic, 2009), 87.

One of the ironies of Trinity Sunday (a festival of the church year celebrated in the Roman Catholic and Anglican communions) is the apology almost always offered by the poor rectors and parish priests who face the daunting task of preaching on the Trinity. The church calendar requires them to focus on this theme, but they often feel overwhelmed and intimidated, faced with the impossible task of making clear and helpful what everyone knows cannot be either clear or helpful. Hence, the sermon usually begins with a fairly lame joke about the impossibility of making sense of the Trinity, and the congregation quietly murmurs in agreement as the preacher descends, step by step, into a murky exegetical and theological black hole. When the sermon finally comes to a conclusion, both the rector and the congregation are apt to feel dissatisfied, confused, and generally thankful that the next Trinity Sunday is a full year away.

Many of these dissatisfied Christians are unwittingly approaching the Trinity in a way not much different from that of Mormon theologian Robert Millet, who gently criticizes classical trinitarian doctrine for its strange arithmetic. "I simply ask: How can $1 + 1 + 1 = 1$? Again, meaning no irreverence, I ask: If we were to invite the Trinity to dinner, how many settings would I need to set? Three persons are three persons. Three persons cannot be one person, nor can I conceive how three persons can be one being."[3] It is not hard to see the problem here, and not hard to sympathize with those who wish that the puzzle could be solved, or else that it would simply go away.

But do we really want this "puzzle" to be "solved"? Readers who have followed our argument in part 1 will be rightly suspicious of such language. The mystery of God—surely expressed nowhere more manifestly than in the doctrine of the Trinity—is not investigative but revelational. It is not a puzzle whose solution eliminates the mystery but a plenitude whose revelation makes known the mystery. As God's image-bearers, we are created to know God, to love God, to enjoy God. God desires and intends to be known and loved, and so he has invited us into his "privy counsel," so to speak. Yet he certainly gives us no promise that we will find him to be less astonishing and wondrous as a result. On the contrary, the invitation is precisely to enter into this glorious wonder more deeply, and to be fed and nourished by what we cannot fully comprehend.

Our aim in this chapter is to give some account of how the mystery of the Trinity fits this description, sometimes in spite of how we have heard the doctrine presented or explained. It should be noted that our aim is *not* to defend the doctrine of the Trinity in any direct way against its various critics (like Dr. Millet). Such a defense lies outside the parameters of this book, and in any case many other books have been written to undertake it.[4] For our

---

3. Robert L. Millet and Gerald R. McDermott, *Claiming Christ: A Mormon-Evangelical Debate* (Grand Rapids: Brazos, 2007), 80.

4. For an extended bibliography of works on the Trinity, along with commentary about the usefulness of different works, see Roger E. Olson and Christopher A. Hall, *The Trinity* (Grand Rapids: Eerdmans, 2002).

purposes, we will simply assume that the doctrine is true; our goal is to see how it can also be meaningful—and meaningful not in spite of, but because of, God's intrinsic incomprehensibility. In other words, we hope to show that *if God is the incomprehensible mystery that Christianity has always declared*, then Christian affirmations about God begin to make more sense and to fit in with other things that we know and understand. Christians can enter into reflection on God as Father, Son, and Holy Spirit without nervous jokes about incoherence, and with an abiding doxological wonder instead.

The Doctrine and Its "Solutions"

Every reader will have some basic grasp of what the doctrine of the Trinity is, but one can hardly do better than to begin with the word itself. The term "Trinity" is not found in Holy Scripture but was coined by the early third-century Latin theologian Tertullian as a way of drawing together the emerging Christian doctrine of God. The word consists of two elements, *tri* and *unity*, and each of these elements is crucial to an adequate understanding of the doctrine.

Take the second element first. Who and what do we worship as we bow our knees to the living God? Loudly and clearly we proclaim that we believe in the *one* and the *only* God. The word "unity"—and perhaps even more obviously the word "unit"—means "one." There are not two gods; there are not three; there is one. This absolutely unique, unclassifiable God has created all things, from the smallest subatomic particle to the vast expanses of the universe and from the tiniest single-celled organism to the highest archangel. All that exists outside of this one God belongs to the created order, and the line between the created and the uncreated is absolute. In this respect, Christians happily agree with ancient Israel that "the LORD our God, the LORD is one" (Deut. 6:4), and they gladly follow Jesus, who famously cites this same text from Deuteronomy in answer to a question about the first or greatest commandment: "The most important one . . . is this: 'Hear, O Israel: the Lord our God, the Lord is one. Love the Lord your God with all your heart and with all your soul and with all your mind and with all your strength" (Mark 12:29–30). Thus, when we worship the Trinity, we worship a *unity*. We are not worshiping three gods.

Yet the doctrine of the Trinity does include a noteworthy *tri*, a very definite threeness, that Christians have always ascribed to the persons of the Trinity. Within the one being of God there is an unexpected metaphysical complexity, a genuine interpersonal plurality, that is particularly associated with the names Father, Son, and Spirit. These three are relationally distinct from each other, such that the Father is not the Son, and the Son is not the Spirit, and the Spirit is not the Father—though each of these three is, without qualification, the one and only God.

How can this be? How can the three be distinct from one another if each is the one and only God? One would expect the fact that each person is identical with the one divine essence to eliminate the possibility of real distinction and relational complexity. Yet the paradoxical conjunction of these ideas is unquestionably what Christians have gone out of their way to affirm. For instance, the famous "Athanasian Creed," written (probably) in the sixth century in honor of the famous bishop Athanasius of Alexandria who was so instrumental in defending the full deity of Christ, reminds us that, since each person of the Trinity is God, every attribute we predicate of God can and should be predicated of each person. So, for instance, the Father is almighty, the Son is almighty, the Spirit is almighty. Yet, as the creed explicitly goes on to explain, "there are not three Almighties, but one Almighty." How can this be? The creed does not answer that question but instead declares the simple Christian conviction: "We worship Trinity in Unity and Unity in Trinity."[5]

This is a pretty pickle. Here is a paradoxical doctrine explicitly taught by Christians throughout the ages, yet apparently amounting not to spiritual nourishment or enrichment but to simple bewilderment. It prompts one to wonder why on earth the church accepted such an unresolved, counterintuitive understanding of God in the first place. Were there no other, more sensible, more straightforward versions of trinitarian theology available? The answer is, of course there were. Many a sophisticated theologian in the early church tried to present the doctrine in a careful, nuanced way that retained its substance while overcoming its paradoxical character. Consider a few of these "solutions," each one proposed to address the trinitarian dilemma, each one pondered by the Christian community—and each one ultimately rejected.

Modalism (or Sabellianism)

According to this early teaching (as early as the third century), the names "Father," "Son," and "Spirit" represented facets or faces of the one true God, masks that God donned as the drama of redemption unfolded in human history—much like a Greek actor might assume multiple roles in a play. Personal names referred not to real distinctions within God but to how God chose to present himself and the meaning of his actions at a particular point in time (i.e., to his "modes" of presentation—hence, "modalism"). God manifested himself as "Father" to Israel; then as "Son" to the new Israel, the church; and presumably also as "Spirit" in certain contexts or settings. Yet it was the same God playing all of these different roles. With this teaching, Sabellius sought to preserve the monotheistic heritage of the early church while still taking seriously the *appearance* of diversity among the divine persons. Yet this diversity was nothing but an appearance, and this is where orthodox Christians were

---

5. Philip Schaff, ed., revised by David S. Schaff, *The Creeds of Christendom*, vol. 2, *The Greek and Latin Creeds*, 6th ed. (Grand Rapids: Baker Books, 1990), 3.66, 14.67.

resistant. Sabellius effectively eliminated the tensions inherent in the doctrine of the Trinity, but at the expense of genuine relational distinctions within God. For modalists, God was not really *tri*-une at all. He was simply "-une," simply a unity. All that was distinctive about the Christian vision of God as Trinity was lost.

Subordinationism (or Arianism)

Subordinationists like the great fourth-century heretic Arius held that Father, Son, and Spirit were genuinely distinct persons, but these distinctions did not compromise monotheism because only the Father was really God in the full, authentic sense. The Son and the Spirit were thought of as lesser "deities," created by God the Father to reign as subordinate "gods" over all other created things. They were, in effect, like the very highest archangels—so high above us ordinary mortals as to be "gods"—yet still created beings infinitely lower than the one true God himself. This approach disposed of trinitarian tensions handily enough, but only by losing sight of the fullness of the Godhead being displayed in Christ. Jesus ended up being just another creature, even if exalted above all others. Therefore this apparently "trinitarian" theology failed to provide the mediator between God and human beings that fallen humanity so desperately needs.

Tritheism

Quite at home in the ancient Greco-Roman world, this third approach bites the bullet and says, plain and simple, that Christians worship three gods. Monotheism may be part of Christianity's Jewish heritage, but on this view, God's new revelation in Christ forces the church to move in a radically new direction. If we accept the implications of Christ's teaching and actions (i.e., if we accept that Christ himself is personally divine in the fullest sense), then it makes no sense to maintain the pretense that Christians worship only one God. After all, the tritheist asks, how can three gods be one God? For the sake of logical consistency, the Jewish foundation of Christianity is jettisoned, and the God who severely punished the Israelites whenever they lapsed into the worship of many gods turns out to be many after all. Once again, the tensions associated with the Trinity are fully resolved by this model, but at the cost of turning away completely from the Judaism that Jesus himself embraced.

Compositionism

This last alternative was not particularly tempting to Christians in the early centuries of the church, for it ran afoul of the almost universally held conviction that God was indivisible, that he could not be divided or separated into components or parts (see the account of divine "simplicity" in the thought of

Thomas Aquinas in chapter 3). But many Christians in our day seem to resort very naturally to the language of "composition" or "partition" to express their understanding of the Trinity: the Father is "part" of God, the Son is "part" of God, the Spirit is "part" of God, and all three together make up the "whole" God. It does not usually take much probing to see how dissatisfying such a view is even to its adherents: does any Christian really want to say that we are meeting only a "part" of God in Christ—just one-third of the deity? In any case, attempts to partition God inevitably end up either assuming that God is a quasi-material entity who can be chopped up into three pieces, or leading us back to tritheism, where each "part" of God is simply one of the three deities who sits together on the divine committee. Either result offers us a fairly simple, logical way of getting past the trinitarian dilemma, but not one that helps us to understand God in a more deeply biblical manner.

Note that each one of these four proposed "solutions" resolves the problem of the Trinity only by falling short, in one way or another, of historic trinitarian orthodoxy. The first two fall short by affirming God's unity at the expense of genuine diversity; the last two do so by affirming God's diversity at the expense of real unity. In either case, full-blown trinitarianism is lost. More recent attempts to "solve" the Trinity make similar problematic moves. Contemporary philosophical theologian James Anderson surveys such attempts and concludes, "No writer from the first century to the twenty-first century has offered an explication of the doctrine of the Trinity that is *both* clearly orthodox *and* free from apparent contradiction."[6] The mystery that characterizes the Triune God cannot be so handily set aside, for every attempt to render the Trinity less mysterious inevitably exhibits a rationalistic bent that forces the unclassifiable plenitude into a logical structure unable to contain its full glory. And our fundamental question remains unanswered. How can we, as the Athanasian Creed implores, "worship Unity in Trinity and Trinity in Unity"?

Back to the Bible?

Some Christians will by this time have grown impatient with the whole business. They will be wondering whether trinitarian doctrine isn't more trouble than it is worth. Is it really even necessary? Can't we stick to the simple biblical portrayal of God and leave it at that?

Sympathetic as we might sometimes be to such questions, they do not finally give us much help. The problem is that "sticking to the biblical portrayal of God" was just what the promulgators of orthodox trinitarianism were doing. Indeed, the "solutions" we have just looked at ended up failing largely on the basis of the biblical testimony itself, a testimony that indicated *both*

6. James Anderson, *Paradox in Christian Theology: An Analysis of Its Presence, Character, and Epistemic Status* (Waynesboro, GA: Paternoster, 2007), 59 (italics added).

comprehensive oneness *and* relational complexity within the being of God. The oneness we have already seen: the unyielding monotheistic heritage of Israel was affirmed by Jesus himself in no uncertain terms, and so the teaching that there was only one true God was nonnegotiable for his followers. But we do well to remind ourselves also of the relational complexity. What was the church to do with the odd way that Jesus and the New Testament authors often talked about God and God's Son and God's Spirit—sometimes employing what we can only describe as "proto-trinitarian" language?

Just a few brief examples must suffice:

- Recall the extensive parallelism between the Father and the Son that Jesus describes in John 5, where the Father's work is also the Son's work (vv. 17, 19), where life belongs to the Son as well as the Father (vv. 21, 26), where the Father's judgment comes exclusively through the Son (vv. 22, 30), where honor or dishonor is necessarily rendered to Father and Son together (v. 23). Yet Jesus clearly distinguishes Father and Son too, for the Son is always imitating the Father (v. 19), receiving from the Father (vv. 26–27), pleasing the Father (v. 30)—never the reverse. Both unity and distinction are evident here.
- More obviously, remember the explicit threefold appearance at Jesus's baptism, where the *Father* speaks from heaven as the *Spirit* descends upon the *Son*, who is being baptized in the Jordan River (Mark 1:9–11).
- Note the triadic structure of much of Paul's writing, such as his famous benediction to the Corinthian church, "May the grace of the Lord Jesus Christ [the Son], and the love of God [the Father], and the fellowship of the Holy Spirit be with you all" (2 Cor. 13:14).
- Observe similar trinitarian overtones in Peter's letters, as when the author of 1 Peter refers to Christians as those who "have been chosen according to the foreknowledge of God the Father, through the sanctifying work of the Spirit, to be obedient to Jesus Christ" (1:2).
- Consider the trinitarian account of Pentecost in Acts 2, where Peter explains, "God has raised this Jesus to life. . . . Exalted to the right hand of God, he [Jesus the Son] has received from the Father the promised Holy Spirit and has poured out what you now see and hear" (vv. 32–33).
- Recall the wording of the Great Commission, where Jesus commands that disciples be baptized "in the name [note the singular—not *names*!] of the Father and of the Son and of the Holy Spirit" (Matt. 28:19).

Suggestive trinitarian hints like these in the New Testament could easily be multiplied, but of course, they remain only suggestive, and in that sense no full-blown doctrine of the Trinity is *explicitly* present in Scripture. Hence one is inclined to ask: How many "suggestive hints" should be required before one is ready to abandon the obvious truths of mathematics, as an explicit doctrine of the Trinity seems to do? How were early Christian leaders able to move forward in their understanding of God, in the light of the logical puzzles that texts like these posed?

The answer, in large measure, is simply that early Christians were not overly concerned with "logical puzzles." Their intention was to be faithful to the God whom Israel had long known in covenant relationship, who had now made himself finally known in his chosen Messiah, and who continued to dwell among them by the Spirit that empowered them to walk daily in the new life of Christ's resurrection. In other words, their ongoing, personal engagement with the living God consistently shaped their theology much more significantly than did concerns about logical rigor.

Consider the case of the apostles themselves. The New Testament writings have remarkably little to say about anything like "logical tensions" in the new and distinctively Christian understanding of Jewish monotheism. Paul can write lyrically about there being "one God and Father of all, who is over all and through all and in all," which certainly sounds like an affirmation of the traditional Jewish perspective. But these very lines form the conclusion of a sentence that is very clearly triadic in its structure: "There is one body and one *Spirit* . . . one *Lord*, one faith, one baptism; one *God and Father* of all" (Eph. 4:4–6). One wants to ask, "Paul, how can these two emphases stand side by side? Are you a monotheist or not?" But Paul seems uninterested in the question.

The same is true elsewhere. Matthew can compose a distinctly Jewish Gospel that cites the Shema from Deuteronomy 6:4 and that builds its discourses in a fivefold structure that imitates the Jewish Torah—yet Matthew's Gospel concludes with the very non-Jewish triadic structure of the Great Commission, which refers to the single divine name shared by Father and Son and Spirit. James can refer at one moment to the one true God as the avenging "Lord [*kyrios*] of hosts" (James 5:4 ESV), an unequivocally monotheistic expression with impeccable Jewish roots—and then three verses later use the same term to refer to "the coming of the Lord [*kyrios*]" (James 5:7 ESV), a phrase clearly referring to the return of Christ. John's Gospel most directly offends our sensibilities, for it takes the very name of God ("I AM"), the Hebrew name that embodies the uniqueness, the incomparability, the stark, monotheistic singularity of the one true God, and places it over and over again on the lips of Jesus. "Very truly I tell you," John quotes Jesus as saying, "before Abraham was born, I am!" (John 8:58). Again, one wants to cry out, "John, do you no longer believe in just one God, namely, the Father to whom Jesus prays? How can Jesus himself also be 'I AM'? How can the Word be 'with' God and yet 'be' God (see John 1:1)? Doesn't this violate the laws of logic?" This line of questioning does not seem to have occurred to the apostle, or at least it does not seem to trouble him. In any case, the only answer he gives is the gospel story itself.

Contemporary New Testament scholar Richard Bauckham has argued persuasively that the closer we look at the apostolic writings, the more it looks as if the authors were very intentionally writing in trinitarian terms—yet without the least hint that they believed monotheism was thereby compromised. On the contrary, it appears that the Jewish monotheism of the apostolic authors was built on a notion of oneness or unity that was much more flexible than our contemporary logical categories ordinarily allow. According to Bauckham, Jewish writers of the Second Temple period (including the time of Jesus and the apostles) who

> envisage some form of real distinction within the unique identity of God . . . are not abandoning or in any way compromising their Jewish monotheism. The Second Temple Jewish understanding of the divine uniqueness does not define it as unitariness and does not make distinctions within the divine identity inconceivable. Its perfectly clear distinction between God and all other reality is made in other terms.[7]

The rigors of a mathematically precise logic were simply not the major concern of Jewish monotheists of the first century, and therefore faithfulness to what they had actually encountered in Christ could push the early Christians in directions that the dictates of logic alone would never countenance.

The Logic of Worship and the Development of a Mystery

The early church continued along this path. Ancient Christians had to make sense of what they found in the apostolic writings (which were still on their way to being recognized as an inspired canon), but these believers were never merely engaging in what we would identify as objective, scientific exegesis. They were also living communally in an intimate relationship with God in Christ, a relationship of such intimacy that Scripture (following Christ himself) can speak of it using nuptial imagery. This imagery is worth pondering for a moment. Christ is the bridegroom, and the church is his bride (Rev. 19:7–9; cf. Eph. 5:22–30; Jer. 3:14). The church's growing knowledge of her Lord is also the bride's growing knowledge of her bridegroom, and so it is a knowledge that is inextricably connected with the personal, relational intimacy of marital union. Remember what this kind of knowledge is like. No groom, however enigmatic he may be, is ever treated by his bride simply as a logical puzzle.

7. Richard Bauckham, *God Crucified: Monotheism and Christology in the New Testament* (Grand Rapids: Eerdmans, 1998), 22. See also the essays included in Bauckham's more recent collection, *Jesus and the God of Israel: God Crucified and Other Studies on the New Testament's Christology of Divine Identity* (Grand Rapids: Eerdmans, 2008).

He is not a puzzle; he is "my husband." To understand him is not to "solve" him, like a riddle in the daily newspaper; it is to live in intimate union and fellowship, and thus gradually to gain a reliable sense of what is true and what is not—a sense that is often difficult to justify to outsiders. "I just know!" says the new bride to bemused inquirers. "I don't really understand it very well myself, but it's true. You'd know what I mean if you were married to him."

The church understood itself to be married to Christ (or perhaps betrothed to him, which also involved a distinctive kind of intimacy in the ancient world). The intimacy of this union allowed the gathered body of believers to do its exegesis and to develop its theology in a way that was deeply shaped, under the direction of the Holy Spirit, by the church's worship. What ancient Christians experienced in worship framed how they read the Bible and the conclusions they reached concerning what specific texts meant or did not mean. When Athanasius, for example, opposed Arius's subordinationist reading of Scripture, he was not approaching the biblical text from scratch, as though any "objective" reader could understand its meaning simply by rigorous independent study. On the contrary, he believed that the text could be understood only in the context of the practices of the church as God's people, lived out—"incarnated" if you will—in their daily life and especially in their acts of worship. As Christians worshiped the mysterious communion of Father, Son, and Holy Spirit, biblical exegesis was guided by the Spirit, and theological insights were birthed and nourished.

Of course, the interpretive grid through which church fathers such as Athanasius read the Scriptures included the careful study of historical background, grammar, authorial intent—all of those elements that we today also associate with exegesis. They read the Bible extremely carefully and reverently. But they also allowed the church's living practice of worship to guide their interpretation of Scripture. This approach to Scripture becomes embodied in a principle often expressed in the Latin phrase *lex orandi lex credendi*, which may be roughly translated as "the law of prayer is the law of belief." In other words, the lived practices of the praying, worshiping people of God rightly shape the doctrine that the church holds. This principle does not mean that the church never goes wrong, or that every prayer of every Christian is an inspired guide to dogma. But it does mean that the meaning of Holy Scripture is opened to us by the Spirit in our worshiping lives, not just in our theological deliberations.

This confidence in the Spirit's guidance of the worshiping church found dogmatic expression in the early Christians' reliance, especially before the establishment of a New Testament canon, on the apostolic rule of faith (*regula fidei*). The rule of faith was a flexible but authoritative summary of the apostles' teaching that shaped and guided the church's reflection and practice from its earliest history forward. Irenaeus, writing in the late second century AD, was referring to this flexible "rule" or standard when he noted that the church, though dispersed throughout the whole world, even to the ends of the earth, has received from the apostles and their disciples this faith: she believes in one God, the Father Almighty, Maker of heaven and earth, and the sea, and all things that are in them; and in one Christ Jesus, the Son of God, who became incarnate for our salvation; and in the Holy Spirit.[8]

This expression of the rule of faith is echoed in other ancient sources as well. Note that the rule does not take the place of Scripture, nor does it stand independently alongside of Scripture. Instead, it is a summary of the faith *of* Scripture, as the worshiping people of God more and more came to understand it.

Consider then, in sum, how the doctrine of the Trinity came to be an accepted part of historic Christianity. First, men and women met Jesus Christ. They saw him doing what only God could do, speaking as only God could speak; they saw him die but then rise from the dead, bearing all authority in heaven and on earth; and they found themselves bowing in worship before him, like "doubting" Thomas who declares in awestruck tones, "My Lord and my God!" (John 20:28). This worship Jesus gladly received. Later, the personal, life-giving power of the Spirit poured out upon them prompted worshiping Christians to treat the Spirit of God, too, just as they treated God himself. Thus the apostolic message came to be expressed in triadic terms, with no indication that the logical difficulties that we so quickly perceive gave the apostles any pause. As the years and then the centuries passed, the threeness of God became more and more evident in the continuing experience of the living, worshiping church, though with the oneness of God consistently enriched rather than overturned as a result. This may seem logically odd, but the church was not looking for logical ways of figuring God out. Instead, it was meeting God, getting to know him, with ever-increasing intimacy, in Christ and by the Spirit. And the God that the living, worshiping church came to know was precisely the *Triune* God.

Was this simply a case of enthusiastic Christians allowing certain ecstatic experiences to lead them astray from logic? Some people may think so, but it is not hard to see the situation in just the opposite way. Led *astray* from logic? On the contrary, Christians were *following* logic. They were being absolutely faithful to the astonishing logic of the apostolic revelation, a logic that pushed their knowledge of God to new and unprecedented heights. At places where superficial human reasoning would have balked, the early Christians pressed on, accepting and delighting in the incomprehensible bridegroom, who increasingly made himself wondrously known to his bride. But were there no

8. Irenaeus, *Against Heresies* 1.10.1; 1.22.1, in *The Ante-Nicene Fathers* (ANF), ed. Alexander Roberts and James Donaldson (Peabody, MA: Hendrickson, 1994), 1:330, 347, slightly modified; cited in *Tradition, Scripture, and Interpretation: A Sourcebook of the Ancient Church*, ed. D. H. Williams (Grand Rapids: Baker Academic, 2006), 68–69.

calm, cool, sensible heads among them to call the church back to the plain demands of mathematics, to the simple and obvious absurdity of "1 + 1 + 1 = 1"? Yes, there were. Every heretic called for just such plain, ordinary sense. Against them all, the church followed its Lord into higher things in the union of worshiping love. So were they rejecting logic? By no means. They were being *supremely* logical, for the living God who was revealing himself was no mere creature on whom to practice mundane puzzle-solving skills. He could be trusted to reveal himself well, even where the revelation tended to draw the church into mysteries that outstrip created minds.

The Explanatory Power of the Mystery

So Christians have affirmed the doctrine of the Trinity, in spite of its logically odd, even contradictory, character, both because the testimony of Jesus and the apostles requires it and because the experience of the worshiping church confirms it. But does our acknowledgment of God as mystery in this peculiar sense—as *triune* mystery—allow us to see other matters in a fresh, new light? When this blindingly bright sun is in the sky, do we see the rest of the landscape more clearly? Does this mystery, in itself so incomprehensible, have the power to make other things *more* comprehensible?

The renewed attention devoted to the Trinity by Christians of all stripes during the last hundred years might suggest that it does. The eighteenth and nineteenth centuries had witnessed a dramatic decline of interest in the doctrine of the Trinity in most Western theology, driven largely by the opinion of many Enlightenment-inspired intellectuals that the logical oddities of the doctrine made it something of an embarrassment to Christian faith. But then the twentieth century arrived, and with it World War I, in which the Enlightenment's naive dream of inevitable, peaceful progress toward a reasonable, unified world came to a catastrophically bloody end. Christian theologians throughout the Western world, led by the indomitable Karl Barth, found themselves rediscovering the trinitarian Christian tradition and finding there a different vision of ultimate good—not a vision of all-powerful monolithic unity but a vision of harmonious community in which diversity can be celebrated rather than stamped out. Many non-Western theologians (from Asia, Africa, and Latin America) have continued to mine the Trinity for a model of human society that can move beyond the modern Western legacy of cultural imperialism and domination, and much Western theology is not far behind. It looks as if historic trinitarian doctrine is not quite so irrelevant as the theological liberalism of the early modern period believed.

However, there are legitimate concerns in some evangelical circles that this "mining" of the Trinity may, at least in some cases, be driven as much by a fashionable social agenda as by heartfelt devotion to the truths of revelation.

So let us set these trends in theological scholarship aside for the moment and think instead about some other indicators that are less subject to the vagaries of the spirit of the age. We find fascinating instances of what might be called the "explanatory power" of the mystery of the Trinity in aspects of human experience common enough that many readers will have encountered them in the last twenty-four hours. Let's consider three of them.

Example 1

First, think about romantic love and its consummation in marriage. Some cynics may argue that erotic love is simply the emotional froth thrown up by waves of sexual desire, and further that sexual desire itself is merely the way that evolution has "selected" the elements in nature that most readily propagate the species. Nothing sacred or transcendent here—all is animal passion and a ravenous drive for satisfaction. But no one in love could ever think this way. Lovers know that it is not sex they want; it is the beloved. The nine-year-old boy who "likes" the red-headed girl he sees on the playground, the wistful teenage girl whose heart flutters because a certain boy walks by her locker, the young newlyweds who are just discovering the ecstasies and frustrations of life together, the empty-nesters who walk quietly together in the neighborhood, the aged widow who still gets tears in her eyes when she thinks about the way her long-dead husband used to laugh—each one of these knows, however inarticulately, the profound meaningfulness of love and of the longing to be loved. And not just of "love" in some generalized sense: to be in love is to long for a *particular* person, as part of a *particular* relationship, and one that, if it is what it ought to be, touches the very heart of what we are as humans.

This experience of, or longing for, the personal intimacy of marital love easily translates into sacred terms. Being in love often whispers to us of paradise. Furthermore, whatever distortions our own culture happens to contribute to the experience of being "in love" (and they are many), the association of sexual, marital love with religious categories is hardly a phenomenon distinctive to our own time or place. In fact, every human culture that we know of shows traces of the same. The bond that we call "marriage" may include one spouse or several, may involve exclusive sexual privileges or more fluid privileges, may be very closely related to the production of offspring or not so closely related—but it is never, ever trivial. On the contrary, it is always related to God, or the gods, or the holy places, or the spiritual world. From ancient fertility cults to contemporary country-western ditties, to speak of sex, of marriage, of erotic togetherness, is to speak of things that take us outside of the ordinary world and into a world tinged with what is transcendently significant. This aspect of human experience gives every indication of being universal to our race.

Now this is an odd thing—perhaps not "bizarre" in any outlandish way, but at least noteworthy. Something important is going on here. We might not feel compelled to "explain" the phenomenon of marital love, but we certainly can see why the cynic's reductionism does *not* explain. Instead, it explains *away* universal human experience as something far less significant than we all know it to be. We would probably rather have this mysterious experience called "being in love" left alone altogether than have it transmogrified into a mere animal impulse that betrays the experience itself.

And then we think about the Christian doctrine of the Trinity. According to Christian teaching, God is both three and one, in a manner we cannot fully comprehend. That is, the foundation of all reality, the unimaginable source of everything that is, is not just a monolithic "I" but also a remarkably mutual "we," a communion of distinct persons supremely united in personal love. Unity defines this God as fully as diversity, but diversity also defines this God as fully as unity. This unity-in-diversity and diversity-in-unity is the creative origin from which all of reality as we know it flows.

Do we not find here a fascinating convergence? Ultimate reality consists in divine persons perfectly united in ecstatic love—and every human person discovers an intrinsic longing for just this kind of interpersonal intimacy. Of course we cannot entirely understand the transcendent communion of persons that God is, but if the ultimate source of reality *were* this sort of God, would we not suddenly find that the human experience of marital love made an awful lot of sense? Think about the primary image that Jesus, following the book of Genesis, uses for marriage: "The *two* will become *one flesh*" (Matt. 19:5). Two persons united in marriage are still two, but they are also bound together in an unfathomable union of intimacy and joy. Such language will be recognized by most lovers as a startlingly exact description of their experience; it will also be recognized by most theologians as a simplified account of orthodox trinitarianism. And what would be more natural than that our deepest experience should reflect the God who created us? Indeed, for the creature who bears the divine image, what else would we expect? This otherwise puzzling feature of human experience turns out to make all the sense in the world if God is the incomprehensibly Triune God that Christians have come to believe.

Example 2

Consider a second example, similar in structure to the first. Think about the bond that ordinarily obtains between blood relatives in a family. Once again, our own culture introduces its own distortions into kinship relations. In this case, the distortion involves a sharply diminished perception, compared to most cultures throughout history, of the significance of what we would call "extended family": many of us may feel far less connected to a cousin a thousand miles away than to a neighbor next door. But even in the contemporary West, we frequently recognize a special connection to those in our "nuclear family"—or if we do not, we acknowledge that our family is somehow broken and we wish it were not so. So think about a nuclear family: or to focus the point even more, think about the peculiar relation that obtains between, say, a mother and a newborn child. There are no doubt lots of physical connections, "need" bonds, but there is also something more. The baby is peacefully cradled in mom's arms, perhaps nursing, perhaps just snuggling. Mom is looking down into her baby's eyes; the baby's eyes are locked on the mother's—and every mother says that there is something indescribable going on in this moment. Here is a love, a tenderness, a self-giving, that she had never imagined before, that penetrates to the center of her being. The mother-child relationship is unlike any other.

And then, as before, we think of the Trinity. We remember again that the Source of all reality is not a solitary Creator but an interpersonal communion of love. Indeed, it is noteworthy that God reveals himself not just as "persons in love" but as a parent and a child, as a Father and a Son, who are one in the unity of the Holy Spirit. There are, of course, dramatic differences between the young mother with her newborn child and the eternal Father with his eternal Son. But the similarities are striking. With the lens of the Trinity in place, we find the life-defining character of motherhood still fascinating, but no longer surprising. If Reality itself, the eternal Creator, has the character of Father and Son united in the Spirit, how could it surprise us that the lesser reality called human persons—image-bearers of the divine—should have a character that is defined, in part, by the loving union of mother and child, of kinship relations?

Example 3

Consider a third example, related this time to the nature of real friendship. Note the emphasis on *real* friendship. The word "friend" is easily used to describe a range of relationships, but most people recognize the immense difference between the multitude of mere *acquaintances* we all have, and the very few special relationships that we cherish as deep, abiding *friendships*. With a real friend, there is a commonality of focus, or of perspective, or of vision, that gradually pierces the superficial layers of self that we readily expose to others, and that allows us and invites us to be more fully, authentically ourselves. A real friendship involves a kind of profoundly casual but deeply attentive intimacy that empowers us to see the world better and to live in it more effectively: it brings out the best in us by redefining us as a mutual *we*, no longer merely as an introspective *I*. In the classic biblical example of true friendship, David and Jonathan come to know and love one another so deeply that the text can tell us that "Jonathan became *one in spirit* with David" (1 Sam. 18:1). This is a description that real friends immediately recognize. As if this were not enough, the verse goes on to say that Jonathan "loved him as himself." We hear textual echoes of what Jesus described as the second great commandment

(Mark 12:31), except that here, loving your neighbor *as yourself* is not a hard-to-reach ideal but a simple description of what the intimacy of true friendship is all about. To have such a friend, to be such a friend, is a marvel.

And then, yet again, we remember our trinitarian doctrine. We are reminded that being "one in spirit" is first of all a characteristic not of created friends like Jonathan and David but of uncreated divine life. Before the world was made, the Father and the Son were one in spirit, one in the Spirit, and out of that incomprehensible unity springs a created order that we might have expected would include echoes, reflections, imitations of the divine unity buried in the deepest heart of every man, woman, and child. And so it is. The intimacy of friendship turns out to be anything but an anomaly; it fits perfectly into the larger picture of what we know to be at the heart of the universe.

Implications

Notice what has happened in all three of these reflections. In each case, we began with features of our own experience that have a deep, almost mystical significance, a significance not just for a few of us but for everyone, not just in our culture but in every culture we know about. We have every reason to think that these are universal aspects of human experience. Considering such experiences in themselves, we have no idea what to make of them. They are interesting, even fascinating, certainly exhilarating, but we leave it at that.

Then through the exegetical and ecclesial experience of the people of God, the surprising doctrine of the Trinity emerges and places all of human experience into a new and more vibrant context—and as an unanticipated result we suddenly find these otherwise inexplicable features of our lives falling into place. We say, "Ah—*that* explains it. If the ground and Creator of all things is not just one but also three and not just three but also one, then it makes all the sense in the world that we, at the deepest, most intimate center of who we are, should find both unity and diversity. Of course! Humanity bears the image of God—how could we *not* reflect God in this way?" Suddenly, and contrary to every expectation, our knowledge of ourselves is enriched, and our vision of the universe as a whole is rendered more coherent. And it all happens as a result of the church's counterintuitive acceptance of an understanding of God that surpasses human comprehension.

It is like an intrinsically unlikely scientific theory that keeps showing itself to have more and more explanatory significance. Think about the law of gravity, which seems on the surface to be a pretty far-fetched notion. "What? Every physical body exerts some sort of attraction upon other physical bodies? How ridiculous! Just look at those two books on my desk—I don't see them slowly snuggling up to one another, do you? Perhaps I won't need nails to build my next house, since the wooden beams are all pulling themselves together anyhow, eh? Ha-ha! How silly!" Yes, how silly—until this surprising hypothesis starts to make sense of so many other things: of the falling of leaves and the trajectory of rockets and the orbit of planets. We cannot *see* gravity tugging at objects, but we eventually realize that, if there *were* such an invisible force in the universe, then the world would have just the kind of character it actually turns out to have. It would all make sense.

And the same is true of the Trinity. At the deepest recesses of human personhood, we find in our daily, perhaps in our hourly, experience that we are surprisingly connected to other persons. Community and relationship seem essential to what we are. We cannot understand how the incomprehensible Lord can be both one and many, but if he *were* both one and many, then our experience turns out to be exactly what we would expect. Suddenly it all makes sense—because of a mystery.

The Vocabulary and Grammar of Glory

So we cannot explain the Trinity, but the Trinity explains much. The Triune God is incomprehensible, and it is that very fact that allows us to take the full biblical witness more seriously, to enter more abundantly into the worshiping tradition of the last two thousand years, and to see facets of our own experience in a new and brighter light. In this respect, trinitarian doctrine bears every mark of being a reliable account of the Creator himself. Here we have knowledge that no creature would ever have come up with on its own, yet it is real knowledge nevertheless—knowledge that springs from the living revelation of God.

Yes, revealed knowledge—yet still creaturely knowledge too. We must take this paradoxical juxtaposition with deepest seriousness. When we speak of the Trinity, we speak of what God has made known to us about himself, and this means that it is absolutely trustworthy (for it is what *God* has made known), yet at the same time it bears the frailty of all human language and thought (for it is made known *to us*). When the living God reveals the mysterious glory of transcendent reality, we may be confident that it is revealed rightly; yet to reveal it to human beings is precisely to express the glory in a human vocabulary, by means of a human grammar—with all of the limitations therein implied. The glory is real, but its expression in words is inevitably an accommodation. A pencil drawing of a ball may be as exact and lifelike as you please, but it remains a two-dimensional representation of a three-dimensional object. To forget that accommodation is to misunderstand both the drawing and the ball.

In this sense, we must always remember how orthodox doctrine works, how the vocabulary and grammar of glory do their job. They do it not by eliminating the mystery but by expressing it in a way we can understand—and true understanding therefore necessarily includes perceiving the limitations in our understanding. This is the reason so much of the Christian tradition has recognized a certain "analogical" character in all theological language. As we saw back in chapter 3, the language we use for the things of God cannot be "univocal" (i.e., meaning exactly the same thing when applied to God as when applied to created things): if it were, then to say that there are three "persons" in the Trinity would mean, plain and simple, that we should set three places at the dinner table, and we would have out-and-out tritheism as a result. But the language we use for the things of God also cannot be "equivocal" (i.e., meaning something entirely unrelated to our ordinary meaning): if it were, then we would know literally nothing at all about God, and we would be reduced to sheer agnosticism. Instead, our language about God is "analogical," which means that it is meaningfully related to our normal usage, though we cannot pin down in ordinary, straightforward terms what exactly the relation is.

C. S. Lewis provides another helpful way of thinking about how our knowledge of God works when he introduces a distinction between a "Master's metaphor" and a "Pupil's metaphor."[9] Imagine, Lewis suggests, a teacher (or, in an older idiom, a "master") who wishes to help his pupils to understand a difficult concept in the sciences, such as the boundedness of infinite space. The teacher might illustrate the concept by inviting his students to consider a globe, which is "bounded" (that is, it is just an ordinary, finite sphere), but which one could walk on in one direction for an infinite distance (i.e., one could keep going round and round the sphere without ever coming to an end). This illustration might very well help the students to get a rough sense of how the concept of an infinite but bounded space works, but it is important to see that they understand the *concept* (space) only by means of the metaphorical *illustration* (the globe). One might say they understand the whole connection between the concept and the illustration only "from below," only in the way that "pupils" understand it. They do not (yet) grasp it in the way that the master does, since he understands the illustration "from above," by first understanding the concept itself. Indeed, he designs the illustration precisely in order to communicate it to those who do not understand it. Approaching the illustration "from above" means that the master understands exactly how it illustrates—and therefore also how it *fails* to illustrate, where the illustration breaks down. The pupils, by contrast, know only that the illustration works, and they know it primarily because of the authority of their teacher. *How* it works, where precisely it applies and does not apply, what its limitations may be—about all of this the pupils have no knowledge whatsoever. That is what it means to be a pupil.

With respect to the things of God, finite human knowers are always in the position of "pupil," never in the position of "master." We understand *that* what God has made known to us is true, and we count on the revelation unreservedly. But we are never in a position to specify *how* it is true in any complete sense.

9. C. S. Lewis, "Bluspels and Flalansferes: A Semantic Nightmare," in *Selected Literary Essays*, ed. Walter Hooper (Cambridge: Cambridge University Press, 1969), 255.

And for that reason, we are utterly, relentlessly dependent on the revelation itself for what we know—not because it reveals univocally, so that the mystery of God is removed, but because it reveals truly, so that the mystery of God may be approached and adored and fed upon. As we noted in chapter 1, the mystery continues to be mysterious even after it has been revealed. Hence, it is too simple to think of revelation as God "lifting the curtain" at some points, as though we now know clearly and distinctly the full, divine reality at those points. On the contrary, we know as creatures, as pupils, as Flatlanders, and therefore we do not know precisely *how* what we know is true. Yet true it is, and we insist upon it by the authority of God himself.

Proceeding with Caution

This awareness of how the vocabulary and grammar of glory function invites both a caution and a confidence. First, the caution. Divine incomprehensibility obliges a certain careful reserve in the way we deal with theological dilemmas and controversies, especially as they are connected to the way that particular theological terms are employed. Specific words do matter, and matter very much. But it is clear that getting the words right does not necessarily mean understanding correctly the reality about which the words speak, and similarly getting the words wrong does not necessarily mean rejecting the reality about which they speak. Many of Christianity's most favored traditional theological terms actually function as technical designations to point to revealed realities that we do not fully understand. The terminology is accepted (usually after much theological wrangling) because it is perceived by the worshiping church to be faithful to the revelation and to protect it from misunderstanding, *not* because it boils down into exact, univocal, two-dimensional language all of the mystery of the multidimensional reality to which it points.

For example, consider the crucial trinitarian term "person" (Greek, *hypostasis*; Latin, *persona*). The whole Christian tradition has relied on this language very heavily, and from earliest times, in its theological reflection. "God in three persons" simply *is* Christian orthodoxy. Furthermore, according to Christian teaching, when we speak in this way we speak meaningfully and truly. The Father, the Son, and the Holy Spirit really are like human persons, and the word "person" is used in a way that reflects ordinary, nontheological usage. Yet while it *reflects* that usage, it is never simply *identical* to it. God is not a "person" in any of the obvious, ordinary ways that would dispel the mystery and leave us, once again, with a pencil sketch instead of a living reality.

Indeed, speaking technically, God is not "a person" at all: God is *three* persons. Should we therefore stand and cry "Heresy!" every time we hear someone refer to God as "a person"? Surely not. We will want to distinguish carefully between those who use such technically unorthodox language casually and incidentally from those who use it precisely and intentionally. Again, we will want to distinguish carefully between those who question the orthodox language because they deny the orthodox Christian doctrine (as Mormons like Dr. Millet do) and those who question the orthodox language because they think it no longer protects the orthodox doctrine from misunderstanding (as do the Protestant Karl Barth and the Catholic Karl Rahner, both of whom resist speaking of God as three "persons" because they think the word "person" no longer means to us what it meant to the church fathers who established it as orthodoxy[10]). Not every statement that runs afoul of traditional usage and technical orthodoxy is *ipso facto* destructive.

The orthodox tradition itself says the same. For instance, Christians have long described the personal distinctions within the one God in terms that reflect the relationships among the persons. Thus the Father is said to "beget" or to "generate" the Son while being himself "unbegotten" or "ingenerate"; the Son relates to the Father as "begotten"; the Holy Spirit "proceeds" from the Father (or from the Father and the Son). Obviously words like these—"generate," "unbegotten," "begotten," "proceed"—mean something that we can understand. They are not used equivocally. Otherwise we could just as easily and appropriately use *any* words to describe the relations, even nonsensical words, and this would clearly be a mistake. No, says Christian orthodoxy, we know that relationally the Son is different from the Father because the Son, as "begotten," finds his source, his "begetting," from the Father. That is what "Father" and "Son," "begetting" and "begotten," mean.

Yet, the moment we say this, we encounter that unclassifiable plenitude whose fullness leaves us with absolutely no adequate categories in the created order. The begetting of the Son is a noncorporeal begetting, a generation that has no beginning and no end. It is therefore a begetting or a generation unlike any we could ever imagine. If we were to employ our normal classifications and connotations for the concept of biological generation—that is, if we were to use our words univocally—we would think that the Father begets the Son as human fathers beget human sons. In fact, this type of begetting was not at all foreign to the Greek or Roman mind-set of the patristic period: Zeus begot many children through having sexual relations with goddesses or with mortal women. But this kind of divine generation is entirely foreign to the Hebrew Scriptures and the New Testament writings, and it utterly fails to understand the limits of the language Christians use to describe God. As Gregory of Nyssa observes, "The inspired teaching adopts, in order to set forth the unspeakable power of God, all the forms of generation that human intelligence recognizes, *yet without including the corporeal senses attaching*

10. See Karl Barth, *Church Dogmatics* 1.1, ed. G. W. Bromiley and T. F. Torrance (Edinburgh: T&T Clark, 1975), 355–68; and Karl Rahner, *Foundations of Christian Faith: An Introduction to the Idea of Christianity*, trans. William V. Dych (New York: Crossroad, 1990), 134–35.

to the words."[11] To think that the begetting of the Son by the Father is like the begetting of human children by a human father would be a ghastly mistake.

Any language that we employ to speak of God will inevitably betray this same fragility. There is in God an abundance—indeed, a superabundance, an overflowing fullness, a plenitude—that we search for in vain within creation itself. Should this surprise us? And therefore, the formal language of orthodoxy is important, but for no other reason than that it faithfully points beyond itself to what transcends human language altogether. Our theological concepts are always an attempt to embody what the church truly knows, without accidentally stumbling into treating these concepts like any other concepts.

The Trinity is no exception to this rule. On the contrary, it may be the rule's clearest exemplification. True knowledge of God as Father, Son, and Holy Spirit is never just awareness of a formalized doctrine expressed in the strict wording of ancient ideologues. The wording is significant, and what it communicates is true—and for that very reason we must look through the words themselves to see the incomprehensible Reality revealed in them. For two-dimensional pupils, knowledge of the multidimensional reality should always be *guided* by the master's words, never *imprisoned* by them.

Doctrine and Nourishment

Finally, the confidence. Knowing that the trinitarian reality of God is too large for our words and categories and yet nevertheless is truly revealed within them summons us to recognize how we can be not just *informed* by the doctrine of the Trinity but also *nourished* by it. Of course, all truth is nourishing in one way or another, since it allows us to encounter reality as it really is. Still, there does seem to be a difference between understanding nutrition and eating a healthy meal. So how do we sit down and eat? Or rather, how does understanding the mystery of the Triune God help us to eat with boldness and hope?

The answer lies, as might be expected, in the nature of divine triunity, for it is a triunity of perfect, unqualified love. "Perfect, unqualified love"—the phrase may sound abstract or idealistic, for it is certainly very far from our day-to-day experience. But we should not be fooled. Call to mind again the very concrete experiences of human love that we were pondering a few pages back. Think of your own experience of love at its best, in whichever form is most personally significant to you—erotic romance or familial kinship or intimate friendship. Is any of this merely a matter of abstract, idealistic cognition? Far from it. Remember the electrifying touch of the lover's hand, or the wondrous trust in the child's eyes, or the peaceful delight of the friend's encouragement. Whenever we are talking about love, this is the substantial, concrete reality that we mean. Even if the doctrine of the Trinity does help us to *understand* these

11. Gregory of Nyssa, *Against Eunomius* 2.9 (NPNF[2] 5:114; italics added).

loves better (by thinking of them as echoes of a divine original), the *reality* of the loves is in no way limited to understanding. The reality is always instead a living, tangible sweetness that flows unhindered to every corner of our existence.

Now add to this picture the supposition that the doctrine of the Trinity is really true. Suppose that these overpowering instances of love in our day-to-day lives are mere echoes of an eternal communion so rich, so ecstatic, that our minds cannot even take it in. Suppose further that the gospel of Jesus Christ is the breathtaking overflow of that unfathomable communion into our prosaic, workaday world. Does this sound like mere metaphysics, mere cognition, mere doctrine? Of course it *is* doctrine, but it is anything but "mere." The trinitarian vision here draws us into a living reality that is unimaginably, almost sensuously rich, vivid, and luxuriant. What would it mean for the fierce, uncreated Love that made the worlds to surge through our tepid, fleeting passions? What would it be like for the men and women of Flatland to find themselves suddenly infused with all the fullness of three-dimensional reality? If even the distant echoes of this music are so magnificent, what are we to make of a dazzling invitation to come into the concert hall itself, to join in the creation and celebration of this spectacular chorus? If the tiny trickle of water we taste at a thousand removes from its source is still so intoxicating, how should we respond when we are called to drink from the fountain itself? The mystery of the Trinity sets all of this before us. Would anyone prefer a simple puzzle that a little cleverness could "solve"?

We can make the same point in another way. Notice that our doctrine of God inevitably has a profound impact on our expectations regarding spiritual life. Someone who tends to think of God primarily as *impersonal* will have no particular interest in the "love" of God, since such a thing is impossible. Impersonal objects do not "love" in any meaningful sense, and Christians have always known that this unrelational, isolated monad, for whom love is a foreign concept, is not their God. If we think of God as *personal*, then love becomes possible, but (as we saw above) the notion of a personal God, taken by itself, may tempt us to think that our love for God somehow completes or fulfills him—as though this supremely relational being had been pining throughout eternity for a creature to relate to. When we move to an understanding of God as "intensely" personal or as *tri-personal*, we counteract that temptation by acknowledging that God has always "had someone to love," that the love of the Father and the Son in the Spirit is an everlasting communion that leaves no room for any silly talk of a divine loneliness that must be overcome.

All of this is good, but the temptation we face when we think of God as complete and fulfilled in his own tri-personal being is to imagine this completeness as debilitatingly *exclusive*. After all, we might think, if we are not "needed" by God, if God is just fine all by his tri-personal self, then you and I may seem to be left out in the cold. We peer in the window, looking at the happy, three-member family gathered round the dinner table, but there is no empty seat at the table, and no sign that we outsiders belong there. They do not "need" us, and so we had better look elsewhere for a relationship of love that will really matter.

But it is not so. God is not just tri-personal; he is *expansively, creatively* tri-personal. The triunity of God is something that unfolds and opens out, not something that curves in and closes down on itself. God's intrinsic relational completeness, the unimaginable eternal intimacy between the Father and the Son in the Spirit, does not *exclude* other relations; it is instead the *ground* of other relations. The unquenchable divine joy that makes creation unnecessary also makes creation possible in the first place, for the love of Father, Son, and Spirit is in no way threatened or imperiled by flowing out beyond itself into a created world. As we saw in the previous chapter, God *is* love, and creation itself is the wholly free outpouring of that love, in generous, gratuitous, open-handed bounty, a bounty that is infinitely hospitable not because it needs us but simply because it is itself.

The implications for the spiritual life are immense. It is a great thing to be invited to a party that is *about us*, where we are being celebrated, where the party will be canceled if we do not attend. We are supremely necessary to such a party, and we can pat ourselves on the back for our sublime significance. But it is a greater thing yet to be invited to a party, to be welcomed into a joy, that is *vastly larger than ourselves*. This party does not wait on our arrival.[12] The music, the laughter, the cheer and delight, do not need us to initiate or to sustain them. They have their own inner dynamism of joy and life and power, a dynamism that is not dependent upon us and that can buoy us up and draw us in and carry us along for just that reason. Far from depending on us for its life, it offers us life. Far from merely celebrating what we are, it celebrates something higher and more glorious, and it carries us to that height and enables us to enter into that glory.

The mystery of the Triune God is just such a life-giving reality. We can enter into the mystery with fulfillment and joy rather than with confusion and frustration, for as we extend our minds and hearts into this inexhaustible, incomprehensible, infinitely personal truth, we find that its incomprehensibility makes other things more comprehensible, even as its inexhaustibility overcomes our exhaustion. Here, mind and heart can rest. True knowledge of the Triune God is thus a holy feast that nourishes, encourages, enlivens, and gladdens. We can expect to be fed by this mystery at levels deeper than the most rigorous logic can penetrate—and fed for all eternity. We will never tire of the trinitarian dishes offered to us by God, nourishment that only a redeemed, re-created humanity can digest. At present, we experience hints of the banquet to come. In the age to come we feast on the full meal.

12. This image comes from the extraordinarily insightful new book on the evangelical doctrine of the Trinity by Fred Sanders, *The Deep Things of God: How the Trinity Changes Everything* (Wheaton: Crossway, 2010), 215.

6

The MYSTERY
of the INCARNATION

Who will measure you, great Sea who made himself small? We came to see you as God. Behold! You are a human being. We came to see you as a human being, and lo! the banner of your Godhead shines forth. Who can bear your transformations, O true One?

Ephrem the Syrian[1]

The Word was made flesh, but how he was made flesh, we do not know. The doctrine from God, I have; the science of it, I do not have. I know that the Word was made flesh; how it was done, I do not know.

Jerome[2]

There is . . . one and the same Christ, God and man, the same uncreated and created, the same unchangeable and incapable of suffering, the same acquainted by experience with both change and suffering, the same equal to the Father and inferior

---

1. Ephrem the Syrian, *Hymns on the Nativity* 13.7–9, cited in *Ancient Christian Doctrine*, vol. 2, *We Believe in One Lord Jesus Christ*, ed. John Anthony McGuckin (Downers Grove, IL: IVP Academic, 2009), 142.

2. Jerome, "Homily 87, On the Gospel of John 1:14," in *Homilies 60–96*, 212.20, cited in *Ancient Christian Commentary on Scripture: John 1–10* (New Testament IVa), ed. Joel C. Elowsky (Downers Grove, IL: InterVarsity, 2006), 40–41.

to the Father, the same begotten of the Father before time ("before the world"), the same born of his mother in time ("in the world"), perfect God, perfect man.

Vincent of Lérins[3]

In a series of insightful sermons on the angel Gabriel's annunciation to the Virgin Mary (Luke 1:26–38), early third-century bishop Gregory Thaumaturgus imaginatively develops how God may first have informed Gabriel about the miraculous conception soon to occur in Mary's womb. "Come hither now, archangel," God commands Gabriel, "and become the minister of a dread mystery which has been kept hid, and be thou the agent in the miracle."[4] The miracle, God explains, is that he himself will enter into the world to redeem it, and the entrance will take place in the womb of the young virgin. Hearing this news, Gabriel finds himself amazed and more than a little perplexed. "Strange is this matter," says he to himself.

> Passing comprehension is this thing that is spoken. He who is the object of dread to the cherubim, He who cannot be looked upon by the seraphim, He who is incomprehensible to all the heavenly powers, does He give the assurance of His connection with a maiden? Does He announce His own personal coming? . . . Can the womb contain Him who cannot be contained in space? Truly this is a dread mystery.[5]

Gabriel goes obediently off to fulfill his commission, but he is still marveling at God's extraordinary ways.

"A dread mystery." It would be hard to find more appropriate words for what takes place in the womb of the Virgin, and for what follows nine months later in the stable in Bethlehem. The coming of Christ is, Gregory says,

> the mystery which transcends all wonders—the Virgin brought forth and bore in her hand Him who bears the whole creation by His word. . . . He found no room [in the inn] who founded the whole earth by His word. She nourished with her milk Him who imparts sustenance and life to everything that hath breath. She wrapped Him in swaddling-clothes who binds the whole creation fast with His word. She laid Him in a manger who rides seated upon the cherubim.[6]

Paradoxical words like these echo absolutely everywhere in Christian preaching and hymnody down through the ages, celebrating the marvelous mystery of the "incarnation," of God becoming "flesh" (Latin, *caro*). And we are not

3. Vincent of Lérins, *The Commonitory* 13.37, in *The Nicene and Post-Nicene Fathers* (NPNF), series 2, ed. Philip Schaff and Henry Wace (Peabody, MA: Hendrickson, 1994), 11:141.
4. Gregory Thaumaturgus, *Four Homilies*, in *The Ante-Nicene Fathers* (ANF), ed. Alexander Roberts and James Donaldson (Peabody, MA: Hendrickson, 1994), 6:66.
5. Ibid., 6:67.
6. Ibid., 6:65.

surprised by this unanimous celebration, for the center of our salvation lies precisely here, in the unimaginable union of God and humanity in Christ.

The doctrine of the incarnation is, of course, very closely connected to the doctrine of the Trinity, and so we should expect to find many points of contact between what we investigated in the previous chapter and what we shall investigate here. But there will also be some distinctions, for we are now interested not only in God himself but also in what God has done to transform the universe—a transformation from *inside*, as God himself becomes a man. How can we conceive of such a thing? Can we conceive of it at all? How have Christians come to speak of the incarnation in the technical language that they have? Does such language matter? We will try to address each of these questions, but the driving conviction behind our whole investigation is the same one we saw in the last chapter: *if God is incomprehensible in the way Christianity suggests*, then the Christian way of speaking about Christ and about God's work in Christ makes all the sense in the world. The affirmation of mystery explains how the natural tensions that the doctrine of the incarnation includes can be acknowledged without abandoning the rational coherence of the doctrine. Indeed, our understanding of the incarnation becomes *more* coherent, simply because we understand why we cannot understand.

The Grand Miracle

As always, we face a certain kind of epistemological difficulty from the outset, for it is plain that the question we must ask cannot be simply, how plausible is it that the incarnation is a mystery like this? If it *is* "a mystery like this," then asking straightforwardly about its "plausibility" is the one thing we cannot do. Scottish theologian Thomas Torrance wisely reminds us what it means to think about the mystery of the incarnation as the "heart of the Christian faith":

> In Christ something has taken place which is so new that it is related to our ordinary knowledge only at its extreme edges; if it is to be apprehended by us it must be apprehended from outside the limits of our ordinary human experience and thought. It is a new and unique reality which has certainly invaded our human life but which we can know only by refusing to categorize it in the sphere of what we already know, and by seeking to know it only out of itself. Even then, we know it remains a mystery.[7]

This is an appropriate reminder, for the words "incarnate" and "incarnation" have long since passed from technical theological parlance into the mainstream of the English language, where they refer to the way some naturally unembodied thing like an idea or a value receives concrete, perceivable form

7. Thomas F. Torrance, *Incarnation: The Person and Life of Christ* (Downers Grove, IL: IVP Academic, 2008), 83.

(as when one speaks of the television or movie "incarnation" of a certain story). In a sense, such popular usage provides another instance of what we saw in the previous chapter regarding the Trinity: the abstract structure of the Christian doctrine sometimes tends to develop a life of its own, and many people (whatever their relationship to traditional Christianity) find it to be convenient or helpful, and sometimes even profound.

However, as we also saw with respect to the Trinity, we want to insist that the significance of the doctrine of the incarnation attaches not merely to its generic logical structure but also to its concrete orthodox content. In other words, it is not just the general notion of "things becoming embodied" that we want to commend. Instead, we want to show that when the doctrine of the incarnation in all of its fullness and particularity is accepted (mysterious though it may be), we find that many other aspects of our common experience end up falling into place.

But how can we consider the incarnation without falling into the error that Torrance has pointed out? How can we resist the temptation to "categorize" the incarnation "in the sphere of what we already know"?

C. S. Lewis famously suggested a helpful strategy in his little book *Miracles*. Chapter 14 of that book is titled "The Grand Miracle," and there Lewis explains that the incarnation is not just one interesting phenomenon among others but is the centerpiece of the whole Christian vision of God's interaction with the world. And as such, the incarnation must be investigated in a distinctive way. Lewis employs the following well-known analogy:

> Let us suppose we possess parts of a novel or a symphony. Someone now brings us a newly discovered piece of the manuscript and says, "This is the missing part of the work. This is the chapter on which the whole plot of the novel really turned. This is the main theme of the symphony." Our business would be to see whether the new passage, if admitted to the central place which the discoverer claimed for it, did actually illuminate all the parts we had already seen and "pull them together." Nor should we be likely to go very far wrong. The new passage, if spurious, however attractive it looked at the first glance, would become harder and harder to reconcile with the rest of the work the longer we considered the matter. But if it were genuine, then at every fresh hearing of the music or every fresh reading of the book, we should find it settling down, making itself more at home, and eliciting significance from all sorts of details in the whole work which we had hitherto neglected. Even though the new central chapter or main theme contained great difficulties in itself, we should still think it genuine provided that it continually removed difficulties elsewhere.[8]

Lewis himself follows this analogy and asks what we find if we allow the incarnation to become the "central chapter or main theme" not just of Christianity or of Christian theology but of the whole mass of what we know and

8. C. S. Lewis, *Miracles: A Preliminary Study* (1947; repr., New York: Touchstone, 1996), 145.

encounter in the world. Do we find aspects of the doctrine explaining or il-
luminating the rest of our knowledge and experience? He thinks that we do,
and he directs us to four specific points of contact.

Points of Contact and Correction

First, let us consider the incarnation's highly counterintuitive notion that
"God" and "man" may somehow be joined in a single entity, for it turns out to
be not quite so outrageous as we might have thought. To be sure, linking these
two notions occasions all sorts of puzzles. How can eternal rational Spirit be
linked with a concrete body? How can necessary Existence be coupled with
the shifting contingencies of ordinary, natural life? These are good questions,
and hard ones to answer. But then, says Lewis, we notice that the incarnation
is not the first or the only place where we encounter such an odd linkage.
In fact, each and every one of us, and every other human person who has
ever lived, is what Lewis calls a "composite" being in much the same sense.
Each of us is an outlandish union of spiritual and corporeal, of rational and
nonrational, one might almost say of supernatural and natural. This union
is baffling enough that philosophers continue to puzzle over the so-called
mind-body problem, the problem of how *res extensa* (an "extended thing," a
body) can be united with *res cogitans* (a "thinking thing," a mind). Of course,
this problem does not simply vanish because we appeal to the incarnation,
but Lewis thinks that it is set in a new light. "Our own composite existence
is not the sheer anomaly it might seem to be, but a faint image of the Divine
Incarnation itself—the same theme in a very minor key."[9] We find ourselves
not so surprised that we should be composite beings if the center of God's
eternal plan for the world is just such an inexplicable composition. It seems
to fit together rather well.

Second, Lewis invites us to attend to the incarnation's picture of the extraordinary condescension of the God who becomes a man. Think about those
words: *God* becomes *a man*. The highest entity there is—not just the highest
creature, but the incomprehensible Reality that *creates* all creatures, the high
Sovereign who is above all height we can conceive—becomes the lowest—not
just a man, but a boy, and before that an infant, and before that an embryo,
and before that a single fertilized cell; or again, not just a man, but a peasant,
and then a despised criminal, and then a corpse in a tomb. From every angle,
this kind of colossal descent is almost unfathomable. And it is matched on
the other side by an equally colossal *ascent*, for the Christian teaching is that
humanity is rescued precisely by being placed "in Christ," by dying with him
and rising with him, by inheriting a new kind of resurrection life, by being
seated in the heavenlies with God himself (Eph. 2:5–6).

9. Ibid., 147.

Such a descent and reascent is indeed remarkable, but Lewis then notes that, contrary to our first impression, it is not particularly unique. On the contrary, all of life seems to follow this arrangement, once we attend to it. It is there in vegetable life, as the full-grown plant casts itself down in the form of a single seed in order to grow again into a new plant; it is there in animal life, as the fully formed organism produces the sperm or egg that, if conditions are right, will grow once again into a mature adult; it is there in human emotional and moral life, as the raging passions of childhood and adolescence are trained and channeled and limited, and thereby enabled to expand into the fuller, richer stability of adulthood. At all of these points, though we had not thought about it before, it seems that the universe follows this pattern of death and rebirth, of descent and reascent. It is as though the incarnation has shown us the archetypal original of which all kinds of common experiences are copies.

Third, the doctrine of the incarnation highlights a feature of Christianity that is not particularly popular in our day, namely, the selectiveness that we see in much of God's work. God becomes not just any man but a very particular man, chosen for a very particular vocation. Indeed, the man himself comes from a chosen woman (the Virgin Mary), who is herself from a chosen family (the tribe of Judah) and a chosen race (the nation of Israel). The whole business of "election," so very common a notion in Scripture and so very uncommon in our culture, seems to be drawn uncomfortably to the fore. Yes, uncomfortably . . . until we recall that, once again, much of our experience involves or confirms this same kind of selectivity all around us. Of the millions of sperm cells released from the male of a species, only a shocking few will fertilize an egg; of the many fertilized eggs in most species (including humans), only a shocking few will survive to birth; of the many offspring born, only a shocking few will survive to reproduce themselves. The whole history of biological advance in the world seems to be built upon a "chosen" few. Hence, selectivity turns out to be not quite the anomaly we had thought. Once again, the incarnation has told us in tones we cannot ignore of something we might have known but had unwittingly overlooked.

Fourth, Lewis observes that the doctrine of the incarnation always points us to how God becomes not just a man, not just a chosen man, but a man chosen for a specific vocation in which he in some sense "stands in" for other people, or in fact for the whole human race. When God incarnate is crucified, he suffers and dies not for his own sins but for ours—he suffers and dies *vicariously*. Again, this is not a very common theme in the contemporary Western world (particularly in the mid-twentieth century, when Lewis was writing): on the contrary, the independent autonomy of every individual is the foundation of our moral vision and of the democratic government that we so cherish. Yet Lewis points out that, upon reflection, it is not hard to see that no one lives or dies as a truly independent or autonomous agent. Every one of us is linked by an extraordinarily complex web to all other creatures, not just in our choices (which always affect people and things besides ourselves), but even in our living itself, where each biological organism lives by consuming other things. In this sense, we are all inevitably involved in a vicarious mutuality in which one thing "dies" in order that another might "live"—just as the doctrine of the incarnation summons us to recall.

Each of these four aspects of the incarnation—the composite character of life, descent and reascent, selectiveness, and vicariousness—turns out to be not just an interesting feature of an obscure religious dogma but a central element in the world we all find ourselves encountering every moment of every day of our lives. We seem to find the incarnation reflecting the natural world quite closely, reaffirming and approving many of the constitutive principles of nature itself.

But this is not yet the whole story, since it is evident that something more than mere *affirmation* of nature is going on in Christianity. The principles of nature may be affirmed, but they are also challenged and enriched, summoned to a higher kind of perfection, as the brokenness of the world is recognized and corrected.

Consider the four principles we have named.

1. The unified composition of soul and body natural to every human being will come to an ignominious end at death, but the incarnation speaks of a deeper union that conquers death rather than being dissolved by it.

2. The natural descent and reascent that we see in plants and animals provides grounds for all sorts of indecencies in ancient fertility cults, but in the incarnation it is united with and purified by a moral rectitude that has no place for a glorified lust or lasciviousness.

3. Nature's selectivity might invite us also to be "selective," in the heartless totalitarian fashion that callously destroys the weak for the benefit of the strong. But in the incarnation the Chosen One is chosen precisely for the benefit of those who are not chosen, to aid and enrich, not to destroy.

4. The vicarious interdependence of all life could be affirmed in a way that undermines individual significance and responsibility, but in the incarnation the one suffers for the many precisely in order to empower the many to regain the responsible freedom that sin had ruined.

At each point, we see how the incarnation and the Christian teachings that surround it provide not a flat reaffirmation of principles we see in our experience but a refinement and purification of them. Though the incarnation itself may be opaque to our vision, we understand the world and our experience more fully as we see the ideal archetype that the world should (but does not perfectly) follow. Here, says Lewis, we find not just repetition of our natural insights, but not just rejection of them either. We find "a real illumination: Nature is being lit up by a light from beyond Nature. Someone is speaking who knows more about her than can be known from inside her."[10] This is just what we should expect if the Christian doctrine of Christ points us to a mystery in the rich, revelational sense. Like the doctrine of the Trinity, the doctrine of Christ explains aspects of our experience by virtue of itself being outside of ordinary explanations.

The Surprising Definiteness of Orthodoxy

Of course, the explanatory fruitfulness of the "grand miracle" will depend upon whether we have understood this Christian mystery correctly in the first place. This statement may strike some of us as a bit surprising, since we usually think of a mystery as something that we do not "understand" at all, much less understand "correctly." But remember again that a revelational mystery is not something that we simply fail to understand; it is something that we *do* understand—and part of what we understand is that it is too big to fit into our normal categories of understanding. This is why such a mystery can be intellectually fruitful and productive rather than repressive and stifling.

So we do need to ascertain what the Christian doctrine of the incarnation actually is. And in a world that seems to become more religiously and philosophically "plural" every minute, this task becomes all the more pressing, for one finds a whole host of different ideas of "incarnation" vying for attention.

Consider, for example, the notion of "incarnation" in traditional Hinduism. As Christians have taken the gospel to the subcontinent of India, they have sometimes been surprised at how receptive the Indian people are to the incarnation of Christ—*so* receptive, in fact, that it makes one suspicious. Longtime missionary Lesslie Newbigin writes of the ready willingness of most Hindus to accept Jesus into their religious world, to grant him a place of honor right alongside all of the other divine incarnations throughout history. But wait a minute. All of the *other* incarnations? This language ought to give Christians pause. As Newbigin says, it gradually became clear that the inclusion of Jesus's portrait in a gallery of the "great religious teachers of mankind," even with worship offered before it on Christmas Day each year, "was not a step toward the conversion of India."[11]

He is surely right about this, and we are thus reminded that it is not just any old talk about "incarnation" that gets Christians excited about God's work in the world. No, the Christian doctrine is a very definite, very particular thing, which insists that the "incarnation" of God in Christ is not just interesting, not just important, not even just of *saving* importance (Hindus would admit

10. Ibid., 159.
11. Lesslie Newbigin, *The Gospel in a Pluralist Society* (Grand Rapids: Eerdmans, 1989), 3.

all this); it is the central event in the whole history of the world, with nothing else like it, nothing else even approaching it.

Why? What is so special? What exactly happened two thousand years ago? The easiest way to answer is to go to the language of the ancient creeds and to declare that, in Christ, the Son of God took upon himself a full, complete human nature, so that he really and truly *became* a man, yet *without ceasing to be* what he always had been, namely, the eternal divine Son. Thus, Jesus is both "fully divine" and also "fully human," with neither of these features undermining or diluting the other. According to the classic statement of christological orthodoxy that comes from the Council of Chalcedon in the mid-fifth century, Jesus is one person with two distinct but inseparable natures: "one and the same Son" stands before us "in two natures, inconfusedly, unchangeably, indivisibly, inseparably," with "the property of each nature being preserved, and concurring in one Person."[12]

This language of orthodoxy is extremely concentrated and focused, and so it might be helpful to unpack it a bit by considering what it *excludes*. What, according to Christians, did *not* happen in the incarnation?

1. First, historic Christianity insists that, in Christ, we do *not* meet simply an exemplary, even a God-inspired, man. It is true that Jesus "incarnated" his love for people in his concrete actions and lifestyle, and this is no doubt a great and godly thing to do. But many saintly men and women have done the same, and so this is not what Christians mean by saying that Christ is God incarnate. To think of Jesus as only a unique, God-inspired man is the ancient *adoptionist* heresy, so called because of its belief that Jesus was an ordinary man who was "adopted" as the Son of God because of his matchless piety. Against such a view, fourth-century defender of orthodoxy Athanasius of Alexandria points out explicitly that the eternal Word (i.e., the Second Person of the Trinity) "*became* man, and did not *come into* a man." Note well this crucial distinction. Athanasius adds that we must "avoid the notion that the Word [merely] dwelled in a man, hallowing him and displaying himself in him, as in earlier times the Word came to each of the saints."[13] Such a notion gives us a certain kind of watered down "incarnation," but in Athanasius's mind it cannot do justice to the uniqueness and finality of Christ's redemptive work.

2. For reasons somewhat similar, Christians hold that Jesus was not, so to speak, a divine creature—that is, an exalted and Godlike being, but one created by God. Early believers were sometimes tempted

---

12. Philip Schaff, ed., revised by David S. Schaff, *The Creeds of Christendom*, vol. 2, *The Greek and Latin Creeds*, 6th ed. (Grand Rapids: Baker Books, 1990), 62.

13. Athanasius, *Against the Arians* 3.30, quoted in McGuckin, ed., *We Believe in One Lord*, 138 (italics added).

by this view in the form of *Arianism*, which taught (as we saw in the previous chapter) that the Son was the first and greatest of the creatures, a veritable "god" compared to the other creatures, but still infinitely less than the one true God who reigns over all. But the church concluded instead that this approach, though it protected an abstract monotheism quite nicely, failed in two decisive ways. On the one hand, it failed to account for the larger scope of biblical teaching, which gives us what Athanasius famously referred to as a "double account of the Savior"—that is, an account that includes both Jesus's subordination to God as a man *and also* his full equality with God. On the other hand, it failed to explain the fullness of Christian salvation, since (as we shall see shortly) the depth and complexity of humanity's sin could be addressed only by a savior who is fully divine—who is God in the same sense that the Father is God.

3. If Christians reject any view of the incarnation in which Jesus was less than fully God, they also reject what might be thought of as the opposite approach, the view that Jesus was less than fully human. On this faulty model, the incarnation is a case of the eternal, unchangeable Word of God entering the world *as if* he were a human being. This view, as it happens, is very close to the classical Hindu notion of "incarnation" that we referred to a moment ago—but it is very far from the orthodox Christian notion. No, say Christians, Jesus did not merely *look like* a human being: he *was* a human being. It is true that the early church was committed enough to Jesus's deity that it toyed for a time with theologies of *Docetism*, theologies that made Jesus out only to *appear* human (Greek, *dokeō*, "to appear") but not really to *be* human. But orthodox Christians consistently set aside such thinking because the docetic view dramatically diluted both the real uniqueness of Christ.

4. Similarly, orthodox Christianity insists that Jesus was not just *physically* human while remaining divine in mind or spirit. This would be the classical heresy of *Apollinarianism*, whose fourth-century originator argued (following John 1:14) that the Word became flesh, *and flesh only*—that is, the Word took only a body to himself rather than a full human nature. This proposed bifurcation was a neat solution to the problem of relating divine and human in Christ (since, quite simply, the bodily element was human and the nonbodily element was divine), but it was rejected by the church because of its unsettling implication that embodiment was the real source of sin in humanity. No, the sin problem was deeper, more comprehensive, than mere weakness of flesh, and therefore it was not merely human flesh that needed to be taken on (or "assumed") by the Son of God. As fourth-century theologian Gregory of Nazianzus put

> it: What is saved is that which has been united with God. If it was half of Adam that fell, then half might be assumed and saved. But if it was the whole of Adam that fell, it is united to the whole of him who was begotten and [thus] gains complete salvation.[14]

This survey of ancient missteps could go on, and (as we saw with the Trinity) it need not include only *ancient* missteps. Contemporary theologian James Anderson systematically investigates the major options in more recent christological reflection and finds that those that attempt to give final resolution to the mystery (or what he calls the "paradox") that is inherent in the incarnation inevitably end up compromising some aspect of the received orthodox tradition. Indeed, they seem to compromise orthodoxy precisely *to the extent* that they insist upon following some logical principle to its necessary conclusion. Anderson's summary of the matter is a provocative one. When one considers the incarnation, "there appears to be no option for the Christian theologian but to grasp one or other horn of the dilemma: to abandon orthodoxy or to embrace paradox and thereby face the charge of irrationality."[15]

Provocative indeed: *either* orthodoxy *or* logic—but never both. To put it this way may well be misleading, for in fact (as Anderson himself goes on to argue in his book) orthodoxy follows a logic of its own that is deeper than our ordinary categories can handle. But it is certainly true that those who demand crisp, clear logical rigor may turn away from orthodox Christology rather frustrated. How can Jesus be both fully divine and fully human in a single person? We simply do not know.

In fact, one may be surprised at how much we *do* claim to know about the metaphysical details of Christ's person. It almost seems that the acknowledgment of mystery carries us too far in the opposite direction, does it not? It seems that one should be happily ignorant about details—but then are we as Christians not surprisingly *insistent* about those details? Chalcedon's "inconfusedly, unchangeably, indivisibly, inseparably" seems to be an awfully thorough description, when we remember that it is a description of something that we constantly insist we do not understand.

The Inadequacy of Explanation

Of course, the Christian answer is that the doctrine of Christ is *revealed*. That is why Christians can accept the surprisingly definite claims of orthodoxy without claiming to understand how those claims fit together logically. Like

14. Gregory of Nazianzus, *The Letter to Cledonius* 101.7, quoted in McGuckin, ed., *We Believe in One Lord*, 148.
15. James Anderson, *Paradox in Christian Theology: An Analysis of Its Presence, Character, and Epistemic Status* (Waynesboro, GA: Paternoster, 2007), 106.

the two-dimensional mathematician from Flatland who accepts our description of a cylinder without understanding how such a figure can exist, we also accept the claims of the orthodox doctrine of Christ, because they have been revealed by the God who tells us that it is so.

But *has* God really told us quite as much as this? If christological orthodoxy is really the nuanced, definitive thing we have outlined, if the details really matter as much as all that, then it may seem rather surprising that the full-blown doctrine is not "revealed" in a more obvious, more straightforward sense—as the commandments at Sinai are revealed, as the principles of the Sermon on the Mount are revealed, directly from the mouth of God. After all, the doctrine of the incarnation did not fall from the sky, with all of its technical vocabulary fully developed and intact. As we have hinted already (and as heretics and skeptics love to point out), the doctrine as we know it today was the outcome of a long and complicated historical process, a process rarely as neat and tidy as defenders of orthodoxy might wish. Why would this be so? What was God up to here? Why did he not simply give us a savior who, on such and such a day and in such and such a place, preached a sermon whose highly publicized topic was "The Incarnation of God, Explained and Illustrated"? It is an interesting question, and it invites us to consider more carefully how the nature of divine mystery influences the kind of answers we give to important christological questions.

We will need to ask both *why* such gradual doctrinal development should have been permitted by God and also *how* such doctrinal development actually took place. Let us begin with the *why* question. If the details of the doctrine are so important, then why did not God declare and explain them in a more obvious, more reputable way? Surely God could have given us an inspired account without the intervention of four centuries of guesswork by theologically fallible Christians. Why, then, did he not do so?

To approach an answer, let us first make a key observation: the mature doctrine of Christ's full deity and full humanity does not emerge out of sheer logical reflection either on the nature of God or on the nature of humanity. This is somewhat surprising when you stop to think about it, but it is very clearly correct. Nowhere in the early church does one find a sophisticated philosopher or theologian who sits down at his desk and follows a line of thinking like the following: "Hmm. I have been thinking a lot about the doctrine of God lately: omniscient, omnipotent, omnipresent, eternal, the whole works. And the more I think about it, the clearer it becomes that this kind of being could be—indeed, should be—united in a single entity with an ordinary human being, who is limited in knowledge, power, and spatial and temporal location. Yes, it all fits together. . . ."

No one followed this line of thinking, and it is fairly easy to see why. Logically speaking, the attributes of God are very nearly the opposite of those of a human being, and the theologians of the early centuries very clearly acknowledged this fact. To take but one example, the famous defender of nascent orthodoxy in the fifth century, Cyril of Alexandria, declared quite forcefully, "Godhead is one thing, and manhood is another thing, considered in the perspective of their respective and intrinsic beings." There it is: stark opposition. When Cyril goes on to say that, in the case of Christ, Godhead and manhood "came together in a mysterious and incomprehensible union without confusion or change,"[16] he is evidently moving beyond the obvious, predictable course of logical necessity. For him, mere analysis of the doctrines of God and humanity simply cannot produce the Christian doctrine of Christ.

And of course, if the Christian doctrine of divine incomprehensibility is true, then this is exactly what we should expect. If God transcends the entire created order, in something analogous to the way a three-dimensional object transcends the two-dimensional world of Flatland, then no amount of created reasoning will allow the creature to understand the Creator, just as no amount of two-dimensional reasoning can allow the Flatlander to understand a cylinder. In any case of real, ontological transcendence, the same is true. The reasoning powers of the "lower" reality cannot adequately conceive of the "higher" reality, precisely because the higher is higher.

For the same reason, no plain, rational explanation of the higher reality can ever be accessible or comprehensible to the lower—even if the explanation comes from the higher reality itself. We see this easily enough in concrete experience (imagine a veterinarian trying to explain veterinary medicine to a dog), but it is all the more true when any sort of ontological transcendence is involved. The very best three-dimensional mathematician on earth, who comprehends circles and rectangles and the relation between them in a cylinder with perfect clarity, will still not be able to explain a cylinder to a Flatlander—not because of the mathematician's lack of comprehension, but because of the Flatlander's incapacity. In the nature of the case, rigorous logical explanation cannot overcome transcendence.

It is important to see that this difficulty obtains even if it is God himself doing the explaining. God does, of course, understand the nature of deity and humanity, and also the relation between the two in the incarnation, and we therefore can trust him without qualification to guide us wisely into the truth that we cannot grasp with logical rigor. But we should not expect his guidance to take the form of a syllogism. Having no grasp of the transcendent mystery that God himself is, we have no resources for conceiving or evaluating how that reality should or could be related to an individual instance of created human nature, and therefore no clear-cut "explanation" of the incarnation will be forthcoming—not even from God. Mere logic (of the creaturely, two-dimensional variety) cannot contain such a thing.

16. Cyril of Alexandria, *On the Unity of Christ*, trans. John A. McGuckin (Crestwood, NY: St. Vladimir's Seminary Press, 1995), 77.

But the problem is even worse. It is not just the limits of creaturely logic that hinder us, for it is not mere creatures that God must "explain" things to. It is *fallen* creatures—creatures, in other words, whose innate sinfulness gives them a vested interest in not perceiving clearly *anything* that their divine enemy might have to say to them. We begin to recognize what a complicated business divine revelation must be, for the recipients of the revelation are infected by a disease that corrupts their minds and wills even as it leads their bodies to the grave. How is the veterinarian to explain veterinary medicine not just to a dog but also to a dog made vicious and ferocious by a new strain of rabies, a dog every minute snapping madly at the one who tries to offer aid? Worse yet, imagine a dog that (by some miracle) has begun in rudimentary ways to think, to reason, to really understand—and whose infection now prompts it to use these elementary reasoning skills to resist, to attack, to undermine all that the veterinarian plans for it. In such a situation, where natural incapacity combines with horribly unnatural resistance, what kind of simple, direct, straightforward explanation—"revelation" in the simple, obvious sense— would have the tiniest hope of success?

It is something terribly close to this dire situation that God must address when he unveils his wildly unprecedented treatment for creation's deep affliction. God himself will intervene in ways inconceivable to any human mind, much less to the unruly, defiant mind of sinful human beings. He will take human nature—unimaginably—into the Godhead, so that the burning brilliance of uncreated Light may remake the created things lost in darkness, so that a death may be died by the deathless One that will kill death itself once and for all. It is this staggering reality that God will reveal to stubborn, bitter, angry, fearful people. How can this revelation be accomplished? How can such an unthinkably exalted hope be communicated? How can the message get through, when the message itself is chock-full of incomprehensible wonders, and the recipients are unwilling to receive messages in the first place? How can such a truth be communicated, when the aim is not merely that it be understood (impossible as that is anyhow), but that it should be embraced, loved, *believed*?

The Revelation of a Marvel

We have come, it seems, to the *how* question. Any scheme for revealing this kind of truth would have to be complex, indirect, unpredictable, even fantastic. It might have to involve concealment as well as revelation, slow recognition as much as immediate clarity, deep faith alongside inspired intellect. As in an old episode of *Mission: Impossible*, subtle hints will be picked up only after the fact; important clues may be delivered and then left to ferment and develop; individual pieces of the puzzle will not be recognized until the whole suddenly falls into place. All of this we find in the gradual development of the Christian doctrine of the incarnation.

But if we are to appreciate this development, we cannot jump immediately to the church's reflection on the doctrine. The real bedrock of the incarnation lies historically not in any logical analysis or argument but in the startlingly direct positing of the marvel itself as an incontestable reality: Jesus Christ appeared among us. Grasping the significance of this enormous event is a complicated affair, for one must consider the long, complex interplay of a whole variety of elements, surely including the unified coherence of Old Testament theology, the formative influence of Jewish tradition, the shocking character of Jesus's own career on earth, the steady unfolding of apostolic teaching, and the church's ongoing experience of life in the Spirit. We have space here to consider only the barest sketch of this exceedingly dynamic process, but a bare sketch may be what allows us to catch a glimpse of the overall picture without being unduly distracted by the messiness of the historical details.

The story begins not with Christians at all, but with the expectations of the Jewish tradition during the years preceding Jesus. These are not very hard to outline. All orthodox Jews chafed under the yoke of the Roman Empire, because all looked back, in one way or another, to the great days of the past when God himself had acted to rescue his people from Egypt and then to establish them in his land as his own kingdom—God's kingdom, ruled over by God's king, the great warrior and poet David, son of Jesse. David has a unique place in God's economy, for God had made promises that David and his offspring would constitute an unending dynasty of kings in Israel, that he would never fail to have a man on the throne of Israel, and that ultimately his house would extend its rule over all the earth (2 Sam. 7:13–16). The conundrum that the people of Israel faced in the years before the coming of Christ was that there was no son of David on the throne, and therefore God's kingdom seemed more a pipe dream than a reality. Yet God's promise to David had been made, and many Jews longed for its fulfillment. So they waited for the promised one, the Messiah, the Son of David, who would arise as God's appointed king to end the long exile, to reestablish God's kingdom with new and unprecedented power, a power that would permanently overthrow the forces of evil.

Then along came a man, an itinerant preacher, about whom strange stories were told: stories of angelic visitations at his birth, and of dramatic deliverance in his childhood, and of unique authority in his words, and of miraculous power in his touch. Gradually, a small group of followers attached themselves to this Galilean. They became more and more convinced that he was the One they had been waiting for. His following grew and with it an excited expectancy that what Israel had long dreamed of was about to be realized.

But suddenly, inexplicably, almost overnight, the dream took a disastrous turn. God's Messiah, God's instrument of power and victory, against whom for three glorious years no opponent had been able to stand, this unstoppable

Son of David . . . was stopped. The religious leaders who hated him penetrated the inner circle of this Messiah-to-be and orchestrated an arrest, a trial, a condemnation. And now the man was being executed—and executed in the worst possible way: he was being crucified, "hung on a tree," which, according to the sacred books (Deut. 21:23 NRSV), was an unmistakable sign of God's curse upon this charismatic dreamer. The stunned disciples were now forced to acknowledge their incredible blunder. Everyone knew, beyond question, that God's Messiah would come to earth to bring the victory they had all longed for, and if a man did not bring the victory, then he obviously was not the Messiah. As their leader died in agony on the cross, they knew that all was lost. They had been wrong. Their man was crucified; he had not been the Messiah after all. One can hear the disappointment in the despairing words of the disciples on the road to Emmaus: "We had hoped that he was the one who was going to redeem Israel" (Luke 24:21). "Alas," they might have added with tears, "we were wrong."

But then the great reversal took place, for on the third day the dead man was raised. The apostles themselves saw Jesus and talked with him—perhaps about unimaginable things that do not come down to us at all in the historical records. What we do know is that, with the resurrection, everything changed for the apostles. They had thought themselves foolishly deceived, but it simply was not so. The resurrection was God's irrefutable stamp of approval on Jesus's message, on his life, and even on his death (Rom. 1:4). Unimaginably, impossibly, the man who had been crucified was shown with power to be the long-awaited Messiah and more. The utterly unexpected had happened, and as a result everything the disciples had thought, everything they had been taught about Judaism, about the kingdom, about the Messiah, had to be reconsidered through the strange lens of the cross and resurrection.

So the apostles returned to their Scriptures and began the reconstruction of their theological vision, with this wildly unanticipated Messiah at the center. Under the tutelage of the resurrected Christ and with the guidance of the Spirit (Acts 1:1–3), they saw Jesus as the new, perfect Israel, who performed flawlessly all that Israel herself had never been able to perform (see Gal. 6:16); they saw him as the Davidic king who rules by serving (John 1:49; 12:13; Luke 22:24–30), who conquers death by dying (Acts 13:34); they saw him as the kinsman-redeemer who makes all of Israel new (Gal. 3:13–14); they saw him as the great high priest (Heb. 9:11–15) who offered, and was, the final sacrifice that would take away sin once and for all (Rom. 3:24; Eph. 1:7; 4:30; Col. 1:14); they saw him as the coming Son of Man, the new Adam (Rom. 5:14–15; 1 Cor. 15:22, 45), who ushers in the age to come right in the midst of this present evil age by his own resurrection (Gal. 1:4; Eph. 1:21). To all of this the holy books bore witness, and the believers' Spirit-led experience gave confirmation.

Christianity was thus born as a faith that believed in mysteries like a Jewish gospel that included gentiles, and in marvels like the eschaton breaking into ordinary time, and especially in impossibilities like a crucified Messiah. If we want to follow the theological logic that was behind the development of ortho-dox Christology, we should begin not with systematic definitions of God or humanity but with the astonishing reality of the cross and resurrection, which became the centerpiece around which every other Christian doctrine was set. The revelatory ethos of the New Testament is rooted not in ratiocination but in wonder, as the early Christians, led by the Spirit, began to understand the unimaginable things that had happened on Good Friday and Easter morning, and began to draw theological conclusions on that basis.

The Marveling Logic of Orthodoxy

So what were these unimaginable, unexpected things? If this marvel of a cruci-fied Messiah was the center of salvation, then what was he doing there on the cross? In answer to this immense question we find a stunning array of New (and Old) Testament images flowing in and out of one another. Over time Christians came to organize this apostolic witness to the work of Christ in terms of three primary patterns of achievement, which can be roughly sum-marized under the well-known headings of Christ's work as *prophet*, *priest*, and *king*, or in terms of Christ's *revealing* work, Christ's *reconciling* work, and Christ's *ruling* work. This is a useful classification in all sorts of ways, though it might be misleading insofar as it sounds so strongly reminiscent of ordinary tasks performed by ordinary people. In the case of Christ, there was nothing ordinary going on. Instead, as the years passed Christians found themselves increasingly aware that what Christ had done was wider and deeper than anyone had ever expected—and they found themselves increasingly willing to accept unanticipated conclusions about who Christ is as a result.

To explore these developments, let us consider a classic example of chris-tological reflection that is located right in the middle of the fervor that led to Chalcedon, and therefore one that can give us a glimpse of what the theo-logical logic of orthodoxy looked like in practice. Think about the well-known treatise by Athanasius of Alexandria, probably composed in about AD 318, titled *On the Incarnation of the Word of God*. We have already noted Atha-nasius's important contribution to the overthrow of Arianism in the fourth century and hence his steadfast commitment to the full deity of Christ. *On the Incarnation* is a reflection that precedes the Arian controversy and that illustrates how Athanasius developed the coherent christological vision for which he is now known.

The short book presents a comprehensive and elegant account of the need for a savior and of how it is that God met that need in the most fitting way, by himself entering onto the stage of human history, by God the eternal Son (or the eternal Word) becoming a man. Why was such a move necessary?

What was the problem that only the scandalous advent of a crucified Messiah could address?

Athanasius understands that problem in terms of the distressing dilemma God faced as a result of human sin. Humanity was the crown of God's creation, having received from God

> a grace which other creatures lacked—namely the impress of His own Image, a share in the reasonable being of the very Word Himself, so that, reflecting Him and themselves becoming reasonable and expressing the Mind of God even as He does, though in limited degree, they might continue for ever in the blessed and only true life of the saints in paradise.[17]

But precisely because of this high position, sin's infection of the human race was the ultimate and intolerable tragedy. How could the creature that most fully resembles God be allowed to disintegrate, to return to the dust from which it had been created? How could what honors God the most be permitted to fall into such dishonor? Athanasius regards the very possibility as "both monstrous and unfitting."[18] Desperate times call for desperate measures, and so something remarkable had to be done.

But what? At least three elements of the human condition need to be addressed, for Athanasius. Fallen humanity is characterized by the deeply problematic traits of *guilt*, having disobeyed the commandment of God and thus incurred the penalty of death; of *corruption*, having damaged human nature itself so that it tends toward vanity and self-destruction; and of *ignorance*, having abandoned the truth of God and therefore lost the knowledge of God. Athanasius suggests that it is precisely these features of humanity's brokenness that call for the dramatic solution provided in the incarnation.

Guilt

First, humanity is guilty. Before sin had ever entered into the equation, God had warned that stern condemnation awaited any who would disobey his light and joyous commands. With that pronouncement, the fate of sinners was sealed, for how could God's "law of death"[19] not have its threatened effect? How could the character of God be stable and consistent if his judgment upon the trespass were not upheld? This, says Athanasius, is a first element in the divine dilemma. Though it seems intolerable that the glorious image of God should be judged in this way, nevertheless "there was a debt owing which must needs be paid; for . . . all men were due to die."[20] This predicament could be

17. Athanasius, *On the Incarnation*, trans. and ed. A Religious of C.S.M.V. (Crestwood, NY: St. Vladimir's Seminary Press, 1996), 1.3 p. 28.
18. Ibid., 2.6 p. 32.
19. Ibid.
20. Ibid., 4.20 p. 49.

resolved only if someone were to come on the scene whose single death could be "a sufficient exchange for all," thus providing "a substitute for the life of all" and "fulfill[ing] in death all that was required."[21] "Here then," Athanasius concludes, "is [one] reason why the Word dwelt among us, namely that having proved His Godhead by His works, He might offer the sacrifice on behalf of all, surrendering His own temple to death in place of all, to settle man's account with death and free him from the primal transgression."[22]

It is important to recognize that this is not the sort of argument that Athanasius (or anyone else) might have made *prior to* the incarnation, as a prediction of what God would have to do to save sinners. On the contrary, who could have imagined it? Or rather, who *that knew the holy God of the Old Testament revelation* could have imagined it? It is true that many cultures have myths about dying-and-rising gods who are tied to agricultural cycles and fertility rites. But the Holy One of Israel is not one of these deities. The Creator of heaven and earth sits on his throne in the heavens. He loves his people, but away with the foolish, idolatrous talk of the pagans! How could the deathless One die? How could Life become lifeless? How could reality exist at all if the Creator and Sustainer of reality were not high above it and independent of its exigencies? Childish absurdities like these are silly at best, tolerable only to pagans who have never heard the voice from Sinai, who have never felt the earth tremble and seen the fire and the smoke and the glory.

No Jew could ever have entertained such notions . . . until a crucified criminal was revealed with power to be God's chosen and victorious Messiah. It is the incontrovertible death and resurrection of Christ that invites—indeed, that *requires*—brand new consideration of God's purposes in the world. And so, in the light shed by Christ's crucifixion and resurrection, the people of God could reconsider Old Testament texts such as Isaiah 53 and Psalm 22, and for the first time wondering believers like Athanasius could think through the reality of sin and recognize how the death of one person, *if it were the right one*, would set everything straight.

But it would have to be the right One. Note the critical christological implications of this question. Who would the one on the cross have to be in order for the plan to work? Who is it that could die and have his death work such a wonder? No one, says Athanasius, but God himself—that is, "the incorporeal and incorruptible and immaterial Word of God,"[23] now made flesh among us. This is what must have happened on the cross: the eternal Word "surrendered His body to death in place of all, and offered it to the Father . . . , so that in His death all might die, and the law of death thereby be abolished."[24]

21. Ibid., 2.9 p. 35.
22. Ibid., 4.20 p. 49.
23. Ibid., 2.8 p. 33.
24. Ibid., 2.8 p. 34.

Corruption

But this is only one aspect of Athanasius's account, for humanity is not only guilty and therefore condemned but also corrupt and therefore tending naturally toward ruin, disintegration, and death. Having been made from nothing and having, because of sin, lost the supreme grace and power of "Likeness to Him Who is," human nature miserably collapses on itself, with weakened body and erring mind and diseased will all alike sliding back into nothingness and death. It was an ignominious fate that "beings which once had shared the nature of the Word should perish and turn back again into non-existence through corruption,"[25] but what could be done?

What indeed, reasons Athanasius, except that death's corruption itself be broken by "this union of the immortal Son of God with our [mortal] human nature"?[26] Though no one could ever have imagined it beforehand, a crucified Messiah who rises from the grave with resurrection power really does make all things new, for in this stupendous event, "the renewal of creation has been wrought by the Self-same Word Who made it in the beginning."[27] Life itself has died, and then in rising he has overturned death and corruption once and for all. Who would have imagined such a thing? And once such a thing is imagined, by whom could it possibly have been achieved? Athanasius answers, "To change the corruptible to incorruption was proper to none other than the Savior Himself, Who in the beginning made all things out of nothing; . . . None save our Lord Jesus Christ could give to mortals immortality."[28] Once again, the christological implications are unmistakable. Who could have saved in this extraordinary way? Only the Son of God, who is the eternal God himself.

Neatly summarizing both of these first two marvelous elements of the gospel, Athanasius says, "By the sacrifice of His own body [Christ] did two things: He put an end to the law of death which barred our way; and He made a new beginning of life for us, by giving us the hope of resurrection."[29]

Ignorance

But this is not yet all. Athanasius perceived a third problem for fallen humanity, and it is human ignorance.

> Men, foolish as they are, thought little of the grace they had received, and turned away from God. They defiled their own soul so completely that they not only lost their apprehension of God, but invented for themselves other gods of various kinds. . . . In a word, impiety and lawlessness were everywhere, and neither God nor His Word was known.[30]

25. Ibid., 2.6, p. 32.
26. Ibid., 2.9 p. 35.
27. Ibid., 1.1 p. 26, italics removed.
28. Ibid., 4.20 pp. 48–49.
29. Ibid., 2.10 p. 37.
30. Ibid., 3.11 p. 38.

Here, from yet another angle, was the same dilemma: the created image of God, now cast away and debased. "What was God to do in the face of this dehumanizing of humankind, this universal hiding of the knowledge of Himself?" asks Athanasius. "What else could He possibly do, being God, but renew His Image in humanity, so that through it humans might once more come to know Him? And how could this be done save by the coming of the very Image Himself, our Savior Jesus Christ?"[31] Observe again how the unassailable reality of Christ's achievement grounds Athanasius's awestruck conclusion regarding Christ's person. If ignorance is our problem, then we need to be taught to know God again. Jesus addresses this need, for in knowing Jesus (especially in his stunning death and resurrection) we do know the Father. And so who must this Jesus have been? Athanasius's answer is unambiguous: "Only the Word Who orders all things and is alone the Father's true and sole-begotten Son could teach humans about Him and abolish the worship of idols."[32]

In summary, consider Athanasius's highly condensed statement of the "things which the Savior did for us by becoming Man." What did Jesus accomplish? "He [1] banished death from us and [2] made us anew; and, [3] invisible and imperceptible as in Himself He is, He became visible through His works and revealed Himself as the Word of the Father, the Ruler and King of the whole creation."[33] These are not the categories of logical deduction. They are simply the wonderful works of God. Real logic is at work here, but it is not the kind of logic that begins with analytical definitions that determine what is possible and what is impossible. When creatures are trying to think about the reality of the transcendent Creator, such premature definitions are never likely to produce much fruit. Instead, Athanasius accepts the revealed account of the marvel that has taken place among us—a final, once-for-all sacrifice; the remaking of humanity beyond sin and death; the full, personal revealing of God himself—as a salvation that rightly overflows both our expectations and our comprehension. And then on the basis of that larger-than-life salvation, he works his way carefully and rigorously to the appropriate conclusions about the kind of being our marvelous Savior must be. Athanasius does not reject reason in the name of mystery, nor does he reject mystery in the name of reason. Rather, he leads us into a reasonable reality that is nevertheless larger than reason, greater than all of life, because it is the reality of God himself.

Development and Doxology

In this respect, the various inadequate Christologies finally judged to be heretical during the formative period of orthodoxy shared one thing in common: they

31. Ibid., 3.13 p. 41. We have slightly modified the translation.
32. Ibid., 4.20 p. 49.
33. Ibid., 3.16 pp. 44–45.

were, if we may put it this way, too rational for their own good. They quickly followed the tenets of a strict logic rather than being patiently, humbly guided by the startling necessities of salvation revealed in Christ's death and resurrection. By contrast, Athanasius never allows a logical issue related to Christ's person to obscure the unspeakable marvel of Christ's work, and it is precisely the marvelous work that *demands* a marvelous person. All of our theological conclusions are therefore conditioned above all by doxology. This explains why the orthodox definition of Christ's person at Chalcedon *states*, but does not *explain*, the Christian doctrine. This is a frustrating business for the rationalist searching for logical answers to analytical questions, but it is just what a worshiping heart desires and expects in the face of the wonder of salvation.

The point, then, is that the gradual historical development of the doctrine of the incarnation turns out not to be an embarrassment for Christian orthodoxy. Quite the contrary: a slow, reflective, worshipful process is exactly what one might expect, if the truths that the doctrine of the incarnation embodies are, so to speak, too big for human language to contain. To think and speak well of the incarnation is not just a matter of knowing the right answers about the person of Christ. It is a matter of knowing the mystery of Christ himself, "in whom are hidden all the treasures of wisdom and knowledge" (Col. 2:3), and this is a knowledge that will always retain its mystery.

But it is real knowledge nevertheless. Christians did not advocate mystery simply to have something marvelous to say in their sermons. If they had been interested in marvels only for the sake of marvels, they could hardly have articulated the *specific* contours of the mystery in the way that they did. Instead, they faithfully acknowledged and accepted an amazing act of God—a crucified Messiah raised from the dead—as the revelation of the very center of God's work of salvation; they steadfastly pursued that clue, in the light of other clues found both in Scripture and in the living experience of the worshiping church; and eventually, the logical implications of the mystery became plain, without reducing the mystery itself one whit.

We might even conclude that the historical *development* of orthodoxy is a crucial part of our genuine *understanding* of orthodoxy. The gradual unfolding of the truth about Christ, the slow but increasing realization over the years of the all-embracing grandeur of God's achievement in Christ, is a necessary part of the teaching itself. Isn't this often the way that our most significant transformations (what some people call "paradigm shifts") occur? We begin by perceiving one important fact or one crucial principle, like a faint glimmer of light in the darkness of night. But then slowly, hour by hour, we become conscious of new applications and new implications. The initial insight expands and increasingly illuminates other areas of understanding. We eagerly and excitedly begin to perceive other things that we had not seen before. Finally, the day dawns with an almost unbearable, and still increasing, brightness—and we find that we are seeing the whole world in a new and different way.

The same thing has happened with the coming of Christ. God planted certain fundamental, revealed truths into the mind of the apostolic church. These basic truths were both life changing and mind boggling, and were immediately perceived to be so (by the power of the Spirit). But lives and minds are lush, complicated things, and so the full transformation ended up being a matter not of moments but of generations, as believers followed the revealed clues more and more deeply into the truth of God.

Questions, Answers, and the Knowledge of God

We are left with an interesting array of questions and answers about Christology—and usually with more questions than answers! Note, however, that the mystery of the incarnation does not involve *only* questions, a sheer absence of knowledge, a sort of "anything-goes" irrationalism. Divine transcendence allows us to understand why we have no comprehension of *how* the incarnation occurred, but the revelation of Christ as the locus of salvation gives us a real and substantial foundation for understanding *what* occurred. On that foundation, orthodoxy is built. Thus, an adequate apprehension of mystery shows us both why we *cannot* know and also what we *do* know—and it invites worship on both counts.

It is crucial, therefore, to insist that our christological questions be approached in humility and worship, not with mere logic-chopping in mind. Every question about Christ is a "question" not merely in the intellectual sense but also in the deeply personal and existential sense. We are never asking strictly out of academic interest, for we are always standing in the presence of the living God himself as we ask—and a sinner's posture before the living God is never merely academic.

One is reminded of the way that 1 Peter speaks of the Old Testament prophets who "searched intently and with the greatest care" into the things of Christ that were being revealed (1:10). The prophets did get their "revelations," their glimpses of Christ and his glory, but these glimpses were hardly complete understanding, nor were they intended to be. Peter goes on to observe (v. 12) that, when they spoke of such things, the prophets "were not serving themselves but you," that is, those receiving the full gospel in the apostles' own day. This is surely a rather pointed rejection of the notion that prophets, then or now, should be aiming to satisfy their own intellectual curiosity. Such satisfaction is a pretty remote hope anyhow, since (as this passage famously ends) "even angels long to look into these things."

If the transcendent God has worked a salvation so stunning, so marvelous, so mysterious that even the angelic host cannot take it in, then it is evidently given to us not for satisfying our curiosity but for saving us from sin and leading us into life. We have received not a set of nutrition statistics meant to be calculated but a life-giving meal meant to be eaten. Hence, the aim of the knowledge of God is never *merely* knowledge: it is the concrete reality of regenerating, re-creating love. Knowledge itself also depends upon and grows out of love. In the end, Paul's celebrated words, "the greatest of these is love" (1 Cor. 13:13), can stand as a rather thorough theological motto.

Meanwhile, christological questions will persist—sometimes *many* questions. Yet while the questions we have may be greater in *number*, the answers (or perhaps the Answer) will unfailingly be greater in *magnitude*. There is always more to Christ than the answers we seek, and to seek only the answers is therefore to miss what we are truly after. Conversely, to seek Christ himself is inevitably to have both questions and answers swept up in the glorious mystery of the eternal God.

7

MYSTERY *and* SALVATION

But a distinction must be observed with especial care between that which is expressly revealed concerning [election] in God's Word, and what is not revealed. For, in addition to what has been revealed in Christ concerning this, of which we have hitherto spoken, God has still kept secret and concealed much concerning this mystery, and reserved it for His wisdom and knowledge alone, which we should not investigate, nor should we indulge our thoughts in this matter, nor draw conclusions, nor inquire curiously, but should adhere [entirely] to the revealed Word [of God]. This admonition is most urgently needed.

"Formula of Concord"[1]

'Tis mystery all: th' Immortal dies:
Who can explore His strange design?
In vain the firstborn seraph tries
To sound the depths of love divine.
'Tis mercy all! Let earth adore,
Let angel minds inquire no more!

Charles Wesley[2]

---

1. "Formula of Concord," art. 11, para. 52. Available at http://bookofconcord.org/sd-election.php.
2. Charles Wesley, "And Can It Be That I Should Gain," available at http://nethymnal.org /htm/a/c/acanitbe.htm.

In the last two chapters, we have seen how mystery helps us make sense of Christian doctrines that, though logically troublesome, have nevertheless been universally recognized as authentically Christian. These doctrines might be hard for some people to swallow, but extensive early debates about the Trinity and the incarnation hammered out a consensus that still defines orthodoxy. No long-standing alternative has been able to maintain a plausible claim to represent the true gospel.

In this chapter, that unanimity is left behind. For now we come to the Christian doctrine of salvation, and we will focus especially on what is often thought of as the most intractable of all divisive theological dilemmas, namely, the exasperating relationship between divine sovereignty and human freedom. It is clear to all Christians that God saves us and we do not save ourselves ("For it is by grace you have been saved," Eph. 2:8); it is also clear that the Bible presents saved human beings as fully, genuinely free ("If the Son sets you free, you will be free indeed," John 8:36). But it is much less clear, when one looks at the history of Christian thought, just how God's saving work and humanity's authentic freedom are related to one another *in the process of salvation itself*. Does God's act of salvation exhaustively determine the human person's response? Does the believer's act of faith decisively influence God's salvific work? These and related questions about the relationship between divine sovereignty and human freedom have vexed Christians for many generations.

We will not have time to review the history of this troubled aspect of Christian doctrine. We must be content to recognize that that history is long and complicated, with major Christian figures and major Christian movements on each side of the debate. Some (such as Augustine, Aquinas, Luther, Calvin, and the Puritans) have emphasized the sovereign work of God in salvation, while others (including Wesley, the Anglicans, the Anabaptists, the Eastern Orthodox, and mainstream Roman Catholicism) have stressed the important role of human response to and cooperation with God. We will focus on the logic of the debate more than on historical detail, and so for the sake of simplicity we will refer to the former as the "Calvinist" position (named, of course, for sixteenth-century Reformer John Calvin) and to the latter as the "Arminian" position (named for Jacob Arminius [1560–1609], the Dutch Reformed theologian who famously challenged the reigning interpretation of Calvinism in the early seventeenth century).

Our goal in the present chapter is not to show that one side or the other is right in this debate. On the contrary, we want to show that *both* sides are "right" in different ways and that therefore the most comprehensively faithful account of salvation consciously refuses to affirm either of these two positions at the expense of the other. Of course, in a rancorous debate like this one, ours will be a difficult case to make. Proponents on each side have a long list of reasons for thinking that their own position requires the rejection of the alternative. But our claim is that *if God is the incomprehensible mystery that*

Christians have always maintained, then the particular contours of this debate regarding the nature of salvation are just what one should expect. Instead of the controversy being bitter and intractable and divisive, it can be regarded as the healthy expression of a fruitful tension that pervades both Scripture and Christian theology. Moreover, an acknowledgment of that tension offers us surprisingly practical resources for dealing with concrete issues of deep pastoral concern.

But the complexity of the debate does mandate some special handling here, for the theological logic that each side follows is very distinctive—including a distinctive approach on each side to the role of mystery. So this chapter is really two chapters rolled into one, with our argument more directly addressing Calvinist concerns at some points and Arminian concerns at others. Readers will find that patient attention to arguments that do not seem immediately relevant to one's own position might help illuminate the overall presentation by the end of the chapter.

The Logic of Sovereignty

We begin with the logical structure of Calvinism, which is straightforward and well known. It may be said to begin with two fundamental, deeply biblical premises. The first is that God is "sovereign," the supreme ruler of all things without exception. As absolute Creator and ongoing Sustainer of all that exists, God also guides all that exists to its proper end, the end that he desires. In the language of Ephesians, God "works out everything in conformity with the purpose of his will" (1:11). Scripture can speak of God's providential guidance of chance events like the casting of lots (Prov. 16:33), of natural phenomena like the weather (Ps. 135:7), of human decisions like those of a king (Prov. 21:1), even of *evil* human decisions like Joseph's brothers choosing to sell Joseph into slavery in Egypt (Gen. 50:20) or like Judas's betrayal of Christ (John 17:12; Acts 1:16–17). In all of these things, God is accomplishing his purpose, for he is the sovereign Lord of all.

The second premise has to do not with God but with humanity, where Calvinists point to the sober biblical truth that human beings are, by their very nature, "sinners." This often misunderstood language means much more than that we all sometimes go wrong; it means instead that we are characterized by an inner tendency that constantly and irresistibly *pushes* us to go wrong. Just as drug addicts take drugs *because* they are addicts, because they are driven by the inner compulsion that we call an "addiction," so also sinners commit sins *because* they are sinners. As Scripture repeatedly says, apart from the unsolicited work of Christ, men and women are dead in sin (Eph. 2:1), under "the dominion of darkness" (Col. 1:13), under "the power of death" (Heb. 2:14), with a "heart of stone" (Ezek. 11:19). Each of these phrases announces in its own way the incapacity of humanity to take even the first step toward God, or even to *desire* to take the first step. Sin is not just an act that we commit; it is a power that has corrupted us and that enslaves us, leaving us helpless either to free ourselves or even to want freedom.

With these two premises in place, we may ask ourselves this question: If ultimate salvation is to come to anyone, whose decision will bring it to pass? It is impossible for human beings themselves to choose salvation, for they are powerless in the face of the sin that has deceived and enslaved them; their "choosing" is the *problem*, not the solution. By contrast, God is the sovereign Lord of all, whose choosing defines reality itself. From both premises, the conclusion is inevitable: God alone must save. If anyone is to enter the heavenly kingdom, it can only be by virtue of the eternal choice of God to save that sinner. This is the simple, compelling logic of sovereignty.

Now we should note three elements here that are especially significant for the way that Calvinists usually give formal expression to this theological logic. First, note that the work of God on behalf of sinners will have to be *irresistible*; it will have to be a work that necessarily and without fail accomplishes its purpose in any human heart it touches. Why? Well, for the very good reason that the human beings who need to be saved are sinners in the full, debilitating sense we just noted. It is not simply that sinful humans occasionally fall short of God's glory. Instead, having been deluded and degraded by sin, they *hate* that glory (John 3:20). They are hostile to God (Rom. 8:7), enemies of God (Col. 1:21), and therefore they oppose God's holy work in one way or another at every possible point. Such is their blindness that they do not *want* to be saved. If God intervenes only in a way that can be resisted, then corrupted sinners can be counted on to resist every time—and therefore God's purpose of salvation will be frustrated every time. However, if God's purpose is *not* frustrated, the reason must be that God's work of grace *cannot be resisted*. And it is that irresistible work of grace, rather than any human decision, that finally determines salvation.

Second, and for similar reasons, God's choice to act savingly toward any particular sinner must be a matter of *unconditional* election. In other words, God chooses or "elects" someone for salvation solely on the basis of his own grace and mercy, not as a result of a sinner having developed some quality or performed some task or even believed some message—not on the basis of any condition whatsoever that the sinner has satisfied. Once again, what condition *could* be satisfied by a hardened heart that naturally hates the light and loves the darkness? What goodness, what faith, what desire could God look for in order to decide whom to choose for salvation? Apart from his own merciful work, there is none to be found (Rom. 3:10–12), and so, for salvation ever to come about, God's choosing must precede all else. Any sinner who turns and follows Christ shows that God has already been at work, since apart from that work the rebellious heart would never have turned in the first place. In sinners, any positive response to God whatsoever—even the bare willingness to believe—must be solely the result of God's gracious, unmerited act of mercy.

Third, note that human freedom enters into this logic in a distinctive way. To be "free" here does not mean that one's choice could go either way, that it is entirely open and unbiased and undetermined. This would be "libertarian" or "contrary-choice" freedom, and Calvinists generally think that it is not even a coherent idea. If a choice is really undetermined, if nothing whatsoever sways us in one direction or the other, then in fact we cannot choose at all—we just stand there in paralyzed indecision. No, "freedom" refers to the ability to do, without hindrance, whatever it is we want to do, and since what we want to do is always determined by our preferences and desires and inclinations, real freedom cannot be hindered by our choices being determined. In other words, the freedom to choose is "compatible" with our choices also being determined—this is therefore the *compatibilist* understanding of freedom, which Calvinists find much more sensible than libertarian freedom.

So with compatibilist freedom, what is it that determines human choices? As we just said, it is our desires and inclinations, for "freedom" means doing what we *desire* to do. And for the believer in Christ, where do those desires come from? According to the logic of sovereignty, the answer is clear: they can come only from God. The sovereign Lord graciously decides to save a certain sinner and then irresistibly acts to transform his or her heart by gradually replacing ungodly inclinations with godly inclinations, replacing the heart of stone with a heart of flesh (Ezek. 36:26). Of course, God's act always accomplishes its purpose, yet with no loss whatsoever of freedom. On the contrary, God's act *results* in freedom. God has sovereignly acted to save the sinner from the bullying effects of sin, and the result is that he or she can finally choose in accordance with right desires. This is the highest kind of freedom, and it is perfectly in accord with God's sovereign work in salvation.

Hesitations and the Appeal to Mystery

There is one more step to take in understanding the logic of sovereignty, and it has to do with the acknowledgment of and response to certain hesitations that inevitably arise. The primary problem is that Calvinism's logic appears to leave us with a troubling account of the character of God, and especially of God's love and justice. Calvinism does not, of course, *deny* God's love or justice, but when we examine the details of the system closely, neither concept ends up being quite what we expected.

We can sketch both of these hesitations fairly briefly. With respect to love, we find that, great and glorious though it may be, the love of God extends only to the elect, not to all the world. According to the logic of sovereignty, God has the power to act irresistibly and change every sinner's heart, thus infallibly saving every human person—yet he does not do it. Why? Would not a loving God want to save everyone he could? One would think so, but *this* loving God does not. He loves some, but others he passes over. "Jacob I loved, but Esau I hated" (Rom. 9:13). This is, to say the least, a surprising kind of love. In fact, to many people it does not look like love at all.

A similar issue arises with respect to justice. Certainly Calvinists believe that God is just: God is righteously angry with sin, and this anger terrifies sinners, as well it should. Yet one cannot help wondering whether the out-pouring of God's wrath upon particular individuals is entirely fair. After all, on the Calvinist model, damnation falls upon sinners who literally could not help being what they were or doing what they did. Every sinner was born with an overpowering sin nature that determined every choice and that could not be escaped—yet God nevertheless holds sinners responsible for their sin, *as if* their actions were up to them, *as if* they possessed the ability to obey and were expected to do so. How can this be? Is this really just? God's justice turns out to be surprising, perhaps even troubling, for it looks quite different from justice as we commonly know it.

It is at precisely this twofold juncture that Calvinists typically invoke the notion of mystery. Scripture tells us of God's good and holy character, and while it may seem odd that the God who could save helpless sinners and will not do it should be called "loving," or that the remorseless condemnation of sinners who had no option except sin should be called "just," it is so never-theless. God is God, and that means sovereign mystery. We should not expect his actions and his judgments to be transparent to us at every point. Aslan is not a tame lion, as C. S. Lewis's Narnians would say. He is good, but he is not "safe." His goodness is fierce, ferocious, untamed—still good, but not in the docile way we commonly understand goodness. Calvinists hold that this kind of incomprehensibility in God is grounds not for unbelief (as skeptics argue) but for submission and worship. God is God, and who are we that we should talk back to God when he has made his ways known to us (Rom. 9:20)? This then is the Calvinist logic of sovereignty: a God who is undisputed ruler of all, humanity that is really enslaved by sin, a gospel of deep, marvelous grace that establishes the only kind of human freedom that is really coherent, and a final, decisive recognition of a holy mystery that we have no right to interrogate.

The Plausibility of Mystery

Now, we have moved through this Calvinist line of thinking rather quickly, both because we expect that it will be somewhat familiar territory for many readers and also because its logic is very straightforward. Furthermore, we want to register now our judgment that this logic provides a deeply Christian account of some fundamental theological principles. Yet, despite its biblical and logical appeal, we do want to raise a question about this approach, and specifically about the way the argument relies upon divine mystery. We do not, of course, object to the notion of mystery itself, but we want to suggest that the particular way that mystery is employed in the Calvinist model should be subjected to deeper scrutiny.

The problem, as we see it, is that the Calvinist appeal to mystery is an appeal to *sheer* mystery, to an incomprehensibility that has no justification or corroboration except that it rescues the logic of sovereignty. Of course, it *does* rescue the logic of sovereignty. That is its great benefit. And it rescues it in the way that mystery always does, namely, by showing why some reasoned objection that would otherwise be unanswerable can be safely ignored in this case. Calvinism's appeal should not be faulted on this score, for appeal to mystery inevitably works in just this way. The Flatlander who objects that the figure called a cylinder cannot logically be both square and round at the same time will be told, "Ah, yes. Your objection would be a good one *if* we were dealing with ordinary, two-dimensional things. But remember that we are now talking about an incomprehensible 'third dimension,' and we cannot expect to be able to understand that." In this way, any appeal to mystery responds to an objection not by answering but by explaining why no answer should be demanded.

Yet, as we noted in chapter 1, it would be foolish for us to stop demanding answers every time anybody cried, "Mystery!" Mystery is not a get-out-of-jail-free card that can be played any time a theologian is in a logical jam. Instead, though we should expect mystery to appear *at some point* in any theology that authentically represents the Lord of heaven and earth, the appeal to mystery at any *particular* point still has to be justified. Paradoxically, we must be given good reason to believe that our reason ought to be transcended at the point in question.

And what should such good reason look like? We have argued throughout this book that a genuine mystery will illuminate other matters while remaining incomprehensible itself. It should "fit in" with other things that we know to be true and make better sense of them by casting them in a new and helpful light. If a certain appeal to mystery fails to do this, then though God certainly *is* a transcendent mystery, the appeal to mystery *at just that point* has the earmarks of special pleading.

So, does Calvinism give us good reason to move beyond reason at the point it specifies? Is its appeal to mystery rendered more plausible by other factors? We suspect that the answer is no. Instead of clarifying and illustrating a theological truth that coherently draws together our whole Christian vision, the Calvinist appeal to mystery seems to function merely as a defensive strategy for bypassing certain logical objections. To see why, let us explore the intrinsic plausibility of the appeal by considering the specific ways that mystery relates to divine love and justice, respectively.

Divine Love

The mystery that is invoked with respect to the love of God is connected very directly to the *nature* of love. Most of us would normally think that love, by its very nature, desires the best for the one it loves, desires excellence, joy, victory, life. Hence, we are surprised that, on Calvinist premises, the love that defines God is fully compatible with his sovereign decision to condemn many, probably the majority, of his human creatures to eternal torment, when he could save them, apparently without the least additional effort. It is true that the creatures in question are unrepentant sinners, and in that sense they merit the judgment that falls upon them. But according to the logic of sovereignty their failure to repent is itself the result of God's will—presumably God's *loving* will. So the mystery lies precisely in the fact that God can be love in his very nature and yet can damn *where salvation is possible.* How does this count as "love"? The Calvinist answer is, *mystery.*

So, is positing mystery at this point warranted by other considerations? Is there something in the nature of love that is obscure or unclear or opaque, something that would prompt us to say, "Ah, yes, it makes sense that mystery would be present here"? It seems not. True, there is plenty of confusion in the contemporary West about what real love is (say, how it relates to syrupy romance or to bodily desire), but this is cultural myopia, not intrinsic impenetrability. True again, we might be uncertain about what really is "good" for someone (e.g., short-term enjoyment vs. long-term benefit) or about how to act when different loves make conflicting claims upon us (e.g., time alone with a spouse vs. time together with the kids), but the fact that love by nature seeks the good and acts in beneficent ways remains as clear as crystal.

What shall we say then? That God loves those he damns, and therefore damnation must be regarded as good for them? This is a hard path to follow. Damnation may be good for unrepentant sinners in the sense that it incontrovertibly confronts them with the sinfulness of their sin, and it is better for them to know the truth than to be eternally deceived. Therefore, given unrepentant evil, eternal condemnation may be a "good" of sorts. Yet how can we confuse this relative good, that of an unrepentant sinner being finally refuted by eternal death, with the far higher good of a *repentant* sinner entering into fullness of life? What father of a rebellious teen, what wife of a wayward husband, would prefer unrepentance and punishment to repentance and restoration?

Or should we say that God does *not* love the damned? How can we? It is true, of course, that a human being who is "loving" need not be thought to love absolutely everyone, everywhere, without distinction. There are people whom we do not even know, and there may be practical limits to how far finite love can extend. But can *God* love some and not others—God who knows all and who *is* love? Remember that love is essential, in some rock-bottom sense, to the very nature of the Triune God. So the question we must ask is not whether it is possible for *a human being* not to love. The question is not even whether it is possible for a *divine* being not to love. The question is, is it possible for *Love* not to love? And the answer certainly seems to be no.

Thus the "mystery" that Calvinism appeals to here seems to stand alone, without independent justification or corroboration of any kind. For just that reason, it sounds like a simple contradiction. This "mystery" does not illuminate; it obscures. Love is something that we encounter every day. It is something we *know*, however poorly we may live according to our knowledge. And there is no sign of the kind of perplexing denseness in the nature of love that would support the radical transmogrification required by the Calvinist appeal. A perfect love that does not desire the salvation of its beloved, or that refuses to love at all in most cases, seems simply impossible.

Of course, it could still be the case, since any mystery will *seem* impossible. In this respect, our aim here is not to disprove Calvinism with some foolproof argument (which would be self-contradictory, since mystery is by definition where argument breaks down); nor is it to discredit the logic of sovereignty and replace it with an alternative (since we have already affirmed the deeply biblical insights that ground the Calvinist logic). We want to show only that appeal to mystery here still leaves some real, abiding difficulties in its wake. One of those difficulties concerns the nature of God's love,[3] and we think appeal to mystery at this point is highly implausible.

Divine Justice

What about God's justice? Is the Calvinist appeal to mystery more plausible here? Recall that the reason mystery must be invoked is that God is said to condemn sinners whose very nature irresistibly compels them to sin. They have no independent choice in the matter—that is, no choice independent of the all-controlling sin nature they have inherited. The compatibilist account of freedom allows for choice in the limited sense that people controlled by a sin nature can and do choose to do what they want—that is, they choose to sin, and they delight in doing so. But they cannot choose to do otherwise. Yet God is said to hold them morally accountable for their choices, even in the absence of any alternative. So it is the nature of moral responsibility that is at issue here. How is God just when he regards sinners as morally responsible even though they cannot do otherwise than sin? The Calvinist answer is, *mystery*.

Separating responsibility from ability in this way challenges strong intuitions about justice, and so we pause once again to ask whether appeal to mystery at this point is justified or corroborated by any other factors. Is there some ambivalence or obscurity in the nature of moral responsibility, something that links it to divine transcendence in a way that would prompt us to expect mystery? It seems not. Most Calvinists are willing to admit that, on a

---

3. See the significantly worded title of the valuable book by Calvinist D. A. Carson, *The Difficult Doctrine of the Love of God* (Wheaton: Crossway, 2000).

practical level, human experience testifies to a significant moral connection between what we are *able* to do and what we are *responsible* to do. Everywhere that praise or blame is commonly ascribed—in our courts, on our jobs, as we parent our children, as we interact with friends or even enemies—we find that responsibility obtains precisely to the extent that the agent has the ability to do what is required. *Ability* to act and *responsibility* for actions are inextricably connected.

Of course, common human experience might lead us astray here. God is not part of the created realm, and so perhaps *ultimate* moral responsibility, where we stand before God, is different from other kinds of responsibility, where we stand before our peers. But why should we think so? Is it because the source of moral duty is the God who is transcendent? But an observation about the source of moral duty has no obvious implications for its nature: duty still seems intimately connected to the ability to obey. Is it because ultimate moral responsibility grows out of our duty to God's transcendent *person* rather than to some impersonal law? But why should this make a difference? The duty of young children to obey their parents is usually formulated in personal terms ("obeying Mom or Dad," not just "obeying the rules"), yet we still see very plainly how responsibility works, and in particular we see that considerations of the children's ability are still very relevant to the discussion. Ability to obey or disobey is assumed. If a parent issues commands that a child *cannot* obey and then punishes the child for not obeying, we are quick to point out the injustice.

We are drawn to the same conclusion as before: there seems to be no independent reason for expecting that mystery should arise at the point where many Calvinists appeal to it. Moral responsibility is something that we deal with all the time, something that we understand clearly, and part of what we understand is that it seems very closely connected to one's ability to act in one direction *or the other*—closely connected, that is, to a libertarian variety of freedom. There are, no doubt, all kinds of determining elements in our decision making, elements arising from our own prior choices and from the choices of others and from our environment and from our passions and from our education and from a whole host of other factors. So we may not know for sure how free a person is in any particular instance. But in our common experience, moral responsibility always seems to require some measure of libertarian freedom, either past or present, by the agent or the agent's representative, however hazily or ambivalently it is expressed. Hence, it is hard to find any independent justification for positing mystery in the nature of responsibility.

Of course, it could still be there. If there is such a thing as mystery (and there is, since God is the transcendent God), it could be that mystery inexplicably obtains with respect to the nature of responsibility, just as it might inexplicably obtain with respect to the nature of love. But one worries that the main reason some Calvinists come to this conclusion is that the logic of

sovereignty requires it: if God is the decisive agent of salvation, then humanity is *not* the decisive agent, and therefore humans cannot *really* decide, cannot exercise libertarian freedom, though God still mysteriously holds them
accountable for their actions. This line of reasoning is possible, but we note
again that the absence of any corroborating factors makes it highly implausible—implausible enough that, for all its strengths, we might be willing to
consider an alternative.

The Logic of Freedom

The most readily available alternative to the Calvinist logic of sovereignty is
the Arminian logic of freedom. Though the conclusions arrived at are very
different, we may approach Arminianism as we did Calvinism, by grounding
its logic in fundamental biblical intuitions about God and humanity.

As before, let us begin with God. According to Arminians, the biblical concept of God is unique precisely in its insistence that the Lord of the universe is
a God of unquenchable covenant love and faithfulness. He is "the LORD, the
LORD, the compassionate and gracious God, slow to anger, abounding in love
and faithfulness, maintaining love to thousands, and forgiving wickedness,
rebellion and sin" (Exod. 34:6–7). Of course, God is holy and just as well as
loving, and he "does not leave the guilty unpunished," as the Exodus text goes
on to declare. But God's is *perfect* love, and he loved the world so much that
he gave his one and only Son precisely in order to meet the demands of holy
justice (John 3:16–17). Jesus comes into the world for no other reason than
"to seek and to save the lost" (Luke 19:10), and so we know beyond doubt that
God is "not wanting anyone to perish, but everyone to come to repentance"
(2 Peter 3:9), that he "wants everyone to be saved and to understand the truth"
(1 Tim. 2:4 NLT).

As for the doctrine of humanity, the Arminian reading takes us back to
the first chapter of the Bible, to the solemn account of God creating men
and women *in his image*. As we noted above, Scripture nowhere directly tells
us what the image of God consists in, but Christian tradition has often connected it with those capacities that allow genuinely responsible human action.
Human persons understand the notion of "ought" and can choose whether
they will do the good that they ought to do or the not-so-good that their impulses and inclinations press upon them. We have the capacity, and therefore
the duty, to choose in the one way rather than the other. In other words, we
are *free* to choose.

It is immediately evident that Arminians have in mind here libertarian freedom, the freedom to act in either of two ways without being rigidly determined
by passions or desires or other factors. If this strikes us as a puzzling kind of
freedom—freedom to do what we *do not* want to do, freedom to act *against*

the inclinations that prompt us to act at all—then we must simply note that, without it, moral responsibility becomes very difficult to understand. On this score, the very arguments brought *against* Calvinism's notion of responsibility count *in favor* of this Arminian counterpart. However odd the notion of libertarian freedom may seem, Arminians insist that we can discard it only by seeing ourselves as pawns driven by motives that we can neither influence nor control. And how then can we be held *morally* accountable for our actions?

So, with these two basic premises in place (the sacrificial love of God and the responsible freedom of human persons), we are ready once again to ask ourselves a question. If any of these bearers of the divine image will be finally and permanently separated from God by damnation, whose decision will bring this about? The answer is plain. Divine love means that it cannot be God's choice; and by contrast, human freedom and dignity demand that it must involve a genuine human choice. Damnation can come only from a dreadful human decision that, shocking as it may be, overrides the intentions of almighty God himself.

This conclusion, that God's gift of grace can be resisted and even overridden, is supported by a variety of biblical texts, which speak of people who "always resist the Holy Spirit" (Acts 7:51) or of religious leaders who "rejected God's purpose for themselves" (Luke 7:30). But it often gives rise to the mistaken impression that the logic of freedom requires a softening of the Christian doctrine of sin. Some conclude that, if sinners have libertarian freedom to *resist* God's grace, they must also have freedom to *accept* God's grace. In this respect, human beings may not be able to *save* themselves, but they can at least *long for salvation*, and when the offer of deliverance comes, they can respond to it naturally.

This view of the human condition is very common in some evangelical circles, but it is consistently rejected by historic Christianity in its Arminian as fully as in its Calvinist expressions. The universal Christian tradition maintains that the fall introduces into all human persons *real* slavery to sin, *real* blindness about truth, *real* hostility to God. Arminians Jerry Walls and Joseph Dongell effectively illustrate the position fallen men and women are in by picturing a terrorist camp in which the prisoners have been tricked and drugged into a condition in which they support their captors and love their captivity.[4] This is a much starker picture of the human condition, a picture in which the sinner's natural internal desires are part of the problem: the sinner *does not desire to be rescued*. Classical Arminians are at one with Calvinists here.

So what is the crucial point at which the two positions part company? That point comes when Arminians insist that God does not allow human fallenness to go unchallenged in *anyone*. God's love for each and every person is

4. See the fine discussion by Arminians Jerry L. Walls and Joseph R. Dongell in *Why I Am Not a Calvinist* (Downers Grove, IL: InterVarsity, 2004), 68–70.

so great that he is unwilling to allow us to be dragged away to hell, witless brainwashed pawns of sin, happily embracing the chains that bind us. That *would* be our fate if we were left to ourselves, but (as John Wesley used to say) God has not left any of us to ourselves. The Spirit of God acts unilaterally, completely apart from what we naturally deserve or desire, with what Arminians usually refer to as *prevenient grace*, that is, grace that "comes before" (Latin, *pre-venire*) any request or willingness on our part. By means of this uninvited intervention, God restores a measure of human dignity and competence in each human person—enough to make a genuinely free choice possible regarding salvation. God enters into the prison camp and awakens us from our drug-induced stupor in order to invite us to join him in escaping from our captivity. On this model, God does not *choose for us* in some irresistible fashion; instead, God's grace is precisely what allows us to *choose for ourselves*. But we can still reject God's loving offer of full deliverance if we choose to, and God himself honors that free choice.

Obviously, on this reading God's sovereign decision in salvation is not as absolute as Calvinists believe. Instead, Arminians hold to what is sometimes called *limited providence*. God *could* irresistibly "provide"—that is, guide or control—the outcome of salvation for each and every creature. He could infallibly determine from the outset who will and who will not believe. But he chooses not to do so. Instead, he limits his own providential control. He chooses to respect the integrity of his image-bearers and not to override their freedom. This is not a limitation that grows out of divine weakness, nor is it a matter of creatures being "stronger" than their Creator. It is God himself who institutes the limitation, precisely in order to make space in the world for the kind of genuinely free, genuinely responsible creaturely action that unqualified divine control would rule out. Moreover, since God does not meticulously control every event, he is in no sense the author of sin or evil or damnation. He may permit sin, but he does not intend it, and so his love and goodness and justice are absolutely inviolate.

The Need for Mystery

Note well that, since God's character is not problematic here, Arminians end up having little reason to invoke the logically suspicious category of "mystery" in order to hold their theology together. It is not that they deny that God is incomprehensible or "past finding out": they are ready to acknowledge mystery in the incarnation or in the Trinity or at any other point where it is genuinely required. But they do not think the doctrines of sin or salvation are among those points. The notion of limited providence allows responsibility for sin and evil to fall squarely on the shoulders of the sinners themselves, and so there is no logical gap for mystery to fill. God is good, humans do evil—period. In this way, human beings, though utterly dependent upon grace for salvation, are still morally active enough to account for their own final damnation. For Arminians, all of the most difficult questions have thus been answered, and pressing the logically objectionable "mystery button" is both unwise and unwarranted.

Or is it? In spite of fundamental intuitions that strike us as deeply faithful to Scripture, and in spite of a simple, direct logic that seems to us very compelling, we find ourselves wondering whether the category of mystery can really be skirted so readily and so completely as Arminians would like. We have already indicated our sympathy with Arminian concerns about the moral coherence of a theology guided exclusively by the logic of sovereignty, and it is the Arminian doctrine of limited providence that purports to solve this problem. But can it really explain salvation in such a mystery-free fashion? At least three important factors suggest that the situation is not so clear-cut.

"Mystery" versus "Contradiction"?

In the first place, one foundational element in the standard Arminian resistance to mystery seems to be logically flawed, namely, the common claim that legitimate expressions of mystery must involve no patent logical contradiction or incoherence. Mystery is just fine, we are told, but logical absurdity is another thing altogether. However, a trouble-free account of this hard-and-fast distinction between "mystery" and "contradiction" is difficult to sustain. The problem can be seen in two ways, the first roughly deductive and the second roughly inductive. In both cases, we find that, if we allow for mystery at all, then we must not be surprised to find that it *looks* like real contradiction.

First, let us return again to our familiar analogy from Flatland. Imagine a group of Flatlanders who are examining (in their two-dimensional world) two figures, one a circle and the other a cylinder whose circular end they perceive. The difference between these two figures will be obvious to any three-dimensional observer, but it will be utterly obscure to the Flatlanders themselves, since all they can see of the cylinder is the circle that defines its base. Even if we communicate to them that one of the figures transcends two dimensions such that, looked at from the side, a certain squareness or rectangularity is evident, they will still be at a loss. They will know (by "revelation") that they are dealing with a mystery in which square and circle are not mutually exclusive, but they will still have no resources whatsoever for distinguishing the cylinder's end from the circle plain and simple. They understand, in principle, that the statement "This figure is both round and square" is true in one case, because a third dimension is involved, and absurd in the other, because no third dimension is involved. In the one case, they have a mystery; in the other, a flat contradiction. But to their (two-dimensional) inspection the mystery and the contradiction are absolutely identical.

So also for us in our efforts to understand the mystery of God. Any attempt to distinguish a mystery from an absurdity simply by asking whether the elements in tension seem necessarily to preclude one another is doomed. To insist that a mystery may be incomprehensible but cannot be incoherent, or that it may be "above reason" but cannot be "against reason," is to insist that an apparent contradiction must not *really* appear contradictory—which is, in fact, to beg the question and deny mystery altogether.

Second, the problematic character of the distinction is revealed by a hard look at the details of those Christian doctrines that are universally accepted as mysteries. For instance, recall the peculiarities of the doctrine of the incarnation (which we investigated in more detail in chapter 6). Jesus Christ is both fully divine and fully human, and this is a mystery. Is it also (apparently) a contradiction? It seems so. While it is true that "divine" and "human" need not be defined over against one another in a way that makes the incarnation into an *explicit* logical contradiction, it is not hard to formulate *implicit* contradictions that have exactly the same force. For example, if God is uncreated and humanity is created, then to be God incarnate is to be both uncreated and created at the same time; or again, if God is omniscient and humanity is limited in knowledge, then to be God-become-man is to be both unlimited in knowledge and limited in knowledge at the same time. The logical "contradiction" is plain, and the only way to avoid it is to exaggerate the division between Christ's two natures, an error into which Nestorius appears to have fallen. Hence, the only resolutions of this "contradiction" turn out to be abandonments of orthodoxy.[5]

Of course, we are not arguing that the incarnation is, in an ultimate sense, contradictory and therefore impossible. But we do want to insist that the notion of mystery is, from a creaturely vantage point, not so neatly separable from logical contradiction as we might wish. If we were making judgments merely on the basis of inspecting internal consistency, the incarnation would not pass muster. It would look like just another contradiction. So we should not too easily dismiss Calvinist alternatives simply because they involve what appear to be logical incongruities. If we allow for mystery at all, then we should be prepared for real logical tensions. And if it appears from Scripture that such tensions are present in the doctrine of salvation, then the logical problems are a part of the package, and we need not cast the whole thing aside as just so much logical nonsense.

A Mystery-Free Bible?

But are such logical tensions present in the Christian understanding of sovereignty and freedom? Both Scripture and orthodox theology suggest that

5. See James Anderson, *Paradox in Christian Theology: An Analysis of Its Presence, Character, and Epistemic Status* (Waynesboro, GA: Paternoster, 2007), 106.

they are, and this gives us a second reason for thinking that a mystery-free account of salvation is too simple.

On the biblical side, a straightforward, nonmysterious reliance on limited providence does not provide quite as self-evidently satisfying a reading of Scripture as we might wish. This is not to say that there are no coherent Arminian readings of the difficult texts, but it is to acknowledge that some texts *are* difficult. The authors of Scripture sometimes say things about the activity or the power of God that no self-conscious advocate of limited providence would ever say. Indeed, some texts leave our sensible, logical understanding of a loving God who is doing his best to save everyone looking decidedly frail.

Let's quickly look at some examples.

- However convinced we may be about the logic of freedom and the shortcomings of Calvinism, is it not surprising to find it said about Paul's gentile converts in Acts 13:48 that "all who were appointed for eternal life believed"? Wouldn't we expect the reverse order: belief and therefore divine "appointment"?
- Do we not find it a bit unsettling to hear Jesus explain the unbelief of his grumbling antagonists in these simple words: "No one can come to me unless the Father has enabled them" (John 6:65)? Is the decision finally up to the Father? Doesn't the Father *want* these grumblers to come to Christ?
- Are any of us not taken up short when we read the following unadorned account of why none of the Canaanite peoples (except the Gibeonites) tried to make peace with the conquering Israelites under Joshua's command: "It was the LORD himself who hardened their hearts to wage war against Israel, so that he might destroy them totally, exterminating them without mercy" (Josh. 11:20)?

We may be able to explain texts like these along standard Arminian lines, but we must admit that the biblical writers sound distinctly Calvinistic at these points.

Indeed, almost any of the "hardening" texts in Scripture may leave us uncomfortable. It is one thing to understand that God finally lets unrepentant sinners go their own way; it is quite another to say that God *hardens* people. Romans 9 is, of course, the strongest of all the hardening texts. It begins with a line that only Calvinists can quote without blanching (God "has mercy on whom he wants to have mercy, and he hardens whom he wants to harden" [v. 18]); it goes on to raise the very question Arminians want raised (how can a just God blame creatures for their hardness of heart if *he* is the one doing the hardening? [v. 19]); but then it answers this question in a way no Arminian ever would ("Who are you, a human being, to talk back to God?" [v. 20]). There are, of course, possible explanations of a text like this on strictly Arminian premises, but one does have to *search* for them. And even with the explanations in place, it remains surprising—and troubling for the Arminian—that the authors of Scripture should speak in the shocking way they do about God's decisive authority, if the reality of the matter is as straightforward and nonmysterious as standard Arminian logic makes out. Why didn't Paul simply take a moment to explain limited providence to the Roman Christians? It would have been so easy to do.

We run into a similar dilemma when thinking in a more comprehensively theological way. For example, a self-limiting concept of divine control may be logical and it may seem morally necessary, but it still implies an overall understanding of the relation between God and the world that is significantly different from what a full-blown doctrine of creation suggests. As we observed back in chapter 2, God is "creator" not simply in the sense that he gets things started or that he sets up the cosmic conditions for the big bang. God is the Creator with a capital C, the incomprehensible Lord whose uncreated Reality stands unimaginably "behind" all that we perceive in the created order. But with this robust understanding of God the Creator in mind, consider again the picture painted by Walls and Dongell of sinners as brainwashed prisoners in a terrorist camp and of God as the stealthy rescuer who sneaks into the camp and tries to convince them to trust him and escape from their prison. This is a wonderful and dramatic picture of loving aid generously offered even where it may be refused, but does it not also sound very suspiciously like the way that one *creature* interacts with another? It sounds not at all like the way a Creator speaks creation into existence or the way a potter shapes clay or the way an avenging Lord judges his enemies.

Note that our goal here is not to overthrow this Arminian picture in order to replace it with a Calvinistic one. It is instead to recognize that the Arminian picture, valuable though it is, seems subtly unsatisfactory if taken as the sole, final account of God's relation to the world. If it *were* the final account, if the logic of freedom *did* tell us the ultimate and quite unmysterious story about God's relation to creatures, then we find ourselves surprised that other elements in the Christian story have the shape they do have. What self-conscious advocate of something as sensible as limited providence would talk in the outlandish way that both Scripture and historic Christian theology do occasionally talk? An understanding of God that is more paradoxical, less easily and straightforwardly explicable, seems to be required.

Foreknowledge as Mystery?

Finally, the more Arminians try to do justice to the elements in Scripture and orthodox theology that seem reminiscent of Calvinism, the further they get from an authentically mystery-free account of salvation. They continue to follow the logic of freedom, but once that logic grows to its full, biblical stature, it turns out to be more like Calvinism than we might initially recognize.

The clearest indication of this tendency has to do with Arminianism's strong doctrine of divine foreknowledge. There are, of course, Arminians (the open theists) who think that any kind of foreknowledge necessarily undercuts the genuineness of freedom, and who reject foreknowledge for that reason. But more traditional Arminians affirm that God knows from all eternity who will respond to the gospel, and precisely on that basis God elects to salvation all who will believe. This approach allows us to understand how God can love and favor believers before they believe—indeed, long before they are even born—without irresistibly *causing* them to believe, which would override their freedom. He can do this by virtue of his foreknowledge of their decision. Similarly, this approach helps us to understand difficult texts about God actively hardening those who oppose him, about God forming them for disaster (Prov. 16:4) and pouring out his wrath on them in the gospel (Rom. 1:17–18), about their being "condemned already" for their unbelief (John 3:18). God foreknew that these sinners would finally prove unrepentant, and therefore from the very beginning God set his face against them—yet not because of his inscrutable unwillingness to save (the objectionable Calvinist notion), but because of their unwillingness to be saved.

Now divine foreknowledge of this kind necessarily entails that the relation between God and time should be rather unusual. If it were not, then the only way God could know ahead of time how Roger or Pamela would respond to the gospel would be (1) for God himself to determine the response, or (2) for God to see how the present circumstances and influences and so on will necessarily produce the response. But the doctrine of free will forbids both of these options. If Pamela is really free, then it is neither (1) God, nor (2) circumstances that will determine her response. It is *she* who will determine it. Therefore, God cannot *predict* what she will do; instead, he must see her actually *doing* it. God knows *now* what she will do *then* only because "then" is not temporally distant for him as it is for time-bound creatures.[6] It is precisely this feature that allows the doctrine of foreknowledge to be so helpful. When God speaks of his plan to harden Pharaoh's heart long before Moses even confronts Pharaoh (Exod. 4:21; 7:3), or when Pharaoh is said to harden his own heart (Exod. 9:34) and then God says just a few verses later, "I have hardened his heart" (Exod. 10:1), we need not be troubled. God can act in advance because God knows in advance. God's response can *precede* Pharaoh's hardening and can

6. There are a variety of technical philosophical accounts of how to understand God's relation to time, and we cannot delve into them here. See Paul Helm, *Eternal God: A Study of God without Time* (Oxford: Clarendon, 1988); Paul Helm, Alan G. Padgett, William Lane Craig, and Nicholas Wolterstorff, *God and Time: Four Views* (Downers Grove, IL: InterVarsity, 2001); William Lane Craig, *Time and Eternity: Exploring God's Relationship to Time* (Wheaton: Crossway, 2001); William Hasker, *God, Time, and Knowledge* (Ithaca, NY: Cornell University Press, 1989).

even *actively contribute* to Pharaoh's hardening, without in any way failing to be a *response* to Pharaoh's hardening.

There is already mystery here aplenty of the logical chicken-and-egg variety, but we are interested in something deeper. Consider how this eternal divine foreknowledge relates to God's love for all the world. We have seen that it is not uncommon for Arminians to criticize Calvinists for portraying God as a deity who cannot candidly say "I love you" to the whole world. On Calvinist premises, God does *not* love the whole world, at least not in the full, complete, rescuing sense; God loves the elect and the elect only. And we have already noted the biblical and theological strain that this thinking produces. Yet Arminianism's strong doctrine of divine foreknowledge pushes in something like the same direction. If we affirm that God eternally knows that certain persons will be finally unrepentant, and if we go further (as Scripture does) and speak of God's concrete antipathy toward his enemies, then in what sense is the offer of salvation to *all* persons a genuine, heartfelt offer? In what sense does God love the sinner whom he knows will never turn from wickedness?

Let's focus the question very specifically: Should we say that God loves Pharaoh? The overall picture of God that is foundational to the logic of freedom makes us want to answer, "Yes! Of course! God does love Pharaoh and would prefer that Pharaoh *not* have a hard heart." Yet it is plain that the classical Arminian affirmation of foreknowledge stands in some tension with this answer. Because of God's foreknowledge, Pharaoh's self-chosen hardening was part of God's eternal plan for the cosmos. There was never an instant in the history of the universe in which God cherished a fond hope that Pharaoh would turn from his hardness. On the contrary, from the very beginning, God regarded Pharaoh as a hardened enemy, and God purposed to contribute to his hardness.

Where, then, is the love of God? Or perhaps we should ask, *When* is the love of God? The answer has to be, it never was. Perhaps God *would have* loved if Pharaoh *would have* been willing. But Pharaoh was not, and so God did not—ever. The whole relationship of God to Pharaoh is portrayed in Scripture as one of unbroken enmity. God plans to harden Pharaoh's heart from the beginning; God actually hardens Pharaoh's heart, even as Pharaoh also hardens it himself; there is no hint of regret or remorse on God's part, for Pharaoh is, from before the foundation of the world, the enemy of God. So does God love Pharaoh? The answer is not so obvious as we might like, for God is not quite so unmysterious as we might like.

Let it be said again that the intention of this argument is not to undermine Arminian intuitions about the priority and integrity of God's love. It is instead to recognize that building on these intuitions by means of an appeal to self-limitation is not the mystery-free enterprise that it might sometimes appear. Divine mystery is unavoidable, and it ends up trickling down into very practical, everyday concerns, even in ways that (as in this case) make it difficult to see clearly the difference between the quandaries raised by this approach and the troubles that beset Calvinism.

A Shared but Dubious Assumption

Let us take a moment to recapitulate the argument to this point. The logic of sovereignty provides a compelling biblical and theological account of salvation, but it does so by putting the moral character of God at risk. It then invokes mystery to resolve this problem, but invokes it in a fashion that seems ad hoc, since it can provide no independent justification for mystery's presence at just that point. Alternatively, the logic of freedom proposes a limitation on sovereignty that promises to eliminate the need for such "contradictions." But the proposal unwittingly rejects mystery simply for being mysterious; it has a hard time doing justice to the entirety of Scripture; and it does not deliver us from mystery in any case. In other words, Calvinism *appeals* to mystery in an implausible way that ends up losing the moral *goodness* of God, while Arminianism *rejects* mystery in an implausible way that ends up losing the sovereign *power* of God. Is there a way of approaching the divine and human elements in salvation that avoids both difficulties?

We think there is, and it begins by acknowledging an important assumption shared by both sides of the debate. That assumption is that *divine agency and human agency necessarily exclude one another.*

Each side clearly makes this assumption. The logic of sovereignty holds that God ultimately decides who will be saved, and so human "choosing" cannot be really free in the ordinary libertarian sense—it must be determined by God's choice. The logic of freedom holds that God allows human beings to decide whether they will accept saving grace, and so God's "choosing" (election) cannot be unconditional—it must be determined by human willingness. In both cases, authentic choosing on one side invalidates authentic choosing on the other.

But is this assumption of mutual exclusion trustworthy? There are at least two momentous reasons for thinking that it is not, one deriving from each side in our debate.

First, from the Calvinist side, we should not accept this assumption *because of the unqualified transcendence of the living God.*

It is true that, in a universe of multiple persons, personal agency allows in the nature of the case for real opposition, since A's intention to do X can easily conflict with B's intention to do Y. If God wants eternal fellowship with so-and-so, but so-and-so does not want eternal fellowship with God, then real opposition is what we seem to have. And whenever there is real opposition, it is necessarily true that only one of the parties can finally decide the case. If A decides, then B does not; if B decides, then A does not. In a case of real opposition, one or the other must have the final, overriding vote, so that either A will trump B or B will trump A.

Yet this conclusion is true only if A and B are "in" the universe in the same sense, only if they are parallel to one another so as to allow this kind of opposition or rivalry. Yet this is clearly not the case when one of the agents under consideration is the living God. As the fundamental intuitions of Calvinism constantly insist, God is most emphatically *not* "in" the world in the same sense his creatures are. God is the eternal Creator, and every human being is but a frail, created thing. We explored in chapter 2 the enormous ontological gulf that separates God and creation—a gulf so enormous that even the imagery of "gulf" is misleading insofar as it suggests a chasm separating two ontologically parallel sides (i.e., each side is a "side" in the same respect). The transcendence of God invites us to recognize that any point at which we smoothly and easily compare God and creatures is bound to be ambiguous or fallacious. As soon as we speak of God's intentions "opposing" our own, we have begun to treat God like just another creature. In the nature of the case, there can be no such "opposition," in the way we normally use the word. Creator cannot exclude creature, nor creature Creator, in the way that creatures constantly exclude one another. Divine agency and human agency cannot stand in competition the way that two creaturely agents can.

But if they cannot compete, then neither of them can win. There is no way to speak neatly or unequivocally of God's choice "trumping" the sinner's, or of the sinner's choice "trumping" God's. It is not that such speech is necessarily wrong; it is instead that we do not know clearly what it *means*. In the blinding light of divine transcendence, we have no way of seeing clearly either the ontological continuity or the ontological discontinuity between God and creation. For this reason, it is not the nature of love or the nature of moral responsibility that should be construed as beyond our understanding in the logic of sovereignty. It is the nature of God himself, and therefore the nature of divine agency itself. The transcendent God is mysterious, and therefore God's eternal choosing is mysterious—and therefore there is every reason to expect that the precise relationship between divine choosing and human choosing will also be a mystery of the most profound kind. Divine choosing and human choosing certainly need not be thought of as simply excluding one another.

Second, from the Arminian side, we should not accept the assumption that divine agency and human agency are mutually exclusive *because of the baffling character of libertarian freedom*.

We noted earlier in the chapter that libertarian freedom is a puzzling thing. We are normally inclined to think that if one state of affairs really is superior to another, then the freer we are from distortions and biases and pressures, the more likely we are to choose the better situation. If we were perfectly free, we would see everything with perfect clarity and we would choose according to what we see—that is, we would choose the better scenario every time.

Choosing the worse over the better could only be the result of some kind of blindness—that is, of some kind of distortion or bias that keeps us from seeing plainly. Freedom ought to result in desiring and doing what is best.

But libertarian freedom does not work that way. Instead, libertarian freedom is precisely what allows us to look at two states of affairs and to understand them perfectly well and yet to choose the inferior over the superior. Theologically speaking, it is what allows those whom prevenient grace has released from the ruthless, unremitting blindness of sin to actively *decide* whether they will embrace sin again or whether they will turn to obedience and life—and many, many of them apparently choose death. Again, libertarian freedom is what allowed our first parents, who walked with God and were not subject to the coercive power of a sin nature, to actively choose to abandon God.

But how could they do it? How could they prefer death to life? Did they not understand that they were choosing death? If not, then it is inexplicable how God could hold them responsible for such an accidental error. So apparently they *did* understand, in some sense. But if they understood, how could they have made the decision in the first place? They must have closed their eyes to what they knew to be true in order to embrace the falsehood that they desired. But why close their eyes? Why make themselves blind? They must have been blind in a deeper sense already in order to desire it. But again, if blind then not culpable; and so this blindness, too, must have been self-chosen; and this choice, too, is inexplicable. We could keep pushing the argument further back, but we would never come to an end. This is the fundamental irrationality of sin, that it *can* be chosen when there is absolutely no reason in the whole universe (literally) to choose it.

But to speak of the "irrationality of sin" is to speak also of the inexplicability of the free choice by means of which sin enters into the world—which brings us back to the nature of freedom. It looks as if we cannot understand free choice as simply the absence of factors that keep us from choosing in the way the situation warrants. It is one of the fundamental intuitions of Arminianism that a deeper, more enigmatic, more ominous freedom must also be posited. For if freedom meant merely the ability to see things as they really are, without distortion, and to make the right choice according to this unclouded knowledge of the actual situation, then Adam and Eve would never have fallen, and no sinner whom God has touched would ever prefer death to life. But they did fall, and sinners do reject God. What does freedom mean then? How does it work? How can the forces that keep us from seeing clearly and doing what is right be removed, *without* the resulting knowledge of what is right removing our ability to choose the worse rather than the better?

Furthermore, if the choice really can go either way—without being determined either by relevant knowledge of the actual situation (which would prompt a decision for the better option every time) or by irrelevant factors that blind us to the actual situation (and thereby never really release us from captivity)—if the choice is really not determined by anything *either* relevant *or* irrelevant, then what is left? Apparently the choice can be determined by nothing whatsoever. There is absolutely nothing that prompts the decision in one direction or the other. It simply happens, without reason, without cause, spontaneously, unpredictably. In other words, free choice here turns out to be just another word for *randomness*. Now to speak of human choosing at its deepest level as just a matter of flipping a coin hardly does justice to the idea of human dignity that defenders of freedom cherish. And in any case, are we left on this model with a picture of the ultimate destiny of the human race being governed by the law of averages, with 50 percent saved and 50 percent damned? We would not, of course, know to which half any particular person belonged (since his or her choice "could go either way"), but should we be confident that in the overall scheme roughly half will arbitrarily choose salvation and roughly half damnation?

This conclusion appears absurd, and the failure of this whole line of reasoning shows us, again, how little we understand what libertarian freedom really is. The fact is, if we follow the logic of freedom at all, the time comes when we have to admit that we are working with a phenomenon that we simply cannot get to the bottom of. We know that to be genuinely free is not to choose randomly; yet we know that it is also not to be determined by some unchosen "cause," whether internal or external. To be free is to be not determined but also not undetermined: it is to be self-determined. Every philosophical analysis of the problem takes us down the one false path or the other, either toward determinism or toward indeterminism. Freedom is the name we give to the inexplicable reality that no philosophical investigation can account for. It is a mystery. And if the nature of freedom itself is mysterious, then we certainly have no grounds for insisting that the mysterious free choice of human beings must exclude the mysterious eternal choice of the transcendent God.

A More Reasonable Point of Mystery

If the mystery of divine transcendence undergirds the logic of sovereignty, and if the enigma of human freedom pervades the logic of freedom, then it is only natural to think that there might be some connection between the two. And we do not have to look far to find it. Recall that free human persons are created in the image of God—in the image, that is, of the God who himself acts freely. The Christian tradition maintains that, both when God brings the world into existence out of nothing and again when he intervenes to redeem the world from sin, he does not act randomly (as if some erratic, haphazard whim momentarily overcame him), but he also does not act out of necessity (as if he were compelled to act, like it or not). Instead, he personally chooses to create and to redeem, and chooses freely, with neither constraint nor caprice.

We can use the same language we employed a moment ago: God is neither determined nor undetermined; he is *self*-determined. Since to be human is to be the image of God, we are not surprised that mystery should attach to human choosing too, for human freedom reflects its transcendent divine original. If God creates freely, should we be shocked or dismayed that human persons enjoy a measure of that same creative freedom?

Note well: that same creative freedom, albeit in a measured or reflected mode. This way of putting the matter takes seriously both Calvinism's explicit commitment to the transcendence of God (for creaturely freedom is *merely* a reflection—God's own freedom is unfathomably high above it) and also Arminianism's implicit commitment to the impenetrability of human freedom (for creaturely freedom is a *genuine* reflection that therefore participates in the mystery of God himself). If we follow this clue, we find that the two paths we were following independently lead to the same source. We are dealing here not with two mysteries but with one.

This is a very important convergence, for it suggests that we are seeing here not just a point at which mystery *could* arise (which could be absolutely anywhere, since it is the nature of mystery to violate our logical expectations), but a point at which we have intrinsic reason to think that mystery *should* arise. Recognizing mystery at this point is not an ad hoc effort aimed at overcoming the weakest link in a chain of theological logic. Instead, it is a direct outgrowth of what Christians have always believed about the transcendence of God, and it is directly related to a notion of freedom whose obscurity we already observed on our own. The nature of transcendence indicates that divine and human agency might turn out to be logically odd; and the difficulties associated with libertarian freedom exhibit exactly that kind of logical oddness. Hence, mystery at this point confirms and elucidates what we already know. It explains why something we see to be inexplicable should be inexplicable. The mystery of God remains utterly incomprehensible, yet it enters into our thinking in ways that make sense of other incomprehensibilities.

This is just the kind of plausible account of mystery that both Calvinism and Arminianism lack when taken on their own. Consider first the Calvinist side. Mystery is usually invoked by Calvinists to explain (or to avoid explaining) how moral responsibility could obtain in the absence of contrary-choice freedom, and also how divine love could happily damn the majority of the human race. We are now in a position to see that neither move is necessary, since positing mystery in the relation between divine and human agency yields the same logical result without the intrinsic implausibility. Those of us who begin with the logic of sovereignty can affirm with all confidence that God, in the wisdom of his eternal counsels, is the active, electing source of salvation, but this eternal divine choosing does not compete with, and therefore need not invalidate, authentic human choosing of the libertarian kind. The human will that is genuinely free is also ontologically sustained by an incomprehensible reality that stands behind it. We cannot understand this ontological discrepancy, and it is exactly that fact that helps us to understand why the relation between divine and human choosing should be opaque to us.

Thus, it is here, at the juncture of God and creation, and therefore of divine agency and creaturely agency, that those of us with Calvinist leanings can most comprehensibly acknowledge the incomprehensibility of God. We can grant a significant portion of Arminianism's case for the logic of freedom without the logic of sovereignty being at all threatened. We can affirm that God is sovereign in the very strongest Calvinist sense without being forced to conclude, with all of its troubling implications, that God's is the only real choosing that goes on. That conclusion turns out to be entirely unwarranted by what we know, and what we do *not* know, about God and ourselves.

Similarly on the Arminian side, mystery was (supposedly) avoided by appeal to a very sensible concept of divine control as self-limited, in spite of the textual and theological difficulties that resulted. But we are now in a position to see that this move, too, is unnecessary, since the mystery of agency preserves our moral intuitions without this stultifying limitation. And the presence of mystery here does for the logic of freedom the same thing that it did for the logic of sovereignty: it allows adherents to concede more to their opponents than they thought possible, without in the least betraying their own convictions. Those of us with Arminian sensibilities can solemnly insist on the irreproachable goodness of God and therefore on the necessity of libertarian freedom for moral responsibility, and we need not fear that unqualified sovereignty will somehow undermine these commitments. For we understand neither what divine agency is (since God is transcendent) nor what creaturely freedom is (since human beings, as the image of God, are *like* God, neither sheerly determined nor sheerly undetermined), and so we have no grounds whatsoever for assuming that one of them must exclude the other. Instead, acknowledging mystery at this point gives us a deeper, richer picture of both.

Summary, and Three Alternatives

Here then, in sum, is our way of addressing the age-old problem of sovereignty and freedom: we submit that appeal should be made very intentionally and rationally to mystery, and at precisely the point at which sovereign divine agency and free human agency meet. This move retains the unassailably Christian intuitions that ground both the logic of sovereignty and the logic of freedom. Further, it enables us to be reasonable without being imprisoned by our reasoning. Just as it would be reasonable for the Flatlander to accept, without fully comprehending, our claim that both squareness and roundness characterize the mysterious thing called a cylinder, so also it is reasonable for

Christians to accept, even if we cannot reconcile, the revealed truths of full divine sovereignty *and* responsible human freedom.

In fact, most Christian traditions (Calvinist and Arminian, Protestant and Catholic, Anglican and Orthodox) make some move like this, recognizing that it is sometimes hard to fit together all that our concrete thought and practice require. The word "mystery" might even be used at such points occasionally. In a sense, the real novelty in our proposal is the contention that this step ought to be taken very consciously and consistently, with the point at which mystery is invoked fixed at the relationship between divine and human choosing, and with the result that full, meticulous sovereignty can be sustained right alongside full, libertarian freedom. It is this juxtaposition, we think, that divine incomprehensibility helps us to comprehend: the strengths of each side are retained, while the weaknesses of each side and the conflict between the two turn out to result very plausibly from the overstepping of creaturely boundaries.

Now, we think this approach has much to commend it, but on an issue as contentious as this one, there is a somewhat unusual danger that it might be wise to address as we conclude. Because so many people have battled over the question of sovereignty and freedom for so long, there is a real danger that peace-loving Christians who see *any* way out of the conflict will be tempted simply to take it, without asking too many questions. We are not advocating that kind of maneuver, and in fact it may be useful to specify three particular versions of the maneuver that we are especially eager to distance ourselves from.

1. In the first place, let it be clear that *we are proposing mystery, not compromise*. We are not advocating what some people vaguely refer to as "balance," which usually involves accepting a little bit (but not too much) of one position and a little bit (but not too much) of another and trying to occupy this middle ground. A compromise position is one that says that God is "relatively sovereign," not quite as sovereign as the Calvinists say, but more than Arminians allow; and human beings are "somewhat free," not as free as Arminians would like, but not so bound by sin as Calvinists think. By contrast, our argument here has been the very *im*balanced one that God is sovereign in the fullest, most robust, most Calvinist sense; and that human persons (by grace) are free with a wildly libertarian, contrary-choice freedom. We cannot see how both of these propositions can be true at the same time, but that is the whole point. A cylinder is not a two-dimensional figure that is "a little bit square" and also "a little bit round"; it is three-dimensional and therefore fully round and also completely square.

2. Similarly, *we are proposing mystery, not relativism or subjectivism*. We are not suggesting that there is no real "right answer" in the sovereignty-freedom debate. On the contrary, there is a very "right answer," because there is a very definite, self-consistent reality

called God, who is Creator, Sustainer, and Lord of the definite, self-consistent reality called the world. Since God is God, it is no surprise that finite creatures cannot grasp the full coherence of this comprehensive picture, but this is not at all the same as saying that "coherence is irrelevant" or that God is "different for every person" or some such drivel. One can imagine a trendy, postmodern Flatlander arguing that the mystery of squareness and roundness in a cylinder shows that "the cylinder has no shape of its own, but we give it shape as we encounter it." Such an argument might initially sound profound, but it is nonsense.

3. Finally, and perhaps somewhat surprisingly, *we are proposing mystery, not ignorance*. When the topic of predestination comes up in our theology classes and we review the two sides and then present our approach, it is usually just a matter of time before some intrepid student decides to cut to the chase. A hand goes up, and a voice says, "You mean, after all this investigation of every side and every argument, the final answer is just that we don't know?" This is a very important question.

Here is our response. From one rather insignificant angle, this terse summary is correct—we don't know. That is, we do not know how divine sovereignty and human freedom fit together. But we want to insist that, from a vastly more significant angle, this summary is exactly wrong. Is the final answer, "we don't know"? No. On the contrary, the final answer, guaranteed by God himself in his revelation to humanity in Christ and in Scripture and in the church, is that we *do* know. We do know that God is sovereign; we do know that God loves us unreservedly; we do know that we are helpless apart from him; we do know that we are responsible before him; we do know that salvation, if it comes, comes exclusively and graciously from the hand of God; we do know that damnation, if it comes, is completely our own doing. All of these things, all of the rock-bottom truths of the Christian gospel, we *do* know, and we can rely on them absolutely, even when we cannot see how they all fit together.

Theological Questions and What Lies behind Them

So if someone still insists on asking a pointed, yes-or-no theological question—say, whether divine grace is resistible (where, as we have seen, Calvinists naturally say no and Arminians naturally say yes)—then it turns out, however inconveniently, that no simple yes-or-no answer will suffice. Instead, it will prove very important to find out what lies behind the question.

- Is the questioner a Christian who is seeking some ever-so-subtle acknowledgment that something about *him* has "contributed" to his salvation? Then the reply is, "You have contributed nothing to your salvation but the sin that must be destroyed. All is of grace, as a sovereign God works in you to will and to do according to his good pleasure" (see Phil. 2:13). (This is, of course, a good "Calvinist" reply.)

- Or does the questioner ask because she is feeling tempted, and she wonders why it should be so difficult if God really wants her to live a holy life? Is she suspecting that she is not really among the elect, and so God is not giving her the strength that she needs? If so, then the reply is, "In the power of the Spirit, you can resist this temptation. No temptation has overtaken you that is not common to all humanity; God is faithful, and he will not allow you to be tempted beyond your strength but with the temptation will also provide a way of escape, that you may be able to endure it" (see 1 Cor. 10:13). (This is a good "Arminian" reply.)
- Or does the questioner ask because he is afraid of his own weakness, afraid that he will let God down, and so he seeks a deeper source of confidence? Then we answer, "Do not fear. The Lord is both the author and the finisher of our faith, and we can be confident of this very thing, that he who began the good work in us will perfect it until the day of Christ Jesus" (see Heb. 12:2; Phil. 1:6). (Calvinism again.)
- Or does the questioner ask because she wonders why a good friend remains immovably opposed to the gospel, and she cannot help wondering whether God is simply refusing to act, refusing to soften the friend's heart? Then the answer is, "Be assured that there is no unwillingness on God's part, for he is not willing that any should perish, but desires that all should come to repentance" (see 2 Peter 3:9). (Arminianism, without a doubt.)
- Or does the questioner ask because her friend's heart seems *so* hard, and so she wonders whether even God is able to change him? Then we reply, "God has melted harder hearts than your friend's and replaced those hearts of stone with hearts of flesh instead. For we were all dead in sin when God made us alive in Christ. Continue to pray that God will remove the blindness and make his own glorious light to shine" (see Eph. 2:1). (Back to Calvinism.)

Note that it is not a Calvinist or Arminian theological agenda that powers the reply in any of these cases. It is, instead, a concrete commitment to all of the truths that the gospel is built upon—even when those truths seem to conflict with one another. This sort of commitment allows the right pastoral medicine to be prescribed for whatever particular ailment the patient suffers from.

In other words, the logic of mystery turns out to give us all of the practical, pastoral strengths of both Calvinist *and* Arminian approaches to sovereignty and freedom. It affirms (with Calvinism) the kind of sovereignty that overthrows our pride and comforts us in our weakness; but it also affirms (with Arminianism) the kind of freedom that challenges our lethargy and reinforces our confidence in God's love. It gives us both!

Of course, some people will say we cannot have it both ways. Staunch advocates of sovereignty are likely to think that any approach that grants real freedom to enslaved sinners has gone wrong; convinced advocates of freedom will probably say that we have still granted to God a monstrous kind of sovereignty. But these criticisms from both sides might tell a significant tale of their own. As C. S. Lewis once pointed out, if the pygmies think you are a giant and the giants think you are a pygmy, then you are probably about the right size.[7] We think that our approach is "about the right size," for it invites us to think rationally but not to be content with a theology that is merely about rational thinking. We do not abandon logic (as if that were even possible), but neither do we need to capitulate to the particular logic of Calvinism or Arminianism. We can be, so to speak, more logical than either one—by refusing to allow a creaturely logic that ignores the incomprehensible mystery of God to back us into a corner.

7. See "Rejoinder to Dr Pittenger," in *God in the Dock: Essays on Theology and Ethics*, ed. Walter Hooper (Grand Rapids: Eerdmans, 1970), 181.

8

MYSTERY *and the*
LIFE *of* PRAYER

If you are a theologian you will pray truly; and if you pray truly, you are a theologian.

Evagrius Ponticus[1]

By prayer I mean not that which is only in the mouth, but that which springs up from the bottom of the heart. In fact, just as trees with deep roots are not shattered or uprooted by storms . . . in the same way prayers that come from the bottom of the heart, having their roots there, rise to heaven with complete assurance.

John Chrysostom[2]

We pray to God to know his passion, death, and resurrection—which come from the goodness of God. We pray to God for the strength that comes from his Cross—which also comes from the goodness of God. . . . All of the strength

---

1. Evagrius Ponticus, *On Prayer* 61 (Philokalia 1.182), quoted in Olivier Clement, *The Roots of Christian Mysticism: Texts from the Patristic Era with Commentary* (Hyde Park, NY: New City, 1993), 184.
2. John Chrysostom, *On the Incomprehensibility of God*, sermon 5, quoted in Clement, *Roots of Christian Mysticism*, 182.

that may come through prayer comes from the goodness of God, for he is the goodness of everything.

Julian of Norwich[3]

Up to this point, each of the chapters in part 2 has investigated a traditional Christian doctrine whose contours become clearer and more meaningful as we understand the significance of God's incomprehensibilty. The time has come in the present chapter for expanding the discussion to include not just traditional Christian *doctrine* but also traditional Christian *practice*. To be sure, we will not be leaving doctrine behind entirely: every Christian practice is rooted in a particular understanding—that is, a particular doctrine—of God or of creation or of salvation or whatever. Still, one can distinguish doctrine from practice, and it is important for us to see how divine mystery affects both. Christianity is never merely a set of truth claims about God and the world; it is also a life to be lived in the presence of God.

A fundamental part of this life is the spiritual practice that we call prayer. If God is supremely, intensely personal, and if we, as divine image-bearers, are personal as a result, then it cannot but be true that God has created us as praying creatures. Indeed, prayer is, in the words of Simon Chan, a "nearly instinctive reflex" for God's image-bearers. "Prayers are the life signs of faith. They occur as naturally as the cries of newborn babies."[4] The spontaneous joy of this instinctive reflex is perhaps familiar to every Christian, at least in some rudimentary way.

But so also certain puzzles are probably familiar to every Christian, certain struggles, certain perplexities. Rare is the follower of Christ whose conscience is entirely clear with respect to his or her own prayer life. Most of us find prayer to be occasionally rich and rewarding, but often irksome and sometimes downright empty. Especially in times of spiritual dryness or in the face of prayers that seem unanswered, we frequently find ourselves asking some fairly basic questions about prayer as the cornerstone of spiritual life. What is really taking place when we pray? Why exactly do we offer up our petitions at all? Do we think that God needs to be informed about our situation? Does prayer change God's mind in some way? Or is prayer merely a subjective exercise to conform my mind to that of God, to improve my spiritual life while God remains basically untouched and unmoved? Why does God so often seem distant, as though he were unable—or perhaps unwilling—to address the hurts that run so deep in our lives? These are basic, practical questions that most

3. Julian of Norwich, *Revelations of Divine Love*, excerpted in Richard J. Foster and James Bryan Smith, *Devotional Classics: Selected Readings for Individuals and Groups*, rev. ed. (San Francisco: HarperSanFrancisco, 2005), 8.76–77.
4. Simon Chan, *Spiritual Theology: A Systematic Study of the Christian Life* (Downers Grove, IL: InterVarsity, 1998), 127.

believers will perhaps admit to asking and that theologians inevitably need to address. Yet they are also questions to which almost every answer seems wrong: anything that we say appears to compromise from one side or the other some of our most basic convictions about God and our world.

Our argument in this chapter is that satisfying answers can be forthcoming for questions like these only when we take with utmost seriousness the mystery of our incomprehensible God. The troubling issues do not simply evaporate, but we discover that, *if God is incomprehensible in the way Christianity suggests*, then we have very good grounds for praying with faith and with humility, even in the midst of our troubles. Prayer need not be regarded as an attempt to convince an unwilling or ignorant God to act, nor is it merely therapy for the pray-er with no objective effect. Instead, as we ponder how our personal and corporate interaction with a surpassingly great God is similar to, but also strikingly different from, our interaction with one another, we can enter more deeply into the life of prayer with the confidence and hope that both Scripture and Christian tradition hold out.

Dilemma 1: What Is God Like?

There are at least two different dilemmas that we face as we consider the role of prayer in the Christian life. Both have deep practical implications, but both grow out of what looks like a more abstract question. That question is, why do we pray?

Why do we pray? Or, to move immediately toward the first problem that this question raises, what is it *about* God that prompts us to pray? How should we think about the God to whom we pray? What is God like? These might still sound like abstractly doctrinal questions, far removed from our ordinary spiritual lives. But many of our stumbling blocks in the life of prayer stem from our distorted views of God. Directed by our own histories, we easily think of God as a regretful parent who is always quietly disappointed with us, or as a severe tyrant who constantly demands more and more and more, or as a distant relative who might occasionally be coaxed into sending a birthday present. Clearly, dysfunctional views of God will make our prayers dysfunctional too, and so our understanding of what God is like becomes a decisive factor in the concrete practice of our spiritual lives.

To remind ourselves of the important practical implications that are waiting in the wings, let us approach these questions about what God is like by beginning with a concrete (albeit somewhat facetious) hypothetical scenario. Suppose you are having breakfast with a small group, say, at a family reunion, and you need the butter for your morning toast. You take a moment to scan the table. If you spot the butter dish all the way down at the opposite end of the table, and if you happen to be in a particularly sour mood this morning, you might pause to ask yourself a few grumbling questions: "Now, why should the butter be all the way at the other end of the table? Didn't Aunt Edna know that I would need butter for my toast? Why didn't she put some butter within my reach in the first place?" Probably you forget such questions quickly, or at least you keep them to yourself as you ask old Uncle Earl to pass the butter down your way. Again, probably he is happy to do so, and so breakfast goes on undisturbed.

But suppose that, when you ask for the butter, it does *not* get passed to you. How would you explain what is going on? The request itself seems reasonable enough—the sort of request that one would expect family members to respond favorably to. Then why has nothing happened? Well, there are at least three possibilities. It might be that the butter is not within the reach of Uncle Earl, especially since he hurt his arm in last night's family horseshoes tournament. Or it might be that he doesn't really *want* to pass the butter to you, because he is still stinging from his loss to you in the final round of that tournament. Or it might be that he didn't hear you ask for the butter, having forgotten to turn up his hearing aid this morning after all the noisy hubbub last night. In other words, Uncle Earl might be *unable* to grant your request, or he might be *unwilling* to grant your request, or he might be *unaware* that a request was ever made. Note well that each of these possibilities signals a certain kind of weakness or imperfection in Uncle Earl—not anything deeply objectionable in a kindly old uncle but something that would become much more problematic if we were thinking about God instead.

And that, of course, is what we need to do. For these same three options are available when we begin to think about requests made as we kneel in prayer. If prayer is a matter (as the apostle Paul taught) of letting our requests "be made known to God" (Phil. 4:6 ESV), then it seems that serious requests that are *not* granted must be explained in one of these three ways. God is unable or unwilling or unaware.

Note that we are talking about *serious* requests here. We probably all acknowledge that plenty of our prayers do not fall into this category, and even that our *relatively* serious requests are often made in the awareness that God might have other, deeper plans in mind. When minor petitions like these are not granted, we may be disappointed, but we usually do not fret much (if we even recall that we had prayed about the matter in the first place).

But about *serious* requests, there seems to be more at stake. Serious prayers grow not out of concerns that are modest or localized or short-range but out of our awareness of fundamental goods rooted (so our faith tells us) in God's own heart. Perhaps we pray for the health of a loved one—yet we are thinking not of some happy though sniffly child but of a desolate, miserable sufferer whose years-long torment of body and spirit has driven both victim and observers to the very brink of despair, outrage, and unbelief. God's failure to answer *this* prayer is not just an inconvenience. It is a capitulation to wickedness and misery; it is letting evil emerge victorious; it is allowing seekers to turn away from faith because faith has not received the confirmation that it desperately needs. Why does God seem deaf to such vital, grave, momentous prayers as these?

In the face of this kind of unanswered prayer, we are confronted very directly with our question: What is God like . . . *really*? And we are pushed right back to the possibilities we envisioned for the breakfast table—except that now, every trace of the facetious has vanished. What is God really like? It seems that either he is unable to grant our requests, or he is unwilling, or he is unaware.

In fact, as we consider these possibilities, things get worse and worse. For a little reflection shows that the same three explanations are available not only as we try to explain what happens *after* a request is made but also as we try to explain the whole context that calls for the request in the first place. Think again about breakfast. Why was the butter placed at the other end of the table, so that you had to ask that it be passed? Well, either Aunt Edna did not have enough butter to put some within everyone's reach (she was *unable* to provide it for you with no request being necessary); or she, too, was irritated by your last-minute defeat of her husband in horseshoes (she was *unwilling* to provide for you); or she forgot that you always like butter on your morning toast (she was *unaware* of your need). It would seem that an aunt without these weaknesses or imperfections would make the request unnecessary. So why do we not say the same thing about God? Even if the desperate request *is* finally granted, why was it necessary in the first place? How can we avoid the conclusion that God, too, must be subject to the same weaknesses and imperfections we detect in the human beings of our acquaintance? Once again, what is God really like?

Classical Biblical Answers

We do not have space here to address a question like this completely, but we can at least trace the trajectory that a satisfying answer will have to follow. And that trajectory begins with the straightforward reminder that historic Christianity most definitely does *not* allow us to draw the troubling conclusions about God that our dilemma initially suggests. There are plenty of voices around us that clamor for such conclusions, the loudest of them (among contemporary evangelicals) probably being that of the "open theists," who argue that the traditional perfections we have been taught to ascribe to God are not really called for.[5] But both Scripture and the theological tradition that grows out of it insist that such an approach cannot work, that the living God is neither unable, nor unwilling, nor unaware—even despite some occasional suspicious biblical language to the contrary.[6]

---

5. See especially David Basinger et al., *The Openness of God: A Biblical Challenge to the Traditional Understanding of God* (Downers Grove, IL: InterVarsity, 1994).

6. For a more detailed discussion of these "suspicious" texts and of many of the other issues surrounding open theism, see Chris Hall and John Sanders, *Does God Have a Future? A Debate on Divine Providence* (Grand Rapids: Baker Academic, 2003).

First, is God unable? Well, it is true that Scripture sometimes speaks of certain circumstances that God would prefer to be different from what they are (e.g., Ezek. 33:11)—that is, it seems that he would change them *if he could*. But the dominant note that Scripture sounds is much different, as it confidently announces, "Nothing is too hard for you" (Jer. 32:17). God is the one who works all things according to the counsel of his will (Eph. 1:11), whose purposes nothing can stop or hinder (Ps. 33:11). In the language of historic Christian theology, God is *sovereign* (possessing supreme ruling authority) over all things, and he is *omnipotent* (all-powerful) by very nature. He is never unable to meet our needs.

Is God unwilling? To be sure, we do find in the Bible some narratives that are surprising on this score—for instance, the story of Abraham having to negotiate with God for Sodom (Gen. 18:22–32) or the story of Moses having to persuade God not to destroy Israel (Exod. 32:9–14). But the biblical testimony as a whole suggests otherwise. It shows a God who is shockingly generous and rich in mercy, a God "slow to anger, abounding in love and faithfulness" (Exod. 34:6), a God who is always ready to care for those in need. For the Christian, Jesus puts an end to all debate when he straightforwardly teaches that the benevolence of human parents is a small and pale reflection of the overflowing bounty of God toward his people: "If you, then, though you are evil, know how to give good gifts to your children, how much more will your Father in heaven give good gifts to those who ask him!" (Matt. 7:11). The Christian tradition describes God here as *omnibenevolent* (all-good) and as *immutable* (unchangeable) in his loving intentions toward us.

Is God unaware? It is true that Scripture occasionally portrays God as seeking information (e.g., Gen. 18:20–21) and that prayer is sometimes described, as we saw above, as making our requests known to God (Phil. 4:6). But, yet again, texts like these are the exception rather than the rule, and they seem to rely on the literary device of "anthropomorphism," which gives us a partial, dramatized picture of God, displayed in the form (Greek, *morphe*) of the human (*anthrōpos*). According to the larger biblical picture, however, God is the one who upholds all things at every moment, who always sees our ways, who counts our every step (Job 31:4). "Nothing in all creation is hidden from God's sight. Everything is uncovered and laid bare before the eyes of him to whom we must give account" (Heb. 4:13). The tradition says here that God is *omniscient* (all-knowing), so that nothing is outside of his irresistibly penetrating gaze.

So the classical Christian answer is no, God is not unable or unwilling or unaware. As we try to figure out what is going on when we pray, any option that simply eliminates one of the divine perfections can be ruled out from the start. And certain conclusions follow. Since God is not unable to meet our needs, it cannot be the case that there is something about our prayers that "empowers" him, that gives him a strength or a capacity that he did not otherwise have. Since God is not unwilling to meet our needs, it cannot be the case that our prayers must convince him to act or must manipulate him into doing what he was otherwise reluctant to do. And since God is not unaware of our needs, it cannot be the case that our prayers are necessary to inform him about our situation. To speak in any of these ways is to speak the language of paganism or of animism or of magic, and it is thus to lose the rich and glorious fullness of perfection that we rightly ascribe to God.

A New Set of Problems

But this conviction about God's unqualified perfection might pose its own distinctive problems for Christian spirituality. When historic Christian theology encapsulates the biblical teachings in terms and concepts like those we have noted above (e.g., sovereignty, immutability, omniscience)—terms and concepts that protect God's infinite perfections—we sometimes get results that are not particularly friendly to the life of prayer. To be sure, God is no longer *im*perfect, but he now seems to have become *so* perfect that he cannot be reached by prayer at all.

Consider the following concerns that arise from some divine characteristics we have already noted, as well as from others that often get mentioned (not very happily) in discussions of prayer:

- When the Christian tradition insists that God is *omniscient*, possessing all possible knowledge, are we not pushed back to asking once again why it is that we must pray at all? Why must we call God's attention to our situation through our prayers, as though he were a distracted businessman who needs a quiet reminder of his children's troubles back home? Is his love for us somehow lacking? Surely not. But then what difference do our prayers really make? In fact, what difference do we *want* them to make? Surely the all-wise God knows better than we do what is best for us?

- Again, when Christians say that God is *sovereign* and *omnipotent*, that he has all power and does whatever he pleases, do we not find ourselves wondering why the world should be in such a mess? And why does God not act with this supreme power when he sees us suffering, or when he sees the world suffering? Can we really believe that a compassionate God watched the horrors of the Holocaust in the mid-twentieth century, and had the power to intervene, but decided not to? Or that a God of kindness and mercy saw the whole Holocaust scenario coming and did nothing to prevent it? This "perfection" in the realm of power seems to go too far, for it tells us that God has *already* exercised his power—in order to produce just the world we are now experiencing. Is this all-powerful God really one we can worship wholeheartedly? Is this the sort of God to whom we would *wish* to pray?

- When the tradition says that God is *immutable*, that he is too great to change or shift since any change would involve movement away from his already-supreme perfection, are we not prone to ask how such a God could ever possibly "answer" our prayers? If the answer we cry out for involves an intervention that would change things, and if God himself is strictly unchangeable, what good can prayer possibly do? How can such a static, immobile God ever go from inaction to action? We may make as many requests as we please, but an "unchanging" granite slab simply lies where it fell. Can an immutable God be any different?

- The Christian tradition has often gone further and affirmed that God is not just immutable but also *impassible*, that is, that he does not undergo "suffering" of any kind. The term "impassible" comes from the same Latin root from which we get words like *passion* and *passive*, a root that has to do with "being acted upon." To say that God is impassible is to say that he is never the "passive" party whom other things act upon or influence from the outside. He is entirely perfect within himself, and so nothing ever causes God to move out of his state of perfect, entire completeness. But what about our suffering, then? Is God entirely immune to it? Is the real reason he does not answer our prayer simply that he does not feel our pain? In this case, what kind of real mutuality or reciprocity is possible between God and creatures? If God cannot feel what we feel, if God remains wholly aloof and untouched by the hurt that so often threatens to consume us, is he really a God we want to worship?

- Traditional Christianity often speaks of God's *infinity*, his un-bounded immensity, his measureless vastness. This teaching may not entail problems by sheer logical necessity, but can we really believe that a God so unimaginably vast, who orders the entire universe, could possibly be interested in the small, petty troubles and hurts of our lives? Do the ocean's fathomless depths concern themselves with the single grains of sand along their edge? Does the builder of a colossal palace worry about the tiny anthill that will be crushed along the way?

- The tradition speaks, too, of God's *eternity*, his existence outside of time as we know it, perceiving what is for us the past, the present, and the future all in one timeless gaze. But can the petitions that we make at a particular point in time truly affect what a timeless God will do? How can they, if he already knows everything that is going to happen? Long before we pray, say, for the safety of our loved ones in their travels, God knows that two particular cars are going to cross an intersection simultaneously and collide, and that two young children's lives will come to a horrific end. How can our prayers change what a timeless God knows?

Other divine attributes could perhaps be added to this list, with other troubles evident as a result, but the point has been made. Divine perfection is a great thing for Christians to affirm, but if perfection involves characteristics like these, then we may very well wonder whether the whole enterprise of prayer has not been unwittingly invalidated. Indeed, it is precisely for this reason that so many modern theologians and writers on the spiritual life have been tempted either to modify these attributes or to jettison them altogether as insurmountable roadblocks to a coherent prayer life. Better an *im*perfect God who is worthy of prayer than a *too* perfect God who is too distant and detached to be responsive to our cries. Better to criticize the tradition in the name of Christian spirituality than to retain these traditional attributes and lose the reality of prayer altogether.

The Attributes of God and Incomprehensibility

But is abandoning historic Christianity really the best solution? It is true that traditional Christian theology gives us a very complex answer to the question "What is God like?"—an answer that appears *too* complex, since it insists *both* that God knows our needs and feels our pain and wants to help us (characteristics that drive us to pray with confidence and hope) *and also* that God is sovereign and impassible and infinite and eternal (attributes that seem to make prayer unnecessary or meaningless). Plenty of contemporary thinkers judge this complex view of God to be hopelessly confused, and they maintain that we should affirm the first set of attributes (the "pro-prayer" attributes) and abandon the second set (the "anti-prayer" attributes).

Yet this revisionist approach ends up causing as many problems as it solves. For instance, it may seem that placing some sort of limit on divine omnipotence keeps us from imagining God as an aloof observer who could overthrow evil in the world if he wanted to but who does not really want to. But is it an improvement to think that God would overthrow evil in the world if he could, and he simply is unable? Is it really better to think of God wringing his hands and saying, "I'm doing the best I can"? On the contrary, it seems wrong to give *either* answer, either the one that says that God is able but unwilling to help or the one that says that God is willing but unable to help. This is the very dilemma that we encountered a moment ago.

Yet is there any alternative? Doesn't strict logic require us to choose one side or the other? After all, a doctor with a chronically sick patient either *can* or *cannot* remedy the patient's illness. If she *can* but refuses to do so, she is very knowledgeable and strong but not very compassionate; if she *cannot*, then she is very compassionate but not as knowledgeable or strong as we would like. Similarly, either the Great Physician can cure our ills but will not, or else he desires to cure our ills but cannot. Logic seems to offer us no escape from this dilemma.

No escape . . . so long, that is, as we are dealing with doctors and patients and other entities *within* the world as we know it. But then we recall that God is not "within" the world. He is not a doctor caring for a patient; he is the Creator and Sustainer of doctors, and of patients, and of all things in heaven and on earth. God is the radically transcendent Reality that stands behind all of reality as we know it, the incomprehensible Ground and Judge of every act, every thought, every longing. The attributes of God are not simply human qualities idealistically pumped up to a superhuman level. They are refracted expressions of a revealed perfection that outstrips all human language and conception.

If we want to know what God is like, then we must always begin by insisting on this transcendent incomprehensibility. God is never grasped by adding one quality to another till we come to the end of our list of really great qualities. He is simply himself, and every attribute is a creaturely attempt to express the unified divine totality from one limited angle. It is pointless to pit the attributes against one another as if they were in competition. It is not God's attributes that struggle with one another for dominance; it is *we* who struggle to put into human words a supremacy that creation itself cannot contain. Of course the attributes are true, and they can be relied upon. But their truthfulness does not reside in an analytical definition so much as in an all-embracing trustworthiness. They effectively point beyond themselves to that superabundant plenitude whose glory spills over into every corner of created reality.

In the actual practice of spiritual life, then, we should always accept the thrust of the biblical metaphors for God, yet not in such a way as to be imprisoned by their extraneous aspects or by their creaturely implications. God is very much like a human doctor, who heals our diseases (Ps. 103:3) and tends to our needs (Matt. 6:8). But none of the failings that might be found in a human doctor can be ascribed to God. He is neither lacking in compassion, like a wicked doctor who shows no mercy to her patient; nor lacking in power or wisdom, like a merely human doctor who can do nothing to help her patient. God is not "like" a doctor at all in these respects, for every doctor is, as we say, "*only* human"—whereas God most emphatically is not. He is the holy Lord of all, the very standard of all that we call compassionate or powerful or wise. To draw the smug conclusion that God "must" be either limited in goodness or limited in ability or knowledge is, in the nature of the case, to treat God as if he were a mere creature—as if he were "only human." Such direct creaturely logic cannot readily be applied to God the Creator.

Reminders of Transcendence

Of course, the appeal of this creaturely logic remains strong, especially in the midst of the crises that drive us to call out to God in prayer. It is strong enough, in fact, that we often need to be reminded of the limits of such creaturely reasoning, so that we can guard ourselves against simplistic answers to our deep, personal questions. Fortunately, the Christian tradition provides exactly this sort of reminder, and in a surprising place: the very attributes we noted above that seem to cause such trouble for our prayer lives. It turns out that these attributes may not be quite what they appear. They may actually serve the very useful function of pointing us, over and over again, to the God who far surpasses our understanding.

It might be worth recalling that we have already seen one example of this phenomenon back in chapter 3, where we noted that the classical doctrine of divine *simplicity* is not what most moderns usually think. Simplicity is the traditional doctrine that affirms that God is not "composite," cannot be divided into "parts"—which seems to many people in our day to have the disastrous implication that there can be no distinction between mercy and wrath in God, no distinction between Father, Son, and Spirit in the Godhead, and so on. This, of course, would be dreadful news, for it would mean that we cannot take at face value any of the relevant portrayals of God in Scripture, lest divine simplicity be compromised. Hence, when we go to our knees in prayer, how can we realistically expect any kind of love or compassion from the God in whom love and hatred are indistinguishable? If there is no mutuality or reciprocity between Father and Son in the Trinity, how can we look for mutuality or reciprocity between God and such puny creatures as ourselves? Here is yet another traditional attribute that seems to be at war with a meaningful life of prayer.

But in chapter 3 we noted that, in the thoughtful work of Thomas Aquinas, the doctrine of simplicity is used less to *affirm* something about God, and more to *deny* that our knowledge of God is ever complete. To say that God is simple is to remind ourselves that all of the ways that we normally analyze or understand reality—ways that inevitably involve breaking reality into its component parts—fall short of the higher, greater, incomprehensible Reality of God. The simplicity of God is, as we put it before, an *apophatic* doctrine, a doctrine that tells us not what we know but what we do not know, a doctrine that reminds us constantly of the limitations of our knowledge. If we apply ordinary categories to God, we will always find ourselves trapped and confused in the long run. Divine simplicity protects us from that error—and it is therefore profoundly good news for Christians troubled by what seem to be unavoidable dilemmas in their understanding of God. We start to understand why complete understanding is—and should be—beyond our grasp.

It is now time to recognize that other apparently difficult attributes of God may be "good news" in the same way that simplicity is. For the sake of space, let us focus on just one, divine impassibility, which is perhaps the attribute in our list above that is least attractive to many contemporary Christians.[7]

---

7. For helpful discussions of impassibility, see James F. Keating and Thomas Joseph White, eds., *Divine Impassibility and the Mystery of Human Suffering* (Grand Rapids: Eerdmans, 2009); Thomas G. Weinandy, *Does God Suffer?* (Notre Dame: University of Notre Dame Press, 2000); Thomas G. Weinandy, *Does God Change?* (Still River, MA: St. Bede's, 1985).

Impassibility, as we saw a few moments ago, is the idea that God cannot be "acted upon" and therefore cannot "suffer." It strikes many people in our day as a very unfortunate notion from ancient Greek philosophy that, like a virus, infected the bloodstream of the early Christian theological tradition. According to the critics, the ancient Greeks always privileged the unchanging stability of "being" over the unpredictable fluctuations of "becoming," and so they were always suspicious that change of any kind whatsoever involved a kind of weakness or vulnerability, a movement away from unwavering, absolute perfection. In an environment influenced by this concern, it is not surprising that the church insisted that God is "impassible," that he experiences no "suffering," that nothing arouses his "passions."

Yet (so the argument goes) the resulting picture of God is devastating: God is absolutely unconditioned, aloof, inert, detached, apathetic, static, unresponsive, lifeless, impersonal. This is a terrible list of descriptors. The critics of impassibility prefer a very different list: they want God to be dynamic, vulnerable, engaged, sympathetic, accessible, responsive, caring, sensitive, involved. After all, they ask, isn't this what we find in the biblical story? Do our pain and heartache touch God? Can the actions of creatures cause God to grieve or rejoice? Can they make God angry, or elicit any other affective response in God? Surely the biblical answer to all of these questions is yes. But the outlandish Greek idea of impassibility shouts a loud, implacable no. Should we not reject such an antibiblical construction of a lifeless God?

Well, much will depend on giving very careful attention to what impassibility has actually meant in the Christian tradition—and also to what it has not meant. Contemporary theologian Paul Gavrilyuk argues that we moderns have unnecessarily confused ourselves on this matter by failing to distinguish ontological and psychological descriptions of God.[8]

Here is what he means. Divine impassibility, as conceived by patristic writers, is not a *psychological* quality that refers to an absence of emotional response to human sufferings, petitions, and so on. How could it be? If God is fully actualized, interpersonal love—the love manifested, as we saw in chapter 5, in the eternal communion of the Holy Trinity—the last thing God can be is apathetic, unconcerned, or cold. Of course not. God is love.

But at the same time, God is love in a manner that surpasses all our conceptions of what love is or could be, since God himself surpasses all of our conceptions whatsoever. Therefore, the theologians of the patristic age were always on the lookout for ways of distinguishing God's transcendent love from common, ordinary human love. Impassibility was one of those ways. When these theologians spoke of God's impassibility, they were speaking not psychologically but *ontologically*—they were making a point about God's *being*. And the

---

8. Paul L. Gavrilyuk, *The Suffering of the Impassible God: The Dialectics of Patristic Thought* (Oxford: Oxford University Press, 2004), 48.

point they were making was chiefly an apophatic one: they were intentionally speaking about what God *is not* so that they could more clearly understand what God *is*. Gavrilyuk speaks of divine impassibility in patristic theology as an "apophatic qualifier on all analogies to the divine life drawn from human experience."[9] In other words, when they said that God is impassible, the fathers meant to remind us that none of our ordinary experiences of emotion or engagement or activity do justice to the supreme reality of God.

It is not hard to see the point here. Roberta Bondi speaks powerfully of the way that sinful human passions and dispositions always threaten to "blind us so that we cannot love." Our passions, she says, "create for us interior lenses through which we see the world, lenses which we very often do not even know are there. When we are under the control of our passions, . . . we are in the grip of emotions, states of mind, habits that distort everything we see."[10] But the living God is never "in the grip" of such things. On the contrary, as G. L. Prestige explains regarding the perspective of the church fathers, divine impassibility guarantees the consistency of all of God's attitudes and actions toward humanity. "Impassibility means not that God is inactive or uninterested, not that He surveys existence with Epicurean impassivity from the shelter of a metaphysical insulation, but that His will is determined from within instead of being swayed from without."[11]

This is clearly a very different understanding of impassibility, and one that allows us to see why many in the early church spoke of God as they did. John Chrysostom, for example, says that God, in his providential governance of creation, "does not simply watch over us, but also loves us; he *ardently* loves us with an inexplicable love, with an *impassible yet fervent, vigorous, genuine, indissoluble love*, that is impossible to extinguish."[12] Here is a combination of descriptive terms that many moderns find utterly unintelligible. How can an impassible God love at all, much less love in a way that is "ardent," "fervent," "vigorous," "genuine"? Chrysostom might be tempted to ask in reply, "How could the love of an impassible God be anything else?" Human love waxes and wanes according to human passions, but God's holy love is utterly free from such creaturely limitations.

Practical Consequences of Impassibility

When we then come back to our broader question—what is God like?—we find ourselves now in a rather new position. We should certainly say that God

9. Ibid., 120.

10. Roberta C. Bondi, *To Love as God Loves: Conversations with the Early Church* (Philadelphia: Fortress, 1987), 65.

11. G. L. Prestige, *God in Patristic Thought* (London: Hollen Street, 1952), 6–7.

12. John Chrysostom, *On Providence* 6.1 (italics added), in Christopher A. Hall, *John Chrysostom's "On Providence": A Translation and Theological Interpretation* (Ann Arbor, MI: University Microfilms International, 1991).

is loving and kind and gracious and so on, as both ancients and moderns agree. But we must also push beyond the limits of human categories—and traditional notions like impassibility can help us to do just that. If we thought we were dealing with a God whose love was comprehensible and familiar, this demanding assertion reminds us that we are instead always in the thick of transcendent mystery. God is gloriously incomprehensible, and so when we are thinking about God, there is always far more going on than our clear-cut logical categories can handle.

Two results follow for our discussion here. First, as we observed before, we find that we have very good reason to reject the ghastly dichotomy that would pit certain of God's attributes over against others in our understanding of prayer. God is neither able but unwilling, nor willing but unable, to come to our aid when we call upon him in prayer. God is neither "doing the best he can," just as any compassionate creature would, nor is he *refusing* to "do the best he can" for us. These categories simply do not work when the object of our attention is the living God.

But, second, the failure of our categories is by no means a regrettable or disheartening thing. We might fear that it is, for we suspect that such failure will leave us nothing but sheer apophatic silence. But it is not so, for the classical Christian belief is that the mystery of God is revelational rather than investigative, and so we can have every confidence that the negations of the apophatic way are provided for no other reason than that we may avoid inappropriately limiting the supremely *positive* truth about God himself. The logical limitations open up the glory; they do not stifle it.

Of course, we have seen this principle already, but it is good to be reminded of it again. Consider our discussion of the Trinity in chapters 4 and 5. Christians say that the one and only God exists eternally in the three *hypostases* ("persons") of Father, Son, and Spirit. We describe Father, Son, and Spirit as "persons" not because they are exactly what we human persons are, for they are not. To be sure, they are not "*im*personal" in our ordinary sense, but neither are they "personal" in the ordinary sense. Instead, God is infinitely more than the term "person" can convey, and in that sense when we call God "three persons" we are speaking apophatically. In actual fact, he is *intensely, unfathomably* personal, more personal than any persons we can imagine, for these persons constitute the Holy Trinity, an eternal communion of love ineffably experienced in the relations between Father, Son, and Spirit in a manner and to a degree utterly beyond any relationship within the created order. The Holy Trinity was dancing the ecstatic rhythms of love before creation ever existed. We concluded, in our earlier discussion, that the apophatic character of "person" language reminds us of a trinitarian glory too great to conceive.

We now see that this same principle holds elsewhere in our theological lexicon. Theological language inevitably consists of terms and concepts and comparisons and metaphors that break down precisely because of the wonder they are asked to exemplify. Language can take us so far, and no further. But this linguistic limitation does not limit the God who has chosen to reveal himself in human language. Hence, even though we cannot comprehend or describe God as he is in himself, we can know that God is more, rather than less, than the revealed metaphors indicate. That is, when we have biblical language that describes God as personal or as loving or whatever, we can always be confident that *God is stronger than our language rather than weaker*. Though God is not personal in the same manner that we are, God is more personal, not less. Though God's nearness to us is utterly unlike the way human beings are present to each other, God is closer to us than we are to ourselves. Though God's love is impassible, it is richer, deeper, broader, higher than all we could ever hope for from another human person. Indeed, God's love is this unimaginable plenitude, not *although* it is impassible, but *because* it is impassible. God is always greater than our brightest, highest hopes: he is never less.

So if we want to know "what God is like," the Christian tradition has responded in two very different theological idioms, one that answers the question directly ("God loves us"), and another that reminds us of how incomplete and therefore misleading any direct answer will be ("God loves us *impassibly*"). Together, this multifunction language gives to our prayers all the support they could ask for. For it both invites us into God's presence in prayer and also summons us deeper. It tells us of the greatness of the love of God, but it simultaneously whispers of the surpassing, incomprehensible greatness of the God of love.

Dilemma 2: Subjective versus Objective

If the mystery of God gives us some assistance in dealing with our first dilemma regarding the life of prayer ("What is God like?"), a second problem awaits, for the question with which we began—why do we pray?—can be focused in a second direction. We might intend to ask not just what it is *about* God that prompts us to pray but also what *in our expectations* prompts us to pray. In other words, what exactly do we intend our prayers to accomplish? What are the concrete effects that prayer aims to bring about? Questions like these give rise to a dilemma that is sometimes expressed in terms of "subjective" versus "objective" understandings of prayer.

The essence of the dilemma is easy to see. Do we intend our prayers to be "objectively" effective—that is, to affect the real, external state of affairs in the world? Or do we hope that they will be "subjectively" effective—bringing about a change in ourselves, the "subjects" who are doing the praying? On the surface, it would seem that the objective approach should be the easy winner. Many of our prayers ask for provision or for protection or for particular blessings, and the concrete aim would certainly seem to be the securing of the provision, protection, or blessing. What could be more obvious?

The trouble with this approach is twofold. First, it seems to presuppose just the problematic view of a limited God that caused us to hesitate a moment ago. Can we not trust the all-knowing one to know our needs? Then why must we ask that they be met, as if we think he is forgetful? Can we not count on the all-loving one to give what is best? Then why do we feel obliged to make recommendations, as if we fear his gift will not be quite what we have in mind? Notice how quickly our understanding of God's attributes—his knowledge, love, and so on—returns to influence our prayer lives from yet another angle.

Second, many people point out that the objective view of prayer seems to value the gifts of God more than the Giver of the gifts. It suggests that our aim in prayer is not God himself but some particular blessing that we want God to give us. In this sense, it seems to be a "mercenary" view of prayer. God is merely the means for securing blessings—perhaps the best and most reliable means, but still only a means. One can almost overhear the supplicant's inner voice: "Hmm. How can I get such-and-such? I could try to work out the problem myself; or I could ask my neighbor for help. No, wait! I'll ask God for help! That is bound to be a more successful approach!" More successful, perhaps (and of course, perhaps not—witness again the problem of unanswered prayer), but this line of thinking hardly grants to God the supremacy and glory that one would expect.

If this objective way of understanding the aim of prayer leads to troubling conclusions, we might be prompted to move in a more "subjective" direction. We might begin to suspect that the ultimate aim of prayer is not the achievement of an objective effect on the world but must instead be a transformation of our own *inner* world, so that our minds are more and more conformed to the mind of Christ. We ask for daily bread, but our aim is not the bread (if God wants to provide that, he will!), but the dependence upon God that asking for bread encourages. We might recall that Scripture itself explicitly connects the granting of requests with conformity to God's will: "This is the confidence we have in approaching God: that if we ask anything *according to his will*, he hears us" (1 John 5:14). The aim is always that we should pray "according to his will," as our Savior did in Gethsemane ("Not my will, but yours be done" [Luke 22:42]). Thus, prayer is not about *getting* things; it is about *becoming* something. Though it may seem odd to put it this way, "praying for something" is not about obtaining that something. Obtaining it should not thrill us; not obtaining it should not disappoint us. The particular thing we prayed for is, in this respect, irrelevant, for the purpose of the prayer is not obtaining that thing. Prayer is about gradually developing a heart that is like the heart of Jesus.

This sounds all well and good, but again there is a problem. This approach seems to posit a deeply ingrained solipsism in prayer—that is, a hard, unyielding, almost necessary focus on the *self*. If getting what we pray for is irrelevant, if prayer is merely a subjective exercise that is designed to affect us (the pray-ers) in certain constructive ways, then it would seem that the practice of prayer is fundamentally at odds with the life of other-centered love that Christianity elsewhere commends. We are encouraged in the New Testament to lay down our lives for our friends: can we not also pray for them—really for *them*, with no concern for any spiritual benefit to ourselves? Apparently not, for the subjective outlook says that our prayers *for* our neighbors are not really *about* our neighbors. Prayer is always *about* ourselves.

In this respect, it is hard to see the difference, for the subjective approach, between prayer and meditation. It certainly is true that prayer and meditation are often linked in Scripture (e.g., Ps. 19:14) as well as in the tradition of Christian spirituality, but to equate them is another thing altogether. For when one meditates, one meditates *on* such-and-such. But many (perhaps most) of our prayers are self-consciously petitionary in character: they ask *for* things, and they really want the things they ask for. Jesus himself seems to encourage this desire, for his command is, "Ask *and it will be given you*" (Matt. 7:7), and he speaks in a parable of the importance of *continued* asking, the kind that never loses heart but persists in bold, settled faith, waiting for God to answer (Luke 18:1–5). This is very clearly a picture of petitioners who want something and of a God who responds to their petitions. A God who merely *observes* us as we perform a subjective spiritual exercise is, biblically speaking, too simple—just as a God who is merely the means to our getting what we want is too simple.

So, as is often the case, both of these approaches to prayer seem to make sense, but each one carries us to conclusions that are hard to swallow. Is there some third option, some way of understanding what the aim of prayer is that avoids the difficulties on both sides? We think there is, and it ends up drawing us back in a surprisingly practical way to the concrete experience of Christians at prayer.

God's Vision for the World

Let us step back for a larger perspective. We want to know what prayer aims at: let us begin by asking a larger question about what God himself aims at. What is God's ultimate vision for the world, and how has he set about achieving it? We can answer that question by taking a look at the comprehensive biblical presentation of the redemptive work of God in human history.

There may be many ways of describing God's cosmic work of redemption, but one of the most ancient is in terms of the great Hebrew notion of *shalom*. Many people recognize this term as the Hebrew word for "peace," and so it is. But much more than mere "peace" is going on. *Shalom* is not just the absence of conflict. It is instead the profound presence of the wholeness and health and vitality that characterize a world that is completely in harmony with itself. *Shalom* is the realization of all the glorious potential that God builds into the world at creation; it is the state of serene concord and orderly creativity that allows the full, unhindered flourishing of all things, both in their individuality and in their interrelatedness. The term is used in Scripture to suggest the completeness or fullness of a number (Jer. 13:19), the physical soundness of one's body (Gen. 43:27), the security or safety of a home (Job 21:9), the prosperity or success of a mission (2 Sam. 11:7), and the welfare of a people or a society (Jer. 38:4). It connotes friendship (Jer. 20:10), stability (Ps. 122:7), and comprehensive wellness (2 Sam. 18:28). When the world is "at *shalom*," it is true in the richest, most vigorous sense that "all is well."

The condition of *shalom* is very often linked to truth and righteousness (e.g., Ps. 85:10; Jer. 33:6), and so it comes to be especially associated in the Old Testament with the coming of the Messiah, who will be the "Prince of *Shalom*" and whose reign will be characterized by endless *shalom*, because he "will reign on David's throne and over his kingdom, establishing and upholding it with justice and righteousness from that time on and forever" (Isa. 9:7; cf. Hag. 2:9; Mic. 5:4–5). God's ultimate aim is frequently described in just these messianic terms, for the day will come, says the Lord, when "I will make a covenant of *shalom* with [my people]; it will be an everlasting covenant. I will establish them and increase their numbers, and I will put my sanctuary among them forever. My dwelling place will be with them; I will be their God, and they will be my people" (Ezek. 37:26–27; cf. Isa. 54:10). May that day come soon.

It is important to note that *shalom* presupposes a right relationship with God as the foundation for healthy, full relationships throughout the world. In the nature of the case, there can be no real, lasting peace without God as its intimate, personal center. This is why God's interest in loving intimacy with his creation, and especially with the human persons who stand as the crown and climax of creation, turns up on virtually every page of Scripture. We see it prior to the fall of humanity, as God enlivens the first of his image-bearers by means of his very own breath (Gen. 2:7), as he lovingly provides a garden for beauty and nourishment (2:9), and as he brings forth a companion perfectly suited for shameless, "one flesh" union (2:23–24)—and then ultimately as the Lord himself walks in the paradisal garden with the man and the woman in the cool of the day (3:8). We see it after the fall, as God sets in motion his unimaginable cosmic plan to reinstate his image-bearers: he calls Abram, he promises "a blessing to all nations," he delivers the law, he appoints a king whose offspring will rule over an everlasting kingdom, he sends prophets to warn the recalcitrant and to recall the wayward. We see it simultaneously in more personal, individual contexts, as God hears the cries of his suffering people Israel (e.g., Exod. 2:24) and responds in mercy to the individual prayers and tears of Abraham and of Hagar and of Leah and of Joseph and of Moses and of countless others. God's engagement with the world seems always to be one of loving provision for and increasingly intimate communion with his people.

Indeed, this aim on God's part helps us to see why the entrance of sin into the biblical story in Genesis 3 is so catastrophic in the first place: at exactly the point where creation should be maximally intimate with God—namely, in the glorious creature who bears God's own image and is therefore "wired" for just such communion—there begins the rebellion that removes all of creation from its exalted place of joyful *shalom*. Having cut themselves off from God, the human pair find that creation as a whole has lost its center and been thrown into chaos. *Shalom* is lost, because loving intimacy with the God of *shalom* is abandoned. This is the great tragedy of our fallen world—and it becomes the driving force in the biblical story line, as the reversal of this broken intimacy is sought. The God of *shalom* is constantly, actively, zealously in pursuit of loving communion with his image-bearers, and through them he intends to draw all things back into the living, loving wholeness that exists within the Triune God from all eternity.

The Personal Character of Redemption

Shalom is, of course, an intensely personal aim, as God himself is an intensely personal God—and for just that reason we find that God's methods are not what we might otherwise expect. If we think of the world in impersonal, mechanical terms, then we might expect that God would deal with its fallenness in a mechanical way—that is, he would repair the system by *replacing* whatever particular elements were fouling it up. Examples of this sort of mechanical repair are easy to come by in common experience. If a machine is broken, then we pull out the faulty part and put in a new one. If a football team is losing because of a weak passing game, then we get rid of the old quarterback and bring in a new one. If the decor of a room does not work, then we toss out the awful painting on the wall and hang something more fitting instead. Note that each of these examples involves the straightforward replacement of whatever is defective or troublesome. It might be difficult to find the right replacement, but the nature of the procedure is pretty obvious and direct.

But what if the aim is not mechanical repair by means of replacement but some deeper, more organic, more *personal* kind of repair—which is not really "repair" at all but is more like a kind of *healing*? This is evidently God's intention, for his redemptive work in the world follows a path that is astonishingly long and convoluted, not nearly as simple and direct as replacement would have been.

Of course, there is some replacement along the way: in Genesis 6, the world's burgeoning population of evildoers is wiped out by a great flood, so that humanity can begin anew with righteous Noah; in 1 Samuel 13:13–14, the wicked King Saul is set aside, to be replaced by David, the man after God's own heart. Yet this sort of move clearly does not solve the deeper, more personal problem that the human race faces, for both righteous Noah and godly David also fall into sin. This pattern makes it clear that no simple, direct replacement operation can really get to the heart of the *personal* problem. Some other solution is called for, some less direct, more radical penetration. The crying need for this deeper remedy is expressed in the Hebrew Scriptures in the oft-repeated longing for a *new* covenant (Jer. 31:31), one that goes deeper than the covenant with Moses, one that writes the law on human hearts rather than on tablets of stone, one that transforms hearts made of stone into hearts made of living flesh (Ezek. 11:19; 36:26). How can such a profoundly personal healing be effected?

This dramatic question prepares us for the even more dramatic Christian answer, an answer that signals our arrival at the climax of God's plan of redemption in the biblical story. How is the transformation effected? By means of that utterly unanticipated, unimaginable, one almost says *impossible* event that Christians describe as the incarnation of the eternal Word himself.

Our reflections in chapter 6 have already indicated what a paradoxical marvel the incarnation is, but we do well here to recall its shocking, almost unthinkable implications—implications far more radical than anyone in the first century expected. The Jews of the day knew that there were problems in the world: this was why they looked for God's Messiah to show God's love and favor by overthrowing the hated Roman government and setting up God's own kingdom (with God's own Davidic king) in its place. This is, once again, a kind of mechanical repair—that is, God replacing the broken part with a new, improved part. It is a fine theory, and (as we have seen) it has some biblical precedent. Unfortunately (as we have also seen), it does not go far enough.

With the Christian doctrine of incarnation, by contrast, we are thinking not of a mechanical replacement but of the profoundly personal healing of the entire cosmos. Since the problem began with humanity, the healing also is to begin with humanity—and so God himself becomes a man. Here we have not merely a message of divine love delivered to the world, not even a series of startling works of love enacted on behalf of the world. Important as messages and works may be, they still affect the world "from outside," and therefore superficially. But full-blooded Christian teaching says that, in some unimaginable way, the Lover is now *inside*. The Author of love—eternal Love himself—has now made his home in our world. The incomprehensible Communion "tabernacles" among us (John 1:14), as one of us. Something wildly new is now going on.

Christ among Us

Here is great mystery indeed. Christ really is *God*, and therefore this incarnate Love is larger than the whole universe, older than the big bang, more solid than the densest slab of granite, more alive than all that we call "living." This unthinkable Reality that is more real than the world has now muscled its way into our quiet precincts. It turns out that all of the messages and works of love were really aimed at this the whole time. All were mere preparations for this ultimate, earth-shattering encounter with Love itself.

And not mere "encounter." God's intention was never merely that we should *meet* him. He did not want to love us in the flat, prosaic, external way that creatures love one another. Instead, his plan from the beginning was to become what we are, in order to draw us into that higher Love that he himself is, the Love that is the source of all creation. We might say that the "three-dimensional" Creator was never content to commune in merely "two-dimensional" ways with his creatures. He purposed instead to stretch or inflate or expand these Flatlanders—impossibly!—into the depths of his own fullness, so that they could taste and drink and live in and become a love that the whole universe cannot contain. The fullness of Reality bursts into the shadowy realm of illusions in order that we, like the Velveteen Rabbit in the old story, might finally become *real* in a sense we had never imagined. To be real in this sense is not utterly foreign to us, for as the image of God we are made for nothing less. Yet the continuity is one we never would have guessed, for Reality itself is not natural to the world of mere images, much less to broken images such as ourselves. To enter into it is like being born all over again.

If we are thinking of the incarnation in this singular way, we are not surprised to find some otherwise-startling elements in it. In Christ, God does not step into the world with power and correct all that is wrong with it (replacement again!). Instead, he steps into the world with weakness and ends up crucified by the wrong that he confronts. Jesus conquers evil precisely by succumbing to it. Thus, love is indeed victorious, but not in the obvious, direct way we might have expected. It is victorious through gentleness and mercy rather than through power and judgment. This victory is like that of a good, wise father who, instead of confronting his angry young son's stubbornness and disobedience directly (with a sharp rebuke or a spanking), takes the boy gently on his lap and holds him, until the young body relaxes and the tension departs and the tears begin to flow. This father's aim is not merely to correct the boy's immediate external behavior: it is to form his heart with an intimacy and love that will result in long-term transformation. In pursuit of this goal, the father's methods will vary from one situation to the next. Sometimes he may very well intervene directly and effectually (e.g., with a spanking). But other times he will not, for his larger, wider goal may often call for less obvious, less direct, more deeply personal methods.

So also, in the incarnation, God bathes the world in the deep, life-changing reality of Love. The immediate effects are varied: the kingdom comes with power (witness the healings and exorcisms that fill the Gospels), yet also the King dies in weakness. In this way it is God's kindness that leads us to repentance, and our ability both to love God and to receive love from God—to enter into real Love—is intertwined and enveloped in the deep mystery of the intensely personal love at the heart of the Trinity. The coming of Christ is not just the external establishment of a political kingdom that God approves of, like David's kingdom of old. How could it be? David's greater Son is more than David himself was, and more than David had imagined. On the contrary, the coming of Christ is that perfect, full embodiment of divine Love that alone can work the marvelous healing that human sin calls for.

Furthermore, we have in Christ not only the perfect expression of *God's* love for *us* but also the perfect example of *human* love for God and neighbor. Thus, we begin to understand how the life of Christian spirituality, as an *imitatio Christi* (an "imitation of Christ"), is related to the mystery of the incarnation. For in Christ we see with our own eyes the untarnished, fully developed humanity that we are all intended to be. Christ is the consummate image of God, the new, second Adam, who is everything that the first Adam failed to be. Indeed, here we have the image of God even more fully expressed than it was in Eden, since in this case we see not just an image but God himself as he bears and displays his own image. The new Adamic DNA that is injected into creation at the incarnation is simultaneously, and in a mystery, the Creator's DNA: it is united with the Creator's own personal life. Thus, in Christ we see and are drawn into the divine Son's love for his exalted Father in the Spirit; and again, we see and are drawn into the Son's sacrificial love for his creaturely brothers and sisters. At every point, Christ makes immediately present and available that eternal intimacy that God desires and is.

Jesus's Life of Prayer

And how is this life-giving intimacy sustained? Here we attend to the other pole in the classical understanding of the incarnation: we remember that Jesus really is *human*, just as we are. As he lived and ministered in Galilee and Judea, he did not function like a divine computer; he did not possess a heavenly hard drive programmed with all the information, insight, and discernment necessary for him to think and live well as a human being. Christ was fully human, and as a human being he found it necessary to live an extremely disciplined spiritual life, with prayer as its chief cornerstone. Prayer and the constellation of spiritual disciplines surrounding its practice consistently nourished the incarnate Son's relationship with the Father, and in turn there emerged the spiritual fruit that is the natural outgrowth of this prayer-filled relationship: love, power, patience, discernment, kindness, self-control, joy, goodness—a panoply of holy qualities produced in Christ through the Spirit (see Gal. 5:22). In this way, the one who has always loved perfectly was learning to love perfectly. The incarnate Word was learning to speak to his Father, to listen to his

Father, to trust his Father, to discern his Father's guidance, sometimes in the midst of great confusion and suffering (see Matt. 27:46).

We do well to pause for a moment to reflect upon the patterns and rhythms that we see at the center of Jesus's spiritual life. We might notice, for instance, *how* Jesus prays. The language he uses—and teaches us to use—is extremely intimate and personal. Growing up as part of a faithful Jewish family, Jesus no doubt learned to pray by habitually repeating the prayers that we now know as the psalms, those inspired poems that give voice to just about every kind of emotion or desire that one might wish to express. The psalms are filled with the language of praise, intercession, complaint, query, give and take: more deeply *personal* dealings with God are hard to imagine. But Jesus goes even further, as he adopts the warm, almost private language of the nuclear family as appropriate in prayer: he addresses God constantly as "Father" (e.g., Matt. 11:25–26), occasionally even as "Abba" (see Mark 14:36), the intimate Aramaic term for "Father" or "Papa." The followers of Christ are also invited to rely on the same family language of respectful, reverent intimacy when they call upon God (see Rom. 8:15; Gal. 4:6).

Again, we might notice *when* Jesus prays. He is no frantic wonder-worker, feverishly driven from one task to another; he never seems to suffer from pastoral burnout. Why not? The Gospels tell us that both before and after times of concentrated, strenuous ministry—and occasionally right in the midst of them—Jesus would withdraw to lonely places to pray (Matt. 14:23; Mark 1:35; 6:46; Luke 5:15–16). The authors of the Gospels often purposely juxtapose Jesus's intense ministry with silence, solitude, and prayer. Luke, for example, encourages his readers to contemplate the connection between Jesus's grounding in prayer and his ability to discern his Father's will as to how he should teach and act in given situations—say, in choosing the twelve apostles (Luke 6:12–13), or in building on Peter's confession of Jesus as Messiah (Luke 9:18–20). For the incarnate Son of God, successful human living seems always to have meant living in the intimate communion that prayer affords.

Part of the invitation to Christ's followers is that we should more and more become human in the full, robust sense that Jesus displayed—which includes the patterns of prayer that sustained him. Jesus's life of prayer teaches us, among other things, that human beings are created for prayer. In prayer, we enter into the intensely personal reality of trinitarian love, just as God has always intended. As God's renewed image-bearers, we partake in God's fully actualized love as it is graciously given to us in the incarnate Son through the Spirit. When we pray, we confront and enter into that same eternal communion that Jesus expressed and sustained in his own prayers. Our lives are parallel to Christ's, because they are dependent on Christ's. In this respect, our aim as disciples is nothing but becoming what Christ is, entering personally into the intimacy with God that Christ embodies and makes possible through his life, death, and resurrection. Prayer is the anchor of that cluster of disciplines whereby we are conformed to the likeness of God's Son, thus whereby we increasingly become in concrete experience God's sons and daughters ourselves.

Here, then, we have a comprehensive picture of God's redemptive work in the world, and of the role of prayer as a crucial element in that work. Prayer, as modeled in Christ's own life, is the concrete point of contact at which intimacy with God is advanced. And intimacy with God is the center of *shalom* and the high aim of all of redemption.

Prayer and Longing

What does this line of thought suggest as we return to our question about the specific intention of our prayers? Clearly, prayer is not simply a mercenary method of getting what we want. Its aim instead is that we should become like Christ, whose intimacy with the Father we imitate. In this respect, the grand picture of redemption we have sketched seems to point toward a more subjective understanding of prayer, for it is *we ourselves* more than our circumstances that need to be transformed. To be sure, the concentration on the "self" is not quite so bad as we might have thought, insofar as prayer involves increasing *intimacy with God*, not just increasing holiness or spirituality in ourselves. Still, the ultimate goal of any prayer we pray would seem to be our likeness to Christ. Every prayer would seem to include an unspoken preface that says something like, "I trust your redemptive work in the world, O Lord, and I desire in this prayer only that I should be conformed to it. I desire not that I should get what I want, but that I should become like your Son. Not my will, but yours be done."

This is a fine prayer, one that trusts in God's sovereignty and submits to God's will. But it is also a prayer that is startlingly out of line with the model we find in Scripture. To be sure, it echoes certain sayings of our Lord, but in its refusal to make specific, concrete petitions, it departs both from Jesus's teaching and from his practice. Jesus's teaching (as we noted earlier) is chock-full of commands to *ask* in prayer: the Lord's Prayer itself includes concrete petitions like "Give us this day our daily bread" and "deliver us from evil" (Matt. 6:11, 13 KJV). And Jesus's practice also includes this element: at Gethsemane we hear not only "Not my will, but yours be done" but also "Take this cup from me!" (Luke 22:42). To entirely abandon what we want when we pray is to make ourselves more spiritual and otherworldly than Jesus himself.

The real problem with such a subjective, petitionless prayer is that our own wants are not the only thing at stake when we pray. *God himself* has wants. God desires that the world should be *objectively* changed. We have seen that the biblical revelation is built around the vision of a God who longs for intimacy with his creation and who is constantly and actively at work to remake the world into a place where that intimacy is a natural, flourishing reality. In this regard, Scripture does very little to protect those divine perfections that might prompt us simply to trust that all is well in the world. Omniscient and timeless and sovereign and immutable God may be. But he constantly indicates that the world as it is is not the world as it shall be, that the new kingdom of *shalom* will come—and God himself longs for and labors for its coming. He summons individuals like Abraham and Paul to perform concrete tasks to advance that purpose (Gen. 12:1; Acts 9:15–16); he intervenes when the Israelites are in bondage in Egypt (Exod. 3:7–10) or when Peter is in prison in Jerusalem (Acts 12:6–10), in order to push that plan forward. The whole career of Christ is built around just such a dramatic intervention: "The kingdom of God has come near," says Jesus (Mark 1:15), and both his preaching and his miracles demonstrate the kingdom commitment to concrete change and renewal of the real world here and now. His followers are called to share that commitment, not least as they pray.

These considerations require us to conclude that more is going on in prayer than mere subjective transformation. Prayer may be a spiritual exercise, but it can never be *merely* a spiritual exercise. Indeed, in light of God's comprehensive commitment to remaking the world, we could almost say that the subjectivist approach is exactly backward. Is the purpose of prayer simply that our minds should be aligned with the mind of Christ, irrespective of whether the world is actually changed as a result? By no means, for the mind of Christ is precisely a mind that *wants* the world to be changed! Should the outcome of prayer be that we are peacefully content to wait as God works out his sovereign purpose? Not at all, for part of God's sovereign purpose is that we should not be content merely to wait! The life of prayer is not intended merely to enhance our spiritual maturity, for part of spiritual maturity is the ceaseless longing for something more, for a world that is more fully and concretely reflective of God and his kingdom. God himself also longs for that "something more."

Undeniably, part of what needs to be changed is the internal state of individuals who desire to follow Jesus. In this sense, our being conformed to Christ really is a part—perhaps even the deepest part—of what God is doing in the world. But the point is that this *subjective* transformation is part of the worldwide *objective* transformation that God is unqualifiedly committed to. He is never content that either we who pray, or the world about which we pray, should be left as is. He intends real transformation in both, and he is always acting on that intention.

Growth in Humility, Growth in Boldness

So, paradoxically, the more we are conformed to Christ's likeness, the less we will be content with a view of prayer that is primarily about being conformed. The more "subjectively" our prayers are effective, the more we will desire for them to be "objectively" effective too. The more deeply we enter into the love that Christ offers and is, the more our love for the world in its present brokenness is also perfected—and thus the more we petition our Father explicitly on behalf of that world.

Of course, we will continue to offer our petitions in humility, with a constant awareness of our own shortsightedness and with a deep confidence in the Father's matchless wisdom. For this reason, we will not be surprised that the answer to some of our prayers is no, and we will receive even such negative answers with joy and praise. But this submission to God is a far cry from the sort of resignation implied by the flawed logic of the subjective view of prayer and the "anti-prayer" attributes. If we let that logic guide us, we get a picture of a God who is perfectly content with the world as it is (after all, he is sovereign) and who wants us to be content too (after all, don't we trust him?)—and thus every petitionary prayer becomes an expression of disobedience and unbelief. But no, it is precisely because prayer has brought us into the intimacy and joy of trinitarian love that we long for a transformed world just as God does. For while there is more to God than the biblical image of a loving father working hard to bring his recalcitrant children to perfection, there certainly is nothing less. With this assurance, we follow Christ in fervently longing and praying and working for change, while at the same time we trust in the Father, who guides all things according to the counsels of his own loving will.

This creative tension between longing and trusting, between boldly working for the kingdom to come and also humbly recognizing that the King already reigns, is a tricky business in the rough and tumble of our daily lives with all of their joys and sorrows. Jesus himself found it so, on at least that one extraordinary occasion to which our reflections keep returning, the midnight vigil in the garden of Gethsemane. At that dreadful moment, even the prayers offered in desperation by the well-beloved Son of God seemed to come up dry.

So let us watch as Jesus prays in the garden. As we gaze, the incarnate Word falls to his knees, begins weeping, and cries out for deliverance from the horrors facing him. What are we to make of this? In his human nature Christ is *us*, each one of us—every mother who has ever prayed for a sick child; every father who has prayed for the safe return of a son or daughter from harm's way; every person who has heard the word "cancer" and felt fear's suffocating embrace; every human being who sees suffering, horror, death on the horizon and longs to be safe, delivered, free. Jesus is *us* and offers *us* his own response in prayer as a model that can take us to the other side of our terror, our disappointment, our disillusionment, our confusion. He prays, he weeps, he asks—yet he does not receive.

Or does he? There is an astonishing text in the New Testament's Epistle to the Hebrews that seems to refer to this remarkable occasion. "During the days of Jesus' life on earth, he offered up prayers and petitions with fervent cries and tears to the one who could save him from death, *and he was heard* because of his reverent submission" (Heb. 5:7). Note well: he was heard. These really are startling words, for as we all know, Jesus did *not* receive what he asked for. The "cup" of suffering and death was not taken from him. Yet he was heard. The idea here seems to be exactly the remarkable juxtaposition that we have just referred to. In the garden, in the midst of deep agony and facing his imminent trial and death, Jesus asks for deliverance. This is real longing, real anguish—real enough that "his sweat was like drops of blood falling to the ground" (Luke 22:44). Yet, as he expresses this longing, he also submits unwaveringly to the will of his Father—the "reverent submission" that Hebrews speaks of. This is real trust, an unrelenting casting of himself into his Father's will. And as the Son of God *both* cries out *and* submits, the prayer is suddenly answered. Jesus is heard. Clarity comes. He is strengthened and can go forward with firmness (Mark 14:42). Even in *not* receiving what he asks for, the man Jesus receives just what he needs. He was heard.

We are likely to find the same in our own lives. Prayer is not a matter of abandoning our wants, but neither is it a matter of God learning from us what is best or of God submitting to our will. Learning and submission always move in the opposite direction. Prayer means longing for what we see as best and then as a result learning to discern what actually *is* best, as we cultivate an ever-deepening relationship with God and submit to the actualization of his loving will in all creation. None of us really wants our own will to be actualized on earth *at the expense* of God's will, do we? We recognize that this would be a disaster for everyone involved, since God's will is infinitely and ineffably wiser. Yet discernment remains difficult, for we seem to see the good so clearly, and we cannot imagine God seeing it any differently. We are like Peter, who saw with utmost clarity that the Messiah should not be subject to shame and death—like Peter, who had to be rebuked as "Satan" in order to be set right again (Matt. 16:22–23). Peter called for triumph, but Jesus was ready for suffering.

So too for us: we may wish for God to dance a jig, when all the while Christ is dancing a slow, sweet waltz. Discernment is like learning to hear the music God is singing into a particular situation and then willingly, lovingly joining the chorus. Yet this kind of submission to God's will does not weaken prayer; it enlivens it. As we discern how God is moving, we increasingly pray in line with God's desires, and God's love ripples through creation as a result. Un-discerning prayer is prayer that goes—oftentimes unknowingly—against the loving grain of the universe.

Following Christ into What We Truly Want

Does this put us back once again in the place of *not* praying for what we want, of simply accepting ("discerning") what God is doing? By no means. What we want is crucial to our prayers, just as submission to God's will is crucial. But it is also true that godly submission steadily purifies our wants, so that our own increasing likeness to Christ is reflected in prayers that are increasingly in accord with God's intentions.

We see the same principle at work where other kinds of growth and maturity are involved—say, in a teenage boy's developing interaction with his parents. As a child, the boy's requests were all about getting and going and doing—were all about short-range pleasures that led (at best) to secondary goods. But increasing maturity allows the boy to be less worried about immediate pleasures and to make requests that are deeper and better and wiser. Note that such requests are not likely to be *desired* any less: if anything, they will be desired *more*, for the young man now perceives their true good in a way he did not in earlier years. But this greater desire is matched by a longer perspective that appreciates *ultimate* goods more and more fully and that sees how his parents' way of achieving those goods may be complex and protracted. Indeed, precisely because he understands his parents better and trusts them more (hence because he is less dependent on having his specific short-term requests granted), for just that reason, he is more likely to make short-term requests that actually *can* be granted! Paradoxically, he can receive immediate answers more because he depends on them less.

In like manner, our prayers are constantly heard by a loving Father who desires our maturity and the increasingly intimate relationship that maturity affords. He answers our prayers (at least in part) according to our maturity. The more like Christ we become, the more our Father can answer, because the better we ourselves are learning to ask.

Our deepest longing for the world, like God's own, is for final *shalom*, and this longing should certainly shape our prayers. Yet we also recognize God's mysterious sovereignty over all things and therefore seek to trust him, and this trust will also shape our prayers. Godly maturity intensifies and perfects both impulses, and teaches us ever so gradually to live in both. The longing without the trust leads to merely objectivist prayers, in which God becomes little more than a blessing-dispenser; the trust without the longing leads to merely subjectivist prayers, in which we placidly accept as "God's will" things that God himself refuses to accept. But when longing and trust come mysteriously together, grounded in the incomprehensible God who sovereignly rules and nevertheless longs for a changed world, then prayer truly has its effect. For the life of prayer is then lived in light of the mystery of Christ, and it is then enveloped in the wider mystery of God. Our prayers are neither pretentiously manipulating God nor resignedly acquiescing to God, for God's own unfathomable reality is neither dependent on ours nor aloof from ours. The living God, the God and Father of our Lord Jesus Christ, has shown himself to be the God of our prayers too.

And so, following Christ's example and heeding his teaching, we can formulate our requests and offer our hearts' desires to God, all the while acknowledging that our desires may be self-centered, distorted, disordered, confused. We present our petitions and intercessions, trusting ourselves to God's fully actualized love, and then we wait for that love to ripple into time, to come to us in our particular place and need. We do so because Christ asks us to trust him, as he has trusted his Father. He invites us into the mystery. He beckons us to follow him to where he has always been, always is, and will always remain—in the bosom of his Father (John 1:18). Prayer is the pathway into this mystery, a mystery that is ineffably personal, thus reflecting our personal nature as God's image-bearers but also summoning us into its own transcendent, trinitarian glory. We pray, we ask, we discern, we weep, we wait. And occasionally—as the age to come manifests its glory in the midst of this present evil age—power breaks forth, love erupts, the answer comes. In light of the incarnation, we understand ever more fully that it is an answer that has always been spoken, an eternal response to our deepest needs and desires.

9

MYSTERY *and* WORLD RELIGIONS

The dogmatician who believes that in Christ "all the treasures of wisdom and knowledge are hidden" (Col. 2:3) and that God "did not leave himself without witness" (Acts 14:17) to the nations around the world will listen to the testimonies of world religions with a receptive mind and hope that by doing so he will gain, whether by their contribution or by their contradiction, a deeper understanding and interpretation of salvation in Christ.

Hendrikus Berkhof[1]

When we see Jesus eagerly welcoming the signs of faith among men and women outside the house of Israel; when we see him lovingly welcoming those whom others cast out; when we see him on the cross with arms outstretched to embrace the whole world and when we hear his whispered words, "Father, forgive them; they know not what they do"; we are seeing the most fundamental of all realities, namely a grace and mercy and loving-kindness which reaches out to every creature.

Lesslie Newbigin[2]

1. Hendrikus Berkhof, *Introduction to the Study of Dogmatics*, trans. John Vriend (Grand Rapids: Eerdmans, 1985), 49.
2. Lesslie Newbigin, *The Gospel in a Pluralist Society* (Grand Rapids: Eerdmans, 1989), 175.

We come now to a chapter that is somewhat different from what has gone before, for here we investigate the fruitfulness of divine mystery *outside* the bounds of Christian theology per se. Specifically, we wish to suggest that an appropriate understanding of God enables us to deal more effectively not only with God himself (as we worship), not only with other Christians (with whom we might agree on much but disagree on certain matters), but also with persons whose most fundamental commitments are radically different from our own. We will focus our attention in this chapter on the fundamental commitments associated with the other major world religions, but the basic principle could be applied to any outlook on life that is significantly different from the orthodox Christian perspective. And that basic principle is this: acknowledging carefully what we do know and what we do not know about God allows us to engage the entire non-Christian world more effectively. We will try to spell this idea out by looking at the relationship between Christianity and non-Christian religions.

In a sense, of course, we are still in the realm of Christian theology. There is a burgeoning academic field among Christians known as the "theology of religions," that attempts to give a reasonable account of the relationship between the various faith traditions of the world, and evangelical reflections on this matter have grown more and more sophisticated as the challenge of world religions has become more immediate.[3] The present chapter does not propose to enter very far into that highly controversial arena; especially, we shall have no wisdom to offer concerning the ongoing debate between "exclusivists" and "inclusivists" regarding whether non-Christians can be saved apart from explicit faith in Christ.[4] What we hope to do here is to consider not the possibility of *salvation* through non-Christian faiths but more generally the possibility of *truth* in non-Christian faiths, and how we ought to investigate that possibility in light of the mystery of God. Our general contention may be put in the following form: *If God is incomprehensible in the way Christianity suggests*, then Christians can learn from other faiths in genuine humility while simultaneously offering an evangelistically compelling witness to the riches of salvation in Christ.

The Problem with Mystery

Let us begin by setting the stage. For the last century or so, Christians of different kinds have adopted a whole host of widely divergent approaches to

3. For a helpful survey of the field from an evangelical perspective, see Veli-Matti Kärkkäinen, *An Introduction to the Theology of Religions: Biblical, Historical and Contemporary Perspectives* (Downers Grove, IL: InterVarsity, 2003).
4. For a constructive example of the interaction in this discussion, see Dennis Okholm and Timothy R. Phillips, eds., *Four Views on Salvation in a Pluralistic World* (Grand Rapids: Zondervan, 1996).

world religions. For the sake of simplicity, we can break them into two very rough categories: those that emphasize the *value* of non-Christian faiths as sincere human attempts to understand God, and those that emphasize the sheer *inadequacy* of any faith that does not grow out of God's revelation in Christ. The first emphasis prompts Christians to speak of *dialogue* with other belief systems, and of what Christians can *learn* from non-Christians; the second highlights the need to *challenge* other belief systems and to *evangelize* non-Christians. Generally speaking, evangelicals have followed Scripture by stressing the second of these alternatives. The high biblical commitment to evangelism and missions tends to make evangelicals suspicious of mere dialogue, since dialogue seems to suggest that believers who interact with nonbelievers are just friends exchanging ideas rather than messengers declaring a life-saving message.

In this context, it is not hard to see why appeal to "mystery" should also be regarded with some suspicion. The more vague or hazy our vision of the truth of God is, the less likely we are to proclaim it with the power and authority that it deserves and that the missionary mandate requires. As the apostle Paul asks in a different context, "If the trumpet does not sound a clear call, who will get ready for battle?" (1 Cor. 14:8). It seems evident that we must know what we are talking about if our message to the world is to be accurate and compelling and winsome, but too much attention to "mystery" seems to keep us from knowing what we are really talking about.

The fear that we might unwittingly lose the authoritative gospel message in the "mist" of mystery is well justified, at least in part. One very popular contemporary model of the relation between religious traditions is the one usually described simply as "pluralism." Advocates of religious pluralism contend that the best approach to world religions is to see them all as different, finite efforts to describe the one great Reality that is central to them all. This Reality would be known to Christians and other theistic believers as "God." But of course, according to the pluralists, everyone knows that the supreme Reality that stands behind the whole universe cannot be grasped in a mere name—in fact, cannot be formulated in human language at all. Dogmas and formulations are mere human attempts to speak the unspeakable, and so the attempts of others (say, Hindus or Muslims or Taoists) have every bit as much legitimacy as our own. By means of this pluralist logic, appeals to mystery have often gone hand-in-hand with outright rejections of what most evangelicals would recognize as the biblical gospel.

Indeed, couldn't the pattern of argument we have developed in this book, and especially here in part 2, be easily molded to serve this agenda? For example, we considered the doctrine of the Trinity in chapter 5, where divine threeness and divine oneness seem to be in conflict with one another, yet divine mystery helps us to see how both can be true simultaneously. Again (and more contentiously), we investigated in chapter 7 the intractable conflict among

Christians over divine sovereignty and human freedom, and we suggested that appeal to mystery allows us to accept both emphases as equally valid elements in a larger Christian vision. Couldn't the pluralist case regarding the major religious traditions of the world be formulated in this same way too?

It would go something like this. Christians maintain that absolute Reality is "personal"—the personal God and Father of our Lord Jesus Christ; Hindus of the Advaita school maintain that absolute Reality is "impersonal"—the ineffable *nirguna Brahman* that transcends any category, including that of personality; Theravada Buddhists declare that absolute Reality does not "exist" at all—there is no "thing" there for our minds to begin to grasp. It is, of course, very natural that Christians who have experienced the ultimate through Jesus Christ should reject with indignation the alternative accounts offered by these streams of Hinduism and Buddhism, for the Christian view and the non-Christian alternatives quite obviously conflict with one another. However, God is a "mystery," is he not? God is "transcendent" and "incomprehensible," is he not? Should we not therefore recognize, here as in the other cases, that we are dealing not with mutually exclusive alternatives but with equally valid expressions that ought to be united in a full-blown (if ineffable) vision of the Absolute? Shouldn't Christians give up their historic mission to "convert the unbelievers" and admit instead that every religion offers its own unique and equally legitimate insight into the nature of the incomprehensible God?

Mystery That Has Been Revealed

This line of argument strikes us as very plausible—indeed, as *dangerously* plausible, given its dire consequences for one's view of Christian evangelism and missions.[5] And for just that reason, we want to make clear where we think the pluralist case is right and where we think it is dead wrong.

First, the pluralist reading of mystery is right in that it takes seriously the fact that God is supremely incomprehensible. No category can do justice to the transcendent Creator, for all of our categories are conditioned by their common application to creaturely things. God is ineffable and inconceivable, and the language and concepts we employ to capture him fall immeasurably short. All of this is true.

What is *not* true is the vast parity among faiths that the pluralist paradigm goes on to demand. The Christian doctrine of revelation suggests that it is not merely *we* who decide to use certain creaturely words and concepts to describe the Creator. It is God who makes himself known, and who does so not just in ineffable experience, but in the concrete historical reality of Christ

5. For an engaging and seductively compelling presentation of the pluralist case, see John Hick, *A Christian Theology of Religions: The Rainbow of Faiths* (Louisville: Westminster John Knox, 1995).

and in the words and images of Holy Scripture. It is true that these words and images come from the pens of human authors; the vocabulary of revelation did not drop from the sky, untouched by human hand or mind. Yet it is also true that God's revelation comes from these authors by the inspiration of the Holy Spirit, who so superintends the composition of Scripture that the result can be described as *theopneustos*, "God-breathed" (2 Tim. 3:16)—the very Word of God. The inspiration of the sacred text may also involve a certain kind of mystery, for it is hard to say exactly how the Bible's divine character relates to the human character that is obviously present too. But *that* God has revealed himself in Scripture no evangelical Christian will doubt.[6] And therefore, there can be no doubt that the central themes, the chief images, the dominant conceptualities of Scripture must be ascribed not merely to creaturely ingenuity but also to the Creator's own decision. If the transcendent God chooses to adopt certain words and concepts to describe himself, we may legitimately believe that the words and concepts so selected do the job they are assigned to do.

Another way to make the same point is to revert to the terminology we have been using throughout this book. The chief error[7] of the pluralist's appeal to mystery lies in the assumption that the "mystery of God" being appealed to is an *investigative* mystery. Pluralists think the mystery that Christians acknowledge is defined by what is *unknown* and that its being *known* would obliterate the mystery altogether. This is why all attempts to describe the mystery are equally doomed to failure. It is also why all of the standard varieties of pluralism in the theology of religions are inevitably "agnostic" in character: indeed, it is precisely this agnosticism that allows them to be pluralistic. After all, if we don't know, then we don't know, and that is that.

But in fact, historic Christianity affirms that the mystery of God is a *revelational* mystery—a mystery that is defined by what we *do* know, because it has been revealed by the God who wants us to know him. It is, of course, logically possible that God's revelation could have revealed only that he was incomprehensible, only that everything we say and think falls short. This seems to be the sense in which Hinduism offers divine "revelation": the truth revealed is that all "truths" are inadequate to the Reality itself.[8] But it is of

6. Of course, others may doubt it. There is no place here for a full defense, but see the fine presentations in Benjamin B. Warfield, *The Inspiration and Authority of the Bible* (Philadelphia: P&R, 1948); James Montgomery Boice, *Standing on the Rock: Upholding Biblical Authority in a Secular Age* (Grand Rapids: Kregel, 1999); Donald G. Bloesch, *Holy Scripture: Revelation, Inspiration and Interpretation* (Downers Grove, IL: InterVarsity, 1993); Telford Work, *Living and Active: Scripture in the Economy of Salvation* (Grand Rapids: Eerdmans, 2002).

7. There may well be other errors as well. See the detailed critiques in Harold Netland, *Encountering Religious Pluralism: The Challenge to Christian Faith and Mission* (Downers Grove, IL: InterVarsity, 2001), esp. 181–246; and S. Mark Heim, *Salvations: Truth and Difference in Religion* (Maryknoll, NY: Orbis, 1995), 13–126.

8. "'Sir,' said a pupil to his master, 'teach me the nature of Brahman.' The master did not reply. When a second and a third time he was importuned, he answered, 'I teach you indeed, but you

central importance to note that God, in the Christian view, did not follow this course. On the contrary, the Christian teaching is that God is a mystery, but also that that mystery has been made known positively and uniquely in God's own Son. "Anyone who has seen me has seen the Father," says Jesus (John 14:9); or again, "No one knows the Son except the Father, and no one knows the Father except the Son and those to whom the Son chooses to reveal him" (Matt. 11:27). So Christianity insists that the Son really does reveal the Father, and that through the Son we really do know the Father. The revelation is not merely *that there is* an unknown mystery (called "God" or "Brahman" or whatever); the revelation is precisely the *making known* of the mystery. The Father is made known by the Son in the Spirit, and Holy Scripture is the inspired, apostolic account of that revelation.

Knowing and Not Knowing

This account will no doubt strike some readers as an attempt to have our cake and eat it too. They will point out that we cannot say, at one and the same time, that all words and concepts are frail creaturely things that cannot grasp God *and* that some words and concepts are better than others. But we reply, why not? A fully, richly Christian understanding of the nature of language and thought seems to push in exactly this direction.

Let us consider language first. We might be inclined to think, in accordance with conventional categories, that language must fall short of God because it is merely a human contrivance, a tool that finite creatures use to try to reach the infinite Creator. Now it is true that *if* language is "merely" a human "tool" that we "use" to "reach" the Creator, then we are bound to fall short. But historic Christianity has always hesitated over this immensely troublesome "if." The fact is, as John Frame rightly points out,[9] human language is *not* merely a human contrivance. On the contrary, Christian theology requires that there was never a time, even before the world was created, when God was without his Word; and the first words ever spoken were not the strained grunts of some prehistoric cave dwellers but the creative words of God himself, "Let there be light" (Gen. 1:3).

Language is God's invention, not ours. It may be true, as Calvin said, that God "lisps" to us when he speaks, like a mother talking baby talk to her infant child.[10] But we do well to recall that the mother is not condescending to speak some language *invented* by the baby. From the beginning, the baby is mimicking the adult talk all around; and the mother accommodates her adult

---

do not follow. His name is silence'" (from a commentary by Hindu theologian Sankara, quoted in Swami Prabhavananda, *The Spiritual Heritage of India* [Hollywood, CA: Vedanta, 1979], 45).

9. John M. Frame, *The Doctrine of the Knowledge of God* (Phillipsburg, NJ: P&R, 1987), 35.

10. John Calvin, *Institutes of the Christian Religion*, trans. Henry Beveridge, 2 vols. (Grand Rapids: Eerdmans, 1972), 1.13.1.

vocabulary to the child's level for no other reason than to initiate the child in this loving and gentle way into the very adult world of verbal communication. On this model, we can admit that human words are not God's most natural mode of communication, but they certainly are a reflection of his own eternal "speaking." And it would be no surprise if he knew best how to use them to communicate the higher realities that transcend the words themselves.

What is true of human language is true of human concepts as well. Every concept of God, taken strictly by itself as simply a human concept, will be infinitely far from the absolute reality it points to. Yet if God, who *is* that absolute reality, chooses to employ some of those limited concepts to reveal himself to the world, then we are not surprised that he can do so effectively. Though the revelation is a kind of condescension or accommodation, it is no less a genuine and credible revelation for that fact, and no less normative for us as we receive it. Human concepts cannot build us an autonomous bridge to God; but if God makes use of human concepts to reveal himself, then they certainly can do the job, for the very good reason that they are themselves created by the God who chooses to use them.

This very strong emphasis on the reliability of God's revelation sharply divides the position we are advocating here from the position of the pluralists. We want to insist, in the very strongest fashion, that we *do* know God as a result of his revelation in Christ and in Scripture, and therefore in the church. To lose that revelation, to abandon the distinctively *revelational* character of the Christian mystery, is to lose the authentic Christian gospel itself.

This is a warning worth taking seriously, especially by those who find "mystery" to be a particularly helpful or attractive category. Any avowal of mystery that is not coupled with a vigorous doctrine of revelation inevitably leads to the doorstep of the pluralists—whether we intend to go there or not. Contemporary theologian Keith Johnson makes this point trenchantly in a recent article investigating the theological work of the late William Placher. Placher was a fine theologian: it might be remembered that we commended his notion of a "radical divine transcendence" back in chapter 2 and his reading of Aquinas and Calvin in chapter 3. Yet it is true that his rhetoric occasionally gives one pause. For example, he writes in his very valuable book *The Domestication of Transcendence*, "In important ways we do not know what we mean when we talk about God."[11] Hmmm. There is much truth in this statement, but it can easily be taken in the wrong way—in a way, in fact, that would land us very quickly in a pluralist account of religious truth. After all, as Johnson asks, "If it is true that God radically transcends all human categories, then who is to say that a 'Christian' interpretation of 'God' is

---

11. William Placher, *The Domestication of Transcendence: How Modern Thinking about God Went Wrong* (Louisville: Westminster John Knox, 1996), 182, quoted in Keith E. Johnson, "Divine Transcendence, Religious Pluralism and Barth's Doctrine of God," *International Journal of Systematic Theology* 5, no. 2 (July 2003): 214.

any more accurate, correct or appropriate than a 'Hindu' interpretation?"[12] The answer obviously is, "No one."

It is unlikely that Placher himself would like this conclusion very much, but the logic holds nevertheless. How, then, can we avoid this slippery slope from transcendence into pluralism? The answer is, by holding tightly to a robustly Christian doctrine of revelation. Placher's approach *might* do this, though Johnson does not seem to be convinced. He writes: "Presumably Placher would argue that his doctrine of revelation cuts off this [pluralist implication]. *The critical question*, however, *is whether his account of revelation is robust enough* to fend it off."[13] Our point here is that this "critical question" is exactly the right one to ask, whatever the answer may be in Placher's own case.[14] Any debility at this point, in the doctrine of revelation, becomes catastrophic for the historic Christian vision of the church's mission to the world, for that mission is built (as we have seen) on the foundation of a very definite "comprehension" of the incomprehensible God.

However, when the doctrine of revelation stands firm, Christians can insist with great boldness both that God is beyond knowledge and that he has made himself known, and known as the very particular mystery that he is. We still know God *as creatures*, yet we also know God as those particular creatures *to whom he has made himself known*, and this difference is all-important. One could say that we know more than mere creatures have any right to know, because God himself has put the unspeakable reality of the Creator into the most adequate terms that creatureliness allows. Are they adequate terms for our knowledge? Certainly, for God has chosen them to reveal himself. Are they *exhaustively* adequate, so that they give complete, unqualified knowledge of the fullness of the divine? Certainly not, for God has revealed himself as the unfathomable Creator of heaven and earth, the transcendent One, who ever remains past finding out.

Two Principles for Encountering Other Faiths

So God has genuinely and fully made himself known; and God has genuinely and fully made himself known *as God*, and therefore as incomprehensible mystery. We must unceasingly emphasize the former, the fullness and adequacy of the revelation, in order to resist the lure of an agnostic pluralism; but with an equal zeal we must also emphasize the latter, the continuing incomprehensibility, in order to resist the lure of an arrogant rationalism. This creative tension has turned up repeatedly in this book, and we must now see how it helps us as we approach non-Christian religions.

12. Johnson, "Divine Transcendence," 216.
13. Ibid., italics added.
14. For Placher's treatment of revelation, see *Domestication of Transcendence*, 185–89.

How should Christians approach people of other faiths, in light of the mystery of God? We suggest two basic principles, with far-reaching implications. First, the fact that God has *revealed* the mystery in Christ and in Scripture enables us to approach those who are outside of Christ in the deep confidence that we have the very words of life. Second, the fact that God has revealed himself in Christ and in Scripture *as mystery* permits us to approach those who are outside of Christ with a genuine, humble openness to what we can learn from them.

The first of these principles is the clear and joyous implication of the revelation that we have just been discussing, and so we need not say much more about it. When God makes himself known and tells us to spread the word to all creation, to all creation we must go. However politically incorrect it may be, we are under the direct command of our Lord to make disciples of all nations, and this discipleship is not to some vague, shadowy mystery diversely expressed, but to Jesus Christ, the Galilean carpenter who was shown with power to be the Son of God. We go to the world with neither embarrassment nor timidity but with the authority of God himself to declare his message, summoning the world to the obedience of faith and commending a Savior apart from whom there is no salvation.

The second principle, on the other hand, needs further investigation, for it initially seems to be incompatible with the first. How can we go to the world with the authoritative message of God and simultaneously go to the world in order to learn what message the "gods" of the world might have for us? What need have we of learning from others if we already have the definitive revelation of God in hand? What affinity is there between Christ and Belial (2 Cor. 6:15), or between Jerusalem and Athens?

These questions are more subtle than they may first appear, for they force us to analyze with great care the relationship between the truth of Christ and the multitude of alternatives that are available in our world. Though it might surprise some readers, not much attention has been given by evangelicals to the question of what kind of truth may be present in non-Christian religions. Evangelical consideration of other faith traditions has been dominated instead by the important and difficult question of whether non-Christians may be *saved*. Of course, the amount or degree of truth in other faiths is connected to salvation, insofar as we must "know the truth" (in some sense) in order to be set free by it. But the question we are asking here is rather different. It is not whether a non-Christian faith offers enough *Christian* insight to provide the possibility of salvation to its adherents. It is instead whether a non-Christian faith offers enough genuinely *trustworthy* insight to justify Christians investigating that faith with seriousness and godly desire. The issue is not, "How much of what we know do they also know, and what is the value of their knowledge for them (i.e., can it save them)?" The issue is instead, "How much of what they know do we *not* know, and what is the value of their knowledge *for us*?"

Note that it is precisely the incomprehensible mystery of God that prompts
us to consider this issue, for that revealed mystery constantly reminds us of
how very much more we have yet to learn about the God we worship. The
acknowledgment of divine transcendence ought to foster in Christians a profound, principled humility that is *always* ready to be instructed—instructed
not because we know nothing but because what we do know points us to so
much more. The riches of God are so vast and our knowledge so shallow by
comparison that we find ourselves expecting to discover some new jewel, to see
anew the flashing brilliance of the great divine Jewel, at every moment. God's
glory is great enough that we hope to encounter it afresh everywhere we look.

Moreover, the historic doctrine of general revelation supports us in this
optimistic quest. This classical Christian doctrine affirms that God has not
only made himself known to *some* people in *some* places at *some* times (in
acts of so-called special revelation), but he has also made himself known to *all*
people in *all* places at *all* times, by means of things like the created order itself
or the human conscience. For instance, Paul declares that God has made certain
things about himself plain to absolutely everyone, for "since the creation of
the world God's invisible qualities—his eternal power and divine nature—have
been clearly seen, being understood *from what has been made*" (Rom. 1:20);
again, Paul notes that even the gentiles who do not know of God's revelation
from Mount Sinai nevertheless show "that the requirements of the law are
written on their hearts," for their consciences bear intrinsic witness to right
and wrong (Rom. 2:15).

But if God's revelation has gone out in some fashion to all people everywhere, then it should come as no great shock to find that all people everywhere possess some aspect of the truth of God. And if this is so, then why
should Christians not seek it out? Why should we not attempt to learn even
from people and cultures who have themselves had no access to the special
revelation of God in Christ?

Hesitations, Moral and Theological

"Because," the answer might be, "those without special revelation misconstrue
even general revelation, to their own destruction." This response embodies
some important theological hesitations that we shall consider in a moment.

But we would be wise to pause first to recognize one aspect of this response
that turns out to be quite problematic morally and that we should be careful
to guard ourselves against. The claim that all those who do not have special
revelation (all of *them*) are morally and intellectually bankrupt in ways that
all those who *do* have special revelation (all of *us*) are not quickly translates
into the perilous belief that one particular person with special revelation (I
myself) is morally superior to any particular person without it. In other words,

it is easy for us to persuade ourselves that, because we have the revelation, we must be holy people; and because they do not have the revelation, they must not be. But both of these outlooks are dubious.

The first, regarding our own holiness, is dubious because (as we saw in chapter 4) a large part of real spiritual growth involves coming to terms with just the reverse, that is, with our own rank sinfulness. We are *not* automatically sanctified by receiving the gospel, and the sooner we admit it, the better. The second outlook, regarding the holiness of others, is called into question by the concrete experience of just about every Christian who ever lived: we constantly encounter a goodness in non-Christians that is at least as real as our own. Indeed, this is exactly the point, or one of the points, at which the religious diversity of contemporary society leaves us most unsettled, is it not? We become aware that wisdom and maturity and virtue appear to be transcultural and transreligious phenomena.[15] Of course, not every appearance of sanctity necessarily reflects reality. But, as longtime missionary and missiologist Lesslie Newbigin puts it, "There is something deeply repulsive in the attitude, sometimes found among Christians, which makes only grudging acknowledgement of the faith, the godliness, and the nobility to be found in the lives of non-Christians."[16] We had better attend to the plank in our own eye before trying to remove a speck from the eye of others.

Yet once this ethical issue has been addressed, the theological problem remains. Isn't it true that the biblical witness presents the general revelation of God as something overwhelmingly misunderstood and even actively rejected by those outside of Christ? How then can Christians expect to learn in significant ways from non-Christian religions?

Part of our answer concerns the meaning of "learning" itself. It is certainly true that Christians cannot "learn" from non-Christians any truth that either overthrows or parallels the truth made known to us in Christ. This is an important point to make, because contemporary pluralism demands that we be ready to learn from other faiths in precisely this sense—that is, without making Christian truth a final, authoritative grid for judging the validity of other religious truth claims. Pluralist Paul Knitter, for example, asserts that "any method for a theological understanding of religions that insists on Christian tradition (the Bible for Protestants, the magisterium for Catholics) as the only or the final criterion of religious truth seems to blind or at least blur the Christian's vision of what the other religions are saying. It prevents a real listening, without which authentic dialogue collapses."[17]

15. Paul J. Griffiths, *Problems of Religious Diversity* (Malden, MA: Blackwell, 2001), 78.
16. Newbigin, *Gospel in a Pluralistic Society*, 180.
17. Paul F. Knitter, *No Other Name? A Critical Survey of Christian Attitudes toward the World Religions* (Maryknoll, NY: Orbis, 1985), 91. Renowned pluralist Raimundo Panikkar describes a readiness to learn in this way as one of the "rules of the game" in genuine interreligious dialogue: each participant must enter into the dialogue "without prejudices and preconceived solutions, knowing full well he may in fact have to lose a particular belief or particular religion

But if Knitter is right, then "authentic dialogue" is an impossibility, at least for those who are genuinely committed to historic Christianity. No one who has sworn allegiance to the Son of God can legitimately step back into the supposedly neutral state of mind that would allow *every* commitment to be challenged. Indeed, anyone who believes in *any* particular religious tradition—Christian or otherwise—will hold that that particular tradition is true in some exclusive sense, and to be required to abandon this commitment in order to talk seriously with others is outrageous. Certainly for Christians, to "learn" in this sense would be quite simply to abandon the bold, confident witness that the Spirit requires and enables and that we have already noted as the first principle for applying mystery to our approach to world religions in a faithfully biblical fashion.

So we do not expect to "learn" a new gospel, or to "learn" facts that would plainly undermine the gospel (such as the "fact" that Jesus was not truly crucified, as many Muslims believe). To be open to "learning" of this sort is to be uncommitted to the mystery of God as it has been revealed in Christ, and this is simply unacceptable. But such uncommitted neutrality is not necessary for every kind of "learning." Let us consider some other kinds.

For example, we might think about the learning of basic, uncontroversial public facts that we simply had not previously been aware of. Is it legitimate for Christians to be open, or even eager, to learn from non-Christians in this sense? Of course it is. A Christian who did not know that Hindus of the Vishishtadvaita school are monotheistic is surely not to be faulted for allowing that fact to enter into his or her consciousness, or for letting it enter in through a lecture that happens to be presented by a Hindu rather than by another Christian. To learn about Hinduism from a Hindu, or by inspecting Hinduism itself, would seem to be the most reliable way to learn, since it gets us closest to firsthand data. Openness to non-Christian faiths in this sense seems to be no problem at all for Christians.

Learning about Spiritual Truth?

What about learning from other religions on a deeper level, learning about God or other spiritual or theological matters? Should we be open in this area? Do non-Christians possess spiritual truths that we might find helpful or edifying? We may have to unpack this idea a bit more carefully.

Contemporary theologian Gerald McDermott suggests that most of what we would ordinarily call "learning" in the theological sphere involves "seeing

---

altogether. . . . He enters unarmed and ready to be converted himself. He may lose his life—he may also be born again" ("The Rules of the Game," in *Faith Meets Faith*, Mission Trends, ed. Gerald H. Anderson and Thomas F. Stransky [Grand Rapids: Eerdmans, 1981], 5:113, quoted in Terrance L. Tiessen, *Who Can Be Saved? Reassessing Salvation in Christ and World Religions* [Downers Grove, IL: InterVarsity, 2004], 455).

old things in new ways" more than "seeing entirely new things."[18] He points out three particular ways that such learning often takes place, each one illustrated by a development in the history of Christian thought:

1. We might learn through a *shift in emphasis*, as when Luther called attention to selected elements in the Augustinian view of salvation and ended up with a "new" or deeper understanding of justification.
2. We might learn by viewing things from a *different perspective*, as when his Aristotelian "lenses" allowed Aquinas to draw medieval Christianity into a deeper, fuller synthesis.
3. We might learn by recognizing a *further implication* of what we already know, as when fourth-century Christians articulated a formal doctrine of the Trinity that was implied in the New Testament but had not been brought to light.[19]

These three ways of learning may very well interpenetrate: recognizing an implication may lead to a shift in emphasis, which in turn may invite a new perspective that has fresh implications of its own. So the important point here is what these three ways of learning have in common, namely, their connection to *what is already known*. In each case, the insight gained involves neither a wholesale rejection of what had previously been accepted nor the embracing of radically new and different ideas, but an enhancement or refining or enriching of the truth already grasped. In other words, most learning is not simply starting from scratch. Instead, it is the kind of deeper understanding that comes when something unexpectedly triggers a fresh insight into what we already know.

So can we, as Christians, "learn" in this sense from other faiths? The answer appears to be yes, in at least three different arenas.

First, in the *personal* arena, it seems clear that Christians can and do often profit from the insights or perspectives or achievements of non-Christians, and there is no reason to limit that profit so that it comes only from non-Christians who do not espouse some particular non-Christian faith. If we can be impressed and instructed even in some limited way by the courage of an atheistic army officer or the skill of a secularistic surgeon or the eloquence of a religionless professor, so also can we appreciate and learn from a Muslim neighbor's devotion to prayer or a Jain friend's commitment to the value of all living things or a Baha'i correspondent's dedication to the unity of all of humanity. Whatever one's comprehensive religious convictions may be, no

18. Gerald R. McDermott, *Can Evangelicals Learn from World Religions? Jesus, Revelation and Religious Traditions* (Downers Grove, IL: InterVarsity, 2000), 14. See also the interesting discussion of how "cognitive structures" undergo "modification" in Julius Lipner, "Philosophy and World Religions," in *Philosophy of Religion: A Guide to the Subject*, ed. Brian Davies (Washington, DC: Georgetown University Press, 1998), 321–22.

19. McDermott, *Can Evangelicals Learn from World Religions?*, 14–17.

one simply *is* a set of religious convictions, and for this reason people with erroneous convictions can sometimes display remarkable virtue and insight, just as people with truthful convictions can often display astonishing malice and stupidity. It is no surprise, then, to find real wisdom and real virtue in adherents of other faiths (or in adherents of no faith at all), and to find ourselves able as a result to see God more clearly or to follow him more closely.

Second, in the *cultural* arena, many, many Western Christians report that their exposure to cultural contexts vastly different from that of typical Western Christianity has been deeply enriching for them: they have "learned" a great deal from alien cultures. It is not hard to see why. The forms and emphases, the strengths and weaknesses, of any particular account of Christian truth are always profoundly influenced by the culture in which one lives. The gospel is always expressed in the "clothing" of some particular culture; or, to change metaphors, the gospel is always perceived through the "lenses" that a particular culture provides. For just this reason, Western missionaries in our day strongly emphasize practices of "contextualization" and "enculturation," in order to separate the authentic gospel message from its standard Eurocentric expression, and to present it instead in a way that fits naturally into the cultural context where it is being preached. The conviction behind this effort is that every human culture, at its best, can and should embody the gospel in its own authentic way. Cultural diversity is a gift in the same way individual diversity is, and the beauty of Christ is rich enough to be perceived and expressed distinctively in every culture on our planet.

But if it is true that we always naturally perceive the gospel through the lenses of the culture we inhabit, then we will not be surprised to find that there are some points at which our own grasp of the fullness of Christian truth is incomplete because of cultural limitations. Even at its very best, one's home culture offers only a single window through which to behold a mystery whose every aspect is worth adoring. But in actuality, no culture is ever at its unfallen best, and so our culture-specific vision of God will inevitably be weak or restricted in some fashion. It is not so weak or restricted that we cannot boldly preach the message, for God's strength is perfected in our weakness, and the infinite value of the priceless treasure is not at all reduced by the brokenness of the vessel that contains it. Still, we must recognize that, for example, we who are American Christians will often have imbibed "Americana" right along with our Christianity. Some of that Americana will no doubt help us to see the gospel better than we otherwise would; but some of it will also keep us from seeing as clearly as we might. Again, this is no surprise: it is another way of acknowledging the very mundane fact that we have much to learn, that there are many points at which our understanding of the truth of God can be improved or enhanced. This is true of each of us as individuals, for we are all finite and broken; and it is true as well of our cultures, for they also are finite and broken.

For this reason—although (as we saw above) we should not be open to purported theological truths or perspectives that overthrow or correct Christianity rightly understood—Lesslie Newbigin is surely right to acknowledge that what he refers to provocatively as "*my* Christianity" may very well need to be overthrown or corrected through contact with other cultures not subject to the same areas of blindness.[20] In the same way that we as individual Christians need each other in the body of Christ, in order to make up for one another's weaknesses and to complement one another's strengths, so also we as *enculturated* Christians need each other, and for exactly the same reason. Each culture will boast strengths that allow it to be the best medium for seeing some aspect of the glory of God, and each will betray weaknesses that require the support of others. As Sri Lankan evangelist and theologian Ajith Fernando states, we are inevitably subject to all sorts of hindrances in our own culture that make our vision of God "biblically defective" in one way or another, while these same blind spots are not present in the same way or to the same degree in a different culture.[21] As we encounter that alien culture and begin to see through its lenses, our vision of Christ can expand in fresh, new ways, which complement and advance the understanding of Christ that captured our hearts in the first place.

Third, in the distinctively *religious* arena, can Christians genuinely "learn" from other faiths? Are there elements in non-Christian religions themselves that might be profitable or edifying? We will look at this question from a historical perspective in just a moment, but a preliminary look at the deep interpenetration between religion and culture certainly hints at an affirmative answer. We noted above how thoroughly religion is influenced by culture, but the reverse is obviously true as well. Every culture naturally asks religious questions and is shaped by religious answers; no culture is sheerly uninterested or detached from spiritual life. In this respect, one could almost define religion as that point at which cultural energy is particularly focused on spiritual matters. This line of thinking suggests that alien religions may be able to offer the same sort of helpful vantage points to Christians that alien cultures offer. If the way non-Christian cultures naturally "see" can be instructive, then it is no great leap to think that the way those cultures naturally see *God* may also have value. Non-Christian reflection on God might be an important (though not an inspired) source of "triangulation" for Christian vision.

Of course, we need not—indeed, we *ought* not—accept non-Christian perspectives uncritically: all must be brought into subjection to Christ. But the point is that non-Christian religious insight need not be rejected simply because it is non-Christian. It may well provide a new and unanticipated angle

20. Lesslie Newbigin, *The Open Secret: An Introduction to the Theology of Mission*, rev. ed. (Grand Rapids: Eerdmans, 1995), 188. See also 182, 186.
21. Ajith Fernando, *The Christian's Attitude toward World Religions* (Wheaton: Tyndale, 1987), 112.

from which to marvel more deeply at, or to live more faithfully in, the mystery of God that we already know in the face of Christ. In this way, attention to mystery really can create in believers a genuine and fruitful openness to the possibility of learning from adherents of other faiths, *without* compromising the finality of the gospel message.

Alien Sources, Edifying Truth

If advocating openness in this fashion sounds like a novel proposal, it is worth recognizing that the people of God have been faithfully involved in exactly this kind of learning project throughout Christian history. Once one begins to look, one finds everywhere the phenomenon of God enhancing or deepening his people's vision by means of tools provided by those who are not his people. From imaginative resources and intellectual frameworks to cultural emphases and spiritual practices, God has often employed countless diverse aspects of non-Christian religion and culture as the means through which he informs and instructs his people.

We have space here to give only a brief sampling of the many realms in which this kind of learning has taken place. We begin with Scripture itself. It is not at all uncommon to find in the Word of God the inspired and edifying use of practices (like circumcision), terms (like the divine name *El*), literary structures (like the poetic form of Ps. 104), ideas (like the wisdom sayings in Prov. 22:17–24:22), and so on that clearly originated outside the Jewish-Christian world.[22] Of course, the inspired use of a source does not entail that the source itself is inspired. The point here is not to suggest some "proto-revelation" that is deeper or prior to the biblical revelation itself. Rather, we simply observe that as the inspired authors were guided by the Holy Spirit, they freely employed concepts and practices that they had learned in pagan religious and cultural contexts and invested them with new and deeper meaning. The non-Christian material was not wholly bankrupt. When we step outside the pages of Scripture and into the church's reflection on Scripture, we encounter even more plainly the same basic pattern: the constructive, edifying adoption and adaptation of insights, images, and examples gleaned from alien sources. The spiritual or theological significance of what is learned from these sources varies widely.

Sometimes what is learned has only a quite indirect theological significance. Contemporary philosopher of religion Paul Griffiths points, for example, to the way that mainstream Christian teaching has been influenced by the work

22. Many of the examples in this section are taken from McDermott, *Can Evangelicals Learn from World Religions?*, 73–90, which presents a substantial chapter of biblical illustrations of the profitable use of sources outside of the Judeo-Christian revelation, including extended references to detailed scholarly discussion.

of scientists regarding the size and structure of the solar system, or by the work of political theorists regarding the value of democratic self-rule. The church, he says, has been "prompted to formulate and teach what it has not previously formulated and taught by coming to know of truths discovered and taught by those outside its boundaries."[23]

We come a bit closer to the spiritual or theological realm when we consider moral insights and practices of non-Christians that have been adopted by Christians. The most obvious contemporary example is that of Martin Luther King Jr., whose leadership in the struggle for racial equality in America was, in his own words, "deeply influenced" by the philosophy of nonviolence articulated by Mahatma Gandhi.[24] King learned from Gandhi not in a way that overturned his Christian faith but in a way that enriched and nourished it. The same pattern could also be detected among ancient Christians. For instance, Eastern Orthodox priest John Garvey recounts the story of early Christian monks who recognized the voice of God in the spiritual admonition they received from a local pagan priest and were "filled with admiration" as a result.[25]

Closer still to the explicitly theological realm is the Christian use of non-Christian philosophical insights and categories. McDermott observes how very often Christian theologians have "plundered the Egyptians" by borrowing from and refashioning non-Christian traditions in the service of biblical truth. Thus, Augustine of Hippo made extensive use of the thought of pagan philosophers Plato and Plotinus; Thomas Aquinas found a baptized but still robust philosophy of Aristotle to be deeply enlightening; John Calvin owed a great debt to his classical training in the tradition of Renaissance humanism; Karl Barth built upon certain aspects of modern existentialism.[26] Of course, as with the biblical examples we have noted, all of these cases illustrate not just how Christians *learn from* non-Christian philosophies but also how the gospel *transforms* those philosophies in the light of Christ. In each case, the non-Christian conceptuality was not just passively accepted but was also converted, so that it became a distinctive means by which the reality of God in Christ could be declared afresh. Thus, Christian theological reflection was (and still is) aided and advanced by the categories and insights of alien communities. The overflowing richness of the divine mystery allows even the revealed truths of the biblical tradition to abide creative exploration so that they can be fruitfully comprehended in these new and unexpected ways.

23. Griffiths, *Problems of Religious Diversity*, 63.
24. See the short clip of original footage of an interview with Dr. King at www.youtube.com/watch?v=PQayMdP79cg. See also Clayborne Carson, ed., *The Autobiography of Martin Luther King, Jr.* (New York: Warner Books, 1998), 67–68.
25. John Garvey, *Seeds of the Word: Orthodox Thinking on Other Religions*, Foundations 2 (Crestwood, NY: St. Vladimir's Seminary Press, 2005), 87.
26. McDermott, *Can Evangelicals Learn from World Religions?*, 121–24, 124–29, 129–32, and 109, respectively.

Learning from Alien Religions

Contemporary Welsh theologian Stephen Williams helps us to take the next step. If it is legitimate to "make theological use of an ontological insight that Plato possessed or conceptual distinctions that Aristotle offered," then "there seems no barrier . . . to the use of Indian or Far Eastern ideas in Christian theology"—even if these ideas come from "'religions' rather than from . . . 'philosophies.'"[27] Of course, religion and philosophy are not always easy to distinguish, especially outside the secularized Western context. But even if the two can be distinguished, it is hard to see what would make "religious" insights utterly worthless if "philosophical" insights have sometimes proven so valuable. Both refer to comprehensive systems that include elements related to the existence of God or the gods, the nature of the cosmos, the significance of humanity, the relationship between good and evil, the possibility of escape from evil, and so forth. The evident usefulness of non-Christian reflection in philosophy seems to argue strongly for the possibility of our "learning" from non-Christian religions too.

Moreover, many contemporary evangelicals explicitly acknowledge how non-Christian religious thought and practice have benefited them, or could benefit Christian theology in general. Testimonials on a relatively popular level are very easy to come by, as when evangelist Ajith Fernando strongly expresses a certain admiration for the "meditative, devotional reverence" of Hinduism, a reverence that is so often absent from the "defective Christianity" of the West with its instrumental, pragmatic attitudes, for instance, toward the natural world;[28] or as when Mennonite ethicist Duane Friesen recounts how encounter with African traditional religions helped to sensitize believers "to the issue of spiritual powers and healing in the New Testament—aspects they had overlooked in their one-dimensional 'scientific' Western culture."[29]

But a look at more scholarly, systematic investigations of other faiths by evangelicals yields similar results. For example, evangelical missiologist and seminary president Timothy Tennent, devoted though he is to the evangelization of India, identifies "several ways in which [Hindu theologian and philosopher] Śaṅkara's writings about theism in the Hindu context have helped me as an evangelical Christian": notably, "Śaṅkara reminds me of how much

27. Stephen Williams, "The Trinity and 'Other Religions,'" in Kevin J. Vanhoozer, ed., *The Trinity in a Pluralistic Age: Theological Essays on Culture and Religion* (Grand Rapids: Eerdmans, 1997), 29. Williams goes on to note, also quite rightly, that the adoption of concepts or insights from an alternative religious framework "does not entail that Advaitic Hindus or Yogacarin scholars are having an experience of God, still less a saving one" (29).
28. Fernando, *The Christian's Attitude toward World Religions*, 112–13.
29. Duane Friesen, "The Discernment of Wisdom in the Encounter between the Christian Faith and People of Other Religious Faiths," *Mission Focus: Annual Review* 8 (2000): 129, quoted in Tiessen, *Who Can Be Saved?*, 435.

evangelicals have neglected the aseity of God in our theologizing."[30] Again, Tennent considers the work of eleventh-century Hindu theologian Rāmānuja, expressing appreciation for Rāmānuja's "emphasis on our utter dependence upon God," and then adds, "Western Christianity, with its emphasis on individuality, could benefit from a reminder of our dependence on God for our very existence and of our connectedness to one another."[31] Perhaps most provocatively, Tennent devotes a full chapter to the highly contextualized Indian Christian theology of Brahmabandhav Upadhyay, a chapter bearing the intriguing title "Can the Hindu Upanishads Help Us Explain the Trinity?"—a question that Tennent chooses not to answer but one that seems to stir in him a cautious sympathy.[32]

Gerald McDermott's award-winning book *Can Evangelicals Learn from World Religions?* is written in a similar vein. McDermott devotes four full chapters to discussion of how concepts in Buddhism, Taoism,[33] Confucianism, and Islam, respectively, shed new light on Christian understandings of God, self, ethics, discipleship, prayer, public life, and so on. For instance, Buddhist doctrines of "no-self" or "no-mind," which appear, for casual critics, to do nothing more than make the ridiculous assertion that "I do not exist," actually do *much* more, according to McDermott. These doctrines, rightly understood, can help us (i.e., evangelicals) guard against the presumption that our thoughts can capture God's being; they can help sharpen our understanding of the radical contingency of all the created order; they can refresh our sense of awe before the mystery of every moment; and they can help us comprehend both our fallen nature and how the life of Christ transcends it.[34]

This impressive list of achievements should in no way be taken to imply that Buddhists do not need to hear and respond to the gospel, but it does strongly indicate that Christians can humbly learn from Buddhists even as we seek to evangelize them.

It is true that Christians could learn many of the general lessons mentioned here through a deeper immersion in our own tradition as easily as through encounter with non-Christian faiths. The fact that we *could* learn from one source, however, does not necessarily mean that we *should not* learn from another, particularly if our encounter with other religious traditions seems inevitable. Besides, there may be particular lessons—particular perspectives,

30. Timothy C. Tennent, *Christianity at the Religious Roundtable: Evangelicals in Conversation with Hinduism, Buddhism, and Islam* (Grand Rapids: Baker Academic, 2002), 47. "Aseity" refers to God's self-existence, his utter freedom from dependence upon anything else as source or origin.

31. Ibid., 55.

32. Says Tennent, "The fact that the church is now predominantly non-Western makes the kind of work by Upadhyay and other non-Western Christians impossible to ignore. We need a more vigorous discussion concerning the viability of these efforts" (ibid., 228).

33. Note that this well-known Chinese faith is also commonly spelled "Daoism"—and it is this spelling that McDermott relies on (as we shall see below).

34. McDermott, *Can Evangelicals Learn from World Religions?*, 155.

particular emphases, particular expressions—that simply do not have Christian counterparts, or at least not in any sense that would make the alien lesson redundant. McDermott notes, for instance, that

> there is nothing precisely like the Daoist *wu-wei* [Chinese for "not doing"] in Christian thought. There are similar notions in Christian mysticism but few that I know of that have quite the pungency of Lao Tzu and Chuang Tzu's admonitions to do nothing. It was through their words . . . that I came to a new depth of understanding of human inability and God's sovereignty."[35]

Note that McDermott's comment here reflects no watered-down, syncretistic Christian-Taoist amalgam. It is instead a full-bodied, traditionally Christian vision of God and humanity—and one that has been informed and enriched by its encounter with Taoism.

To repeat, it remains absolutely true that Taoists (and other non-Christians) still desperately need the gospel. *Wu-wei* is not a substitute for Jesus Christ, and from the vantage point of full-blown Christianity, even the most helpful insight will prove to be off the mark in various respects. But from the vantage point of full-blown Christianity, it may also prove to be *on* the mark in certain respects—and in respects that are apparent *only* from the perspective a non-Christian vantage point offers. Calvin commented that it is only by wearing the "spectacles" of Holy Scripture that fallen human beings can perceive the glories of nature aright,[36] and this image may be an apt one here too. The "spectacles" of Christian revelation put Christians in a position to perceive the true profundity and power of ideas that originate elsewhere. We dare not become patronizing or cocky from this lofty vantage point, for we also are sinners, and our use of the "spectacles" is not nearly so error-free as we would like to suppose. Nevertheless, the actual value of every insight will ultimately be perceived only in the full light of Christ. Hence McDermott remarks, "Just as Christians saw more in Judaism than Pharisees did, Christians can see things in other religions that devotees of the religions have missed."[37] When God reveals himself in Christ, everything looks different as a result.

Correcting Christian Truth?

So significant is the Christian revelation of God, and the revelation of God as mystery, that we might even want to consider the possible value of non-Christian claims that seem to *contradict* Christian faith. This is dangerous

35. McDermott, *Can Evangelicals Learn from World Religions?*, 208. He adds in a footnote that the spiritualities of Meister Eckhart and Margaret Porette might be parallel, though these can hardly be construed as household names in evangelical circles.

36. *Institutes* 1.11.1.

37. McDermott, *Can Evangelicals Learn from World Religions?*, 117–18.

ground, for a false step into some blathering nonsense about "all religions saying the same thing" or "no real difference between truth and falsehood" would be an unmitigated disaster. But, as always, there is a real danger in the opposite direction too. The danger is that believers enthusiastic about the truth of God tend to forget that the truth of God *as they perceive it* is never quite the pure, undefiled thing that we would like it to be. Remember Newbigin's warning from a few pages back about the hazards of what he calls "*my* Christianity." While God's revealed truth needs in no way to be corrected by anyone or anything, there may be all sorts of ways in which *my particular grasp* of the truth needs to be challenged and refined. Whenever we think about God, and especially when we think *truly* about God, we inevitably risk substituting for God himself our "true thoughts" about him.

Of course, we all recognize the problem when we think about it. The God who is "inconceivable" is, by strict necessity, far greater than even the truest of our true concepts. The God who is "past finding out" always exceeds whatever it is we have found. To appeal once again to the imagery of Flatland, the three-dimensional object is inevitably more than any two-dimensional sketch or photo can show—and with a "more" that a two-dimensional thinker cannot grasp, however accurate the photo may be. If a grandmother pulls a photo out of her purse and says, "Look, here is my new grandson," none of us pauses to marvel at how thin the child is—so thin, in fact, that if we turn him sideways we cannot see him at all! Why? Because we know that the paper-thinness that we see before us is a function of the photograph, not a characteristic of the child. We mentally adjust to take into account the lack of a third dimension in the photo, and we adjust so quickly that we are not even aware that we are adjusting. But a Flatlander cannot make this mental adjustment. However perfect the photo may be at representing the child in two dimensions (perhaps Grandma will exclaim, "This is the best photo ever!"), the Flatlander who clings to the photo as an exact representation of the child will inevitably go astray.

In a similar way, the ideas we have of God, even ideas rooted in divine revelation, always point beyond themselves. Indeed, they are accurate precisely *to the extent* that they point beyond themselves. The concepts we have, even the most orthodox, are penultimate rather than ultimate, the means rather than the end, a two-dimensional picture rather than the living, three-dimensional reality itself. Hence, we must cling to the revealed ideas and images; yet if we cling to them in the wrong way, as though the ideas and images were indistinguishable from the reality itself, we unwittingly cling to what *is not* God. And "clinging to what is not God" is one very simple definition of idolatry.

But exactly here it may be that certain non-Christian or even anti-Christian doctrines can perform the great service of reminding Christians of this danger. Like the reflections we pursued on the holiness (i.e., the radical "otherness") of God in chapter 2, or like the apophatic emphasis that we saw in early Christianity in chapter 3, or like the uncomfortable insights of contemporary postmodernism that we noted later in chapter 3, certain non-Christian claims may be able to help us get at the truth of God precisely by challenging conventional "truths" that Christians have become a bit too cozy with.

Here is an example. It is commonly thought that one of the watershed issues that divides the truth of Christ from many Eastern alternatives is the issue of divine personality. God has revealed himself in Scripture and in Christ in unambiguously personal terms, and so when other faiths *deny* divine personality, they run afoul of this plain Christian truth. It seems that this is a case where you simply have to choose one side or the other: yes or no, right or wrong, personal or impersonal.

But is it really so clear? It is undeniable that God's revelation shows him to be personal, and therefore Christianity affirms divine personality to the highest degree. Yet the *very* highest degree—that is, as "personal" rightly describes God's own being, as known only to God himself—is well beyond our frail sight. The mystery of God far outstrips the category of "personality" as we normally understand it. In fact, the trinitarian claim that God is *intensely* or *exponentially* personal (as we were describing it in chapters 4 and 5) is one way of recognizing our limitation, one way of setting our ordinary understanding of personalness in proper perspective. If we cling to *mere* personalness, then we are quickly pressed into one or another of the classic trinitarian heresies. For we know what a "person" is, and you can't be one and also three of *those* at the same time—and therefore we inevitably ask (perhaps unconsciously), "Well, is God *really* one person, or *really* three?"

But orthodox Christians know that that kind of thinking will not work, that it domesticates the truth about God's "personality" rather than submitting to it. Of course we need not—we dare not—cast aside the revelation: if God has chosen personal categories for his own self-description, then the ultimacy of personal categories is established. "Personal" is, by God's own express pledge, the *best* way that creatures can think about God. But it is still *creatures* doing the thinking, and so it is good for us to be occasionally pushed beyond mere personalness. We are pushed in this direction sometimes by revelation itself, as when we remember that God has shown himself to be not just personal but also incomprehensibly, *tri*-personal; we are similarly pushed by the Christian apophatic tradition to remember that God is always ineffably different from what we mean by "personal."

Might it be possible to take, say, Buddhism's outright denial of ultimate personality in this same way, as a kind of corrective against our natural tendency to domesticate the revelation of God? Can we be profitably pushed by Buddhists to remember that a God who is "personal" in the ordinary sense (or who even "exists" in the ordinary sense) is not *really* the ultimate that we seek? It is a surprising idea: to think that our Buddhist friends may inadvertently be provoking us to think more Christianly about the Trinity! But note that they do it not by instructing us in some concept that is better and higher than personhood (there is no such thing, for God has revealed himself as personal), but by shocking us into remembering just whom we are talking about. McDermott observes, "We evangelicals sometimes regard God idolatrously as a bigger version of ourselves. The Buddhist traditions, in a way not completely dissimilar to Barth and Isaiah, admonish us to recognize that . . . we are creatures and He is the Creator."[38]

Again, this is dangerous ground. Someone will perhaps ask: "Wait—how is this acknowledgment of 'value' in claims that 'contradict' the Christian revelation different from the pluralist position that you rejected earlier in this chapter? Pluralism insists that every concept is inadequate, and it therefore sets the Christian claim that ultimate reality is personal right alongside the Buddhist claim that ultimate reality is not personal, recognizing a certain sort of 'penultimate' truth in both. How is your scenario different?"

This is an excellent question, and the answer is this: pluralism requires that both Buddhist and Christian claims are penultimate *in the same sense*. Both are limited, both are incomplete—and therefore they are entirely parallel to one another, with neither able to boast any priority or precedence of any kind. They are "different" claims, but neither is "better" than the other. By contrast, our proposal is one that very happily grants priority and precedence to God's revelation in Christ. The truth of God has been expressed by God himself in human terms. This does not remove the mystery, for the terms are still human, and if we affirm them *merely* as human terms, then we inevitably go wrong. In the face of divine mystery, every mere statement, every mere concept, falls away into silence: as Aquinas said, it is all like straw.[39]

But when we acknowledge our weakness and let the revelation of God point beyond itself to the incomprehensible God therein revealed, we are on a path that leads to glory. The value of non-Christian claims is in rightly challenging us when we stray off that path. In no way are the two sets of claims equally valuable or equally authoritative, for the one has its own final value, while the other boasts solely an instrumental value. The one affirms the truth of God in the fullest way it can be affirmed; the other reminds us along the way that God himself is greater than every affirmation. To employ another image from C. S. Lewis,[40] the one is like a good, refreshing drink of water that nourishes us, while the other is like a mouthwash that rinses out what is not so good or so nourishing.

38. McDermott, *Can Evangelicals Learn from World Religions?*, 139. See also Garvey, *Seeds of the Word*, 121.

39. See Josef Pieper, *The Silence of St. Thomas: Three Essays*, trans. John Murray and Daniel O'Connor (New York: Pantheon, 1957), 40.

40. Walter Hooper makes reference to Lewis's conversational use of this image in the introduction that is included in C. S. Lewis, *Present Concerns* (San Diego: Harcourt Brace Jovanovich, 1986), 7.

Prospects—and Warnings

By taking divine mystery seriously, we have come a long way from the simple affirmation that "Christianity is true, and therefore other outlooks, and especially other religions, are false." In a sense, the movement beyond this simple formula has been forced upon us by the complications of a twenty-first-century world, a world in which Christian faith will not be insulated from encounter with a wide variety of long-lived, ardently held alternatives. But this encounter should not strike us as unfortunate, for it is the long-awaited outcome of the ancient Christian vision of taking the gospel to the very ends of the earth.

At the ends of the earth, we find tremendous, desperate need of that gospel, with much error and distortion that must be overcome. But we also find new expressions of wisdom that may be able to challenge our own inadequate grasp or application of the Christian truth. In such a diverse world, as Pentecostal theologian Amos Yong observes, evangelicals must guard at every turn against any "irresponsible religious syncretism," but we must also be prepared "to ask what the gospel might look like if its primary dialogue partners are not Plato, Aristotle, Kant, Hegel, or Whitehead, but rather the Buddha, Confucius, Lao-tzu, Chuang-tzu, Nagarjuna, Shankara, Ramanuja, Chu Hsi, Dogen, Wang Yang Ming, and so on."[41] Addressing this complex question appropriately will require great wisdom and great discernment, so that neither the confident boldness of our witness nor the humble genuineness of our inquiry is compromised. But the whole world, including ourselves, stands to profit wondrously from this new work of God. As Timothy Tennent put it in a recent address, "This is an exciting day to [be] hammering away in God's theological workshop."[42]

The bulk of this chapter has pointed to the need for continuing, humble inquiry in light of the transcendent mystery of God. Perhaps we can summarize by offering a very brief, single-sentence response to some of the apprehensive questions we encountered earlier in the chapter.

- How, we asked earlier, can we go to the world with the authoritative message of God and simultaneously listen for the message the "gods" of the world have for us? We answer: we are not listening for the gods of the world, but for the one true God, whose glory has been declared by the very heavens to all nations (Ps. 19:1), the very God whose gospel we also proclaim.
- Why should we seek to learn from unbelievers when we already have the definitive revelation of God in hand? We answer: no one on earth

41. Amos Yong, *Beyond the Impasse: Toward a Pneumatological Theology of Religions* (Grand Rapids: Baker Academic, 2003), 189–90.
42. See "The Translatability of the Christian Gospel," available at http://timothytennent .com/?s=upanishads.

has the transcendent God or the revelation that reveals him "in hand";
We make known the normative message, but the glory is refracted
anew everywhere it shines.

- What likeness is there between Christ and Belial, or between the things
of God and the things of the world? When Paul asks this question
in 2 Corinthians 6:15, his implied answer is, none whatsoever—and
for just that reason we must be very slow indeed to cast aside as
demonic anything that gives unexpected testimony to the presence
and activity of the living Christ.

At each one of these points, we find that the glorious mystery of God is so
surpassingly great that we cannot afford to overlook the new opportunities
for learning that world religions provide.

But it would be a mistake to let the possibility of learning from other faiths
make us blind to at least three other factors that need to be taken seriously.
First, we must not skip lightly over what is dangerous or even demonic in
other religious traditions. As Newbigin notes, "The sphere of the religions
is the battlefield *par excellence* of the demonic."[43] It would be wonderfully
convenient to believe that interreligious conversation and engagement are just
a matter of intellectual sparring among happy, friendly colleagues. Wonderfully convenient—but also terribly naive. Our fallen world is a spiritual and
supernatural war zone, and when theology ignores that fact, it unwittingly
contributes to the number of casualties.

Second, the biblical model overwhelmingly emphasizes not what we can
learn from unbelievers but what we can offer to them—namely, the fullness of
the gospel[44]—and so the logical priority of evangelism over a benign "interreligious dialogue" is nonnegotiable. We need not be rude or offensive, but we
dare not allow our good manners and civility to swell into an implicit denial
of our true allegiance.

Finally, it cannot be emphasized strongly enough that the encounter with
other faiths, though required by the Great Commission and though potentially
invigorating and even instructive, can be deeply hazardous for Christians
whose own faith has not been profoundly nourished by the communal riches
of historic Christian theology and spirituality.[45] A novice who is introduced,
with honesty and humility, to one of the great, centuries-old non-Christian
religious traditions of the world, meets an intensely winsome, intellectually
coherent, religiously compelling vision of reality that—whatever its flaws—
has the demonstrated ability to offer profound religious satisfaction to its
adherents. This is (at least partly) why it has become a great world religion!
Even if its vision of reality is ultimately wrong, it is not just the silly nonsense

---

43. Newbigin, *Open Secret*, 170.
44. See Tiessen, *Who Can Be Saved?*, chap. 14, for a fine overview.
45. See ibid., 437; McDermott, *Can Evangelicals Learn from World Religions?*, 216.

that far too many evangelicals presumptuously assume. Hence, our point in this chapter is definitely *not* to encourage everyday Christians to go and study exotic world religions as simply a stimulating way to grow spiritually. Interaction with these alternative traditions can pose an enormous threat to those of immature faith who glibly stroll in just to see what they can see.

But having said all of this, the question still has to be asked: must we encounter other faiths sheerly as competitors to be overcome or as primitives to be instructed or as enemies to be feared? Or can we combine bold, authentic witness to Christ with humble, respectful inquiry into other faiths? Our contention here is that the latter path is the better one, and that a traditional affirmation of the mystery of God shows how we can follow that path cautiously and faithfully. God has made himself known, and God has made himself known as the incomprehensible Lord. Therefore, we speak with confidence of the Savior whom we have seen and know, and we also speak of him as the one whom we need to see afresh from every possible angle, with an ever richer vocabulary, with new and beautiful images that reinvigorate our weak imaginations.

EPILOGUE

Seeking, Finding, and Seeking

The mind advances to ever greater and more perfect attentiveness and so comes to understand what the understanding is. . . . The closer it comes to the vision of God, the more it realizes just how invisible he is. The true vision of the seeker is that the invisible is seen, because the quest goes beyond what is visible and is enclosed on all sides by incomprehension, which is a kind of sacred darkness.

Gregory of Nyssa[1]

When we speak of God, we do not say all that we might (for that is known to him only) but only what human nature is able to receive and our weakness can bear. We do not explain what God is but candidly confess that our knowledge of him is not exact. Where God is concerned, confessing our ignorance is the sign of greatest knowledge.

Cyril of Jerusalem[2]

1. Gregory of Nyssa, *Life of Moses*, quoted in *Ancient Christian Doctrine*, vol. 1, *We Believe in One God*, ed. Gerald L. Bray (Downers Grove, IL: IVP Academic, 2009), 49.
2. Cyril of Jerusalem, *Catechetical Lectures* 6.2, quoted in Bray, ed., *We Believe in One God*, 48.

A book like this one never quite comes to a close, for there is always more to say. Yet it is exactly here that we may need to remind ourselves that theology is not primarily about "saying." It is about knowing, and it is about that particular kind of knowing that is inseparable from a full, rich life of worship. This is what the task of "knowing the unknowable" (as the subtitle of our book puts it) inevitably involves.

We can see this task from another angle if we relate it to the famous description that the apostle Paul gives of Christian knowledge of God in 1 Corinthians 13. Expressed in the classic King James idiom, the text says, "For now we see through a glass, darkly; but then face to face: now I know in part; but then shall I know even as also I am known" (1 Cor. 13:12 KJV). Considered in its totality, this statement is conspicuously double-edged. On the one hand, Paul insists that even now, we faithful followers of Christ *do* see God; we *do* know God. We are not swept away in the ignorance of the world, in the vain speculations of those for whom God is a "mystery" in a sheerly agnostic sense. How could we be? God has made himself known in Christ, and we follow that great Savior. We know.

On the other hand, we know now only "in part"; we see only "darkly." There is an opaqueness now that must one day be overcome. One day, it *will* be overcome. The time will arrive when we at last see clearly, when we at last know fully, even as also we are known by God himself. On that day, we will know.

Here is a knowledge worth waiting for. Preaching from this same text in 1 Corinthians, Augustine of Hippo declares, "We will see the truth without its wearying us but with eternal delight, and since we will behold it plainly and surely, we will be set afire with the love of truth itself." We will be satisfied, he says, "with a satisfaction that never satiates."[3] Isn't this just the opposite of our ordinary experience? In this life we are very rarely *fully* satisfied, and yet we fairly commonly find ourselves weary with the seeking. What if we could be satisfied to the uttermost and simultaneously energized to seek all the more? What mystery could allow such a marvel? What besides the mystery of God, which, says Augustine in another place, "is both sought in order to be found and found in order to be sought? It is sought in order to be found all the more delightfully, and it is found in order to be sought all the more avidly."[4]

To seek God, to find God, to know God, to worship God—these are the expressions of an intensely personal learning process that reflects the active involvement of the intensely personal God himself, who creates us for himself, draws us to himself, demands our open and receptive response, empowers us by his Spirit to offer it, and guides us as we seek to become more holy and to understand more fully and to worship more truly. He is intimately involved at every step. How can the result be anything but extraordinary?

---

3. Augustine, Sermon 359A (*PLS* 2:759–61), quoted in Judith L. Kovacs, trans. and ed., *The Church's Bible: 1 Corinthians; Interpreted by Early Christian Commentators* (Grand Rapids: Eerdmans, 2005), 227.

4. Augustine, *The Trinity* (Brooklyn: New City, 1991), book 15, prologue (396).

Here, then, is theology's true aim: not just knowledge about God, but the knowledge that God himself *is*. If we seek this knowledge, then Jesus promises that we will find it (Matt. 7:7–8). But to find it is to find nothing less than the Father and the Son and the Holy Spirit. Such knowledge comes by diving in to the fathomless ocean of the Triune God himself, an ocean that refreshes us in an exhilarating and unexpected manner while also descending beneath us to an unimaginable depth. To *think* about that depth means learning to *live* in it boldly, humbly, and joyously. As bearers of the divine image, we are made for exactly this. In a wider sense, the universe as a whole is made for exactly this. For in the last day, "the earth will be filled with the knowledge of the glory of the LORD as the waters cover the sea" (Hab. 2:14). In that day, we will know fully what we now know truly but partially. In that day, the sun will perfectly shine, and the landscape will be perfectly illumined, and all the world will be filled with light and life.

Subject Index

Scripture Index

2 Timothy

3:16 211

Hebrews

1:1–2 77
1:3 78
2:14 149
4:13 182
4:15 79
5:7 203
9:11–15 138
10:15–16 79
11:3 23
12:2 174
12:14 95

James

3:1 94
3:17 94
5:4 106
5:7 106

1 Peter

1:2 105
1:10 145
1:12 145

2 Peter

1:16 36
3:9 157, 174

1 John

4:8 72
5:14 192

Revelation

1:20 5
4:8 27
4:11 26
10:5–6 26
15:4 27
17:7 5
19:7–9 107
19:10 27
20:11 xiv
22:9 27